Artists, ART, & Story:

Southern California

2015-2016

Coordinated by Karrie Ross

Foreword by Hilarie Kelly

Our Ever Changing World ~ Artists, ART, & Stories:
Southern California
Coordinated by Karrie Ross
Foreword by Hilarie Kelly

All rights reserved
Copyright © 2016 Karrie Ross

A Be-It-Now! Book

Printed in the United States of America
Books are available for special promotions and premiums.
For details contact:
Published by Be It Now!®, Los Angeles, CA 90066
email: books@beitnow.com
book website: www.karrieross.com

Book Design: www.KarrieRoss.com
ALL imagery is © per respective artist. All rights reserved by artist.

ISBN 13:9781532845246

To my native state, California.

To all the Artists, who participated.

For all the wonders of the world.

Thank you

Other Books by Karrie Ross

The Big Little Book of Thoughs

My Breasts Talking
My Hands Talking
My Trees Talking

Coaching Parent Coaching Child:
3x award winning book on Parenting

The Bebuddies.com Books

Be Watchful: EnviroNate (*award winning book*)
Be Healthy: Doc
Be Kind: CareyAngel

Got Shui?
(*in progress*)

Books by BzzzBee.com the Bee
BZZZed
You Have My Heart
SnowBee

Our Ever Changing World:
Through the Eyes of Artists:

Book One: What are you Saving from Extinction?
Book Two: Couples and Collaborations
Book Three: *in progress*
Book Four: Artists, ART, & Story

The Story of Art is the Art of Stories

Hilarie Kelly, Anthropologist

WE ARE COMPELLED TO LISTEN TO THE STORIES THAT ARTISTS HAVE TO TELL. Archaeologists and art historians are equally enthralled by exquisite rock paintings produced thousands of years ago. We marvel at the artistry, and are fascinated by this small glimpse at a human world that existed long ago, but – alas – we know nothing about the artists or why they created these masterpieces. Speculation is rife on this topic, because the art itself – the physical piece – does not satisfy by itself. We must have the story!

The enduring and captivating mystery behind ancient rock paintings – and behind the works of more recent and contemporary artists – is why they were created. What was the inspiration, the purpose, the message? From what wellspring of joy, pain, anger, or hope did the artists draw these unique expressions? Human art, from the very earliest forms, appears distinctly imbued with a sensibility and a vision that speaks to us, even now, and we are moved, we strive to fully understand.

Arthur Kleinman, an esteemed medical anthropologist and psychiatrist, once said, "We are…storied folk. Stories are what we are; telling and listening to stories is what we do." His work often focused on the healing and therapeutic value of stories.[1]

Isn't art in itself a form of story-telling?

If art is a form of story-telling, and if stories can heal, then what and who is being healed? Is it the artist? Or is the artist acting as a kind of shaman, attempting to heal others, perhaps even whole communities? Archaeologists have often surmised that this could be what was behind many ancient rock paintings, a magical and ritual artistic attempt to make things right. People living in the Kalahari in Africa, the San, have apparently been using rock art in connection with healing for a very long time.[2] Their notions of dis-ease, as they explain to contemporary anthropologists, focus not just on the bodies of individuals, but also holistically on the "body" of social, environmental, and spiritual relationships that have kept them all alive and well through challenging circumstances. Are their rock paintings akin to therapeutic texts?

Famed evolutionary zoologist Desmond Morris (who is also a surrealist painter) has proposed an interesting theory about art.[3] He thinks of art as a form of playful experimentation that takes risks and often upsets the routine way of doing things. He further argues that such envelope-pushing creativity is necessary to our species' survival. That is the survival imperative: adapt or die; stagnation is death. How is this reflected in the stories of artists themselves?

In our society, artists are often imagined to be especially sensitive souls, and we are therefore bound to be somewhat curious about what has moved them to express themselves in ways out of the ordinary. (Isn't this one of our most basic definitions of art?) What do artists know and see that the rest of us don't, and how does it matter to us? Or is it just that artists have exceptional talents for expressing visions that we all possess? Many scholars have noted an interesting connection in the modern Western art tradition between art and social conscience.[4]

What is the relationship between our society and its artists? Like shamans in some other societies, are they appreciated and respected, but also sometimes feared and shunned?

Given a sufficient abundance of resources available (education, supplies, inspiration, material support), are we all potential artists of one sort or another? To answer any of these questions, we need to know more about the stories of artists themselves.

BIO: **Hilarie Kelly** received a Ph.D. in anthropology from U.C.L.A. in 1992 and formerly taught at California State University, Fullerton and Long Beach campuses. She currently teaches at University of La Verne. She has done ethnographic and applied research in Africa and North America. Areas of specialization include gender, economic development, transnationalism and globalization, health and nutrition, aging, performance and visual representation. In her spare time she dances, gardens, cooks, travels, and does photography.

---

[1] Quoted from Kleinman's Prologue to the book, Patients and Doctors: Life-Changing Stories from Primary Care by Jeffrey M. Borkan et al, eds., University of Wisconsin Press, 1999: x.
[2] See Deciphering Ancient Minds: The Mystery of San Bushmen Rock Art by David Lewis-Williams and Sam Challis, Thames and Hudson Publishers, 2011. See also http://www.ruf.rice.edu/~raar/Theories.html
[3] See http://www.aestheticamagazine.com/interview-with-desmond-morris-on-the-artistic-ape/
[4] For example, LACMA (Los Angeles County Museum of Art) provides a resource guide on this topic for its visitors. (http://www.lacma.org/sites/default/files/FINAL%20FOR%20WEB%20Artist%20as%20a%20Social%20Conscience_0.pdf) See also this online guide to an art studies textbook: http://www.wwnorton.com/college/art/gatewaystoart/ch/36/outline.aspx

*~ an introduction deals with the subject of the book,
supplementing and introducing the text and indicating a point of
view to be adopted by the reader. ~*

I BELIEVE THAT ARTISTS ARE IN SOME WAY HISTORIANS...that
their work saves something from becoming forgotten. And,
artists more than just create art—they are also a product of it
—it's a way they filter things, their experiences, thoughts,
actions, that show up everyday, exposed in the art they create.

Why only Southern California?

First because it's my native home and — second, I choose to
have my books document the lively, varied, not only the locals,
but those from all over the world who come to live here for
more than the sun, waves, and entertainment ... but for the
opportunity to be a part of a thriving uniquely different way of
living, art-making...and the diversity of it all — one hell of a
vibration.
    The title *Artist, ART & Story* brings together the whole of
art. Each is represented, the ARTIST by their name, ART by
the image, and Story by their recounting of something that
"happened" in their life that has nothing to do with, or the
mention of ART. Completing the whole.

Stories are very powerful.

I look at life as there is joy in making a difference. I'm pretty
sure I always have. My mother was very community oriented
and so is my sister... I, on the other hand, and maybe it's due
in part to my being in advertising for my whole life career...

I want to create historical moments. My ART PROJECT Books do that. Book One started with a question and when I noticed that it changed the lives of the artists that participated I've been hooked ever since.

I once had a conversation with a close friend about what is more important — to be seen or to participate. I was the participate side of the conversation, he was the be seen part. Both have merit and are important parts of being in this world.

My experience has been that I've not had trouble being seen, but nothing really ever happened until I started participating, doing something. His experience was that he was always doing something and for him he needed to be seen. AND now through the magic of Story we all can be heard. Everyone has a different life story that most often gets lost in the process of writing bios and artist statements. Therefore, this book and it's focus on bringing it all into life.

This was a process, learning, and journey for me.

Crazy artists... one doesn't get the full meaning until you start making projects, especially ones that need the help of others... but, we still do it... right?

I was so deep in the project that not until I woke up one day towards the end, did I realize that never before in my life have I needed to solicit so much for help from others—in my past, I've always created something that I could do myself.

A little over twelve years ago, seems like yesterday, I started getting more active in the Los Angeles art scene and realized I wanted to do something, make a difference... and since I write, design, publish books and catalogs they seemed a natural. Each book I create brings a new insight and learning... each currently with a focus on Southern California.

The Art Project Books will go nowhere if I don't work on getting artists to join in and the joining in of the artists bring them and me, more awake to what we are doing. So in reality its a win win for us all. And I've bared my soul throughout the project as I know personally how wonderful sharing change can be. And the more focused one is, the greater the movement, so I'm getting more and more focused as I write.

Being seen, heard, and participation are at the base of these books — for me, the artists connected to them, as well as the people who buy them... you.

Please take time as you read and consider the following stories. They will make you cry, laugh, be amazed, be sad, mad and still want more. The stories you will read are brave. They are thought provoking. They are the other part of an artists life most never have an entry into.

Thank you.
Karrie Ross
http://www.karrieross.com

Note: The artists are listed in the order if when they submitted their stories. I appologize if I left anyone out anywhere or misscoppied anything. The book has not been edited or proofed, so sentence structure is purely of the artists own words and adds to the quality of the sharing. THANK each and every one of the artists that I asked to change a word here-or-there OR to rewrite the whole story. Your efforts have not gone unappreciated and help to make this book the best it can be...and on focus...!

Artists, ART, & Story:

Southern California

2015-2016

Listing of Artists in Order of Appearence

Kathi Flood

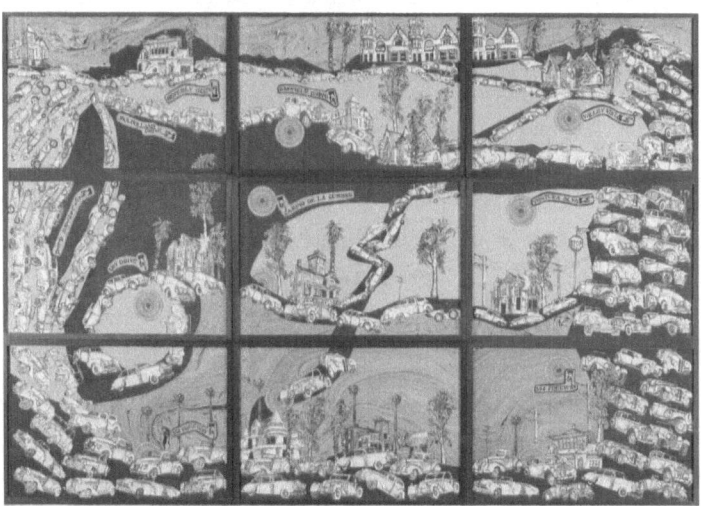

<u>Bottleneck</u>: 7:10 a.m. and the beeping begins. Some beeps are timid, high-pitched quick Repetition Beeps, banged out by overly cautious hardworking citizens. Then, of course, the Anger Beeps, deep-breath-long and wobbly. And yeah, there are those who lean on the horn all the way down the hill, just in case. Whether intermittent or maxed out roadhog style, the adrenalin rushes I feel as I am jolted awake sour my gut for the coming day.

You see, I live in a canyon on a hairpin turn, and instead of slowing down, many commuters going from the San Fernando Valley to the Westside of L.A. protect themselves by beeping as they round the curve. Even though it is illegal to come up this road 7-9 a.m., scofflaws, desperate to clock in to their jobs on time, gladly become instant outlaws, praying that they hit it on a day without police at the corner.

There are 250 homes on the hill, and most folks' bedrooms are close to the road. I also live in a wildlife view-shed area with deer and bobcats, and many of us take the responsibility of being stewards to the land seriously. There have been too many accidents on 'Snake Road', including four people hit by cars, a death or two, head-ons, and back-up at the top of the hill preventing residents from leaving their homes for hours.

So Big Mouth here blurted out, "I'll be the facilitator of the Traffic Committee!" In that heroic instant, I forgot the dynamics of committees. Committee meetings are generally time-drainers in which everyone opinionates and not much action is taken, in the name of politeness and egotism. We threw around ideas like convoluted cul-de-sac designs, traffic calming measures, and plenty of good ole vigilante flash mob actions.

And the more I tried to make things better, the more clogged up they got. Let's just say that our 'hood is a conglomeration of Deniers, Girl Scouts, and Alpha Dogs. We talked and surveyed and researched possibilities. We made convenience versus safety lists. We numbered the ideas and crossed them off one by one.

We had a big ole meeting in a big ole room with the community and government officials. The room was slam-jammed and volatile. At one point, nostrils flared, a neighbor stood up a la a miner's strike with PMS. Even after being asked to stay on the subject of traffic, she defiantly declared, 'I'm going to talk about it anyway!' She segued into an accusatory tirade about neighbors who let their bushes grow too high. It was the Libertarian Conservationists versus the Safety Committee, providing us with a giddy moment of high drama in an otherwise bureaucratic jumble of cliches.

Hilarious vigilante pranks ensued. One man got a large video camera and trained it on drivers who were stuck in line going uphill, boldly marching up to their cars and brazenly bawling them out. Someone else donned a black outfit and motorcycle, impersonating an officer and eventually getting bawled out by a real cop. One man even blocked the road with his car, folded his arms, and offered commuters a big, fat smirky pout.

Then another inevitable turn of events: bifurcation of our 'hood. Upper Road versus Lower Road. Carefully couched NIMBY-esque oratories degraded into tit-for-tat support. There were gossipy sub-committees hastily formed the next morning. Local institutions were enlisted to sponsor desperate, random self-protective plans. People vacillated between positions of self-protective convenience and public safety, citing statistics willy-nilly to support their assertions. There were winks, there were tears. At some point, we receded into our air conditioned homes to mull it over, holding onto a strange combination of empowerment and defeat.

Life happened, and I found it necessary to bow out of The Traffic Committee. Efforts continue to protect our neighbors, wildlife, and sanity around here. At one point, we had three women in their ninth month of pregnancy at the top of the hill, and if they were ready to deliver their children during the commuter rush, it would have happened in their driveways. We are typical of the Los Angeles canyon roads that are impacted by the constant swelling of our commuter population. We try not to make eye contact with the 4-wheeled invaders that crawl by our homes as we introspectively water our bushes and wash our cars.

And as I write this, someone else just beeped. But it was a cute, little, polite chirp. I didn't mind. I released all of my frustrations by becoming absorbed in making a large, goofy, cartoony etching collage of the situation. I drew tilty, bloated antique cars, foliage, freeway signs, canyon homes and some random Where's-Waldo-esque animals. I went from scowling to smirking. No, I didn't run out to my driveway in my bathrobe and flip them off. I am lost in my own personal, self-invented, goofy reality. Art works.

http://www.KathiFlood.com

Stefanie Vega

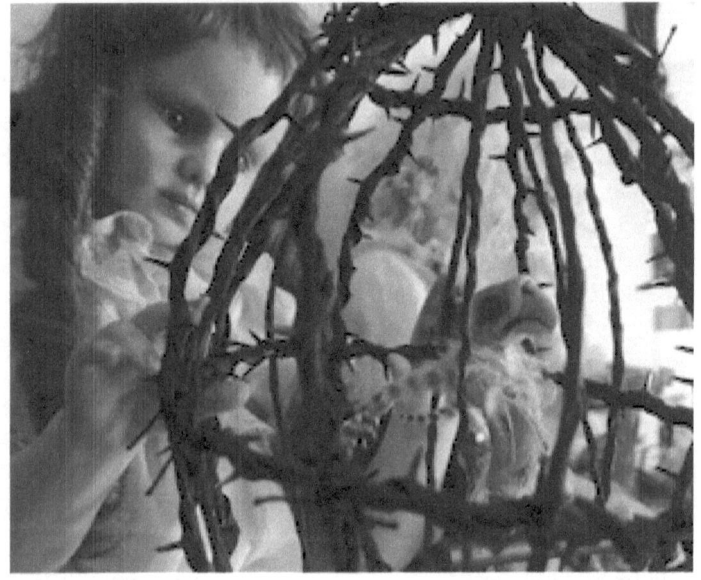

The Secret Thorn

My mother died.

While sorting through her belongings, I found a doll I had long forgotten. My childhood dolls were the totems of my dreams. Upon them I projected my greatest self...my future self. But was this particular doll purposely forgotten, as was the secret we had shared so many years before? This was my grandmother's doll—the very one that had survived my mother and her mother before her. Over one hundred years old, this was the doll that held generations of secrets, but none as culpable as the burden I expected her to carry. I would name her my caretaker of regret. And as fate would have it, she would resurface in my life. I could not escape my keeper of secrets. As I held her small porcelain body, I was flooded with memory. The dark corridor of veiled recall was once again in focus. Like a haunting lullaby, I was serenaded by the forgotten past.

I was only allowed to play with this doll at Grandma's house. In the 1960's, the area of Brooklyn where we lived could have been the dark faerie tale forest taken right from the pages of the most frightening of children's tales. This was a place where the disastrous consequences of misbehavior were reality. It was a gloomy, sinister abode of the unrevealed. The mysterious and secret language of the street dictated the drama that played out like Shakespeare... blood and death.

How does a child understand murder? What are the circumstances that can make her feel responsible? At what age does one come to realize the power of words? How many secrets can one doll hold? In these surroundings I learned to be sneaky and imaginative. I became crafty and clever. Like a garden in my mind, I buried the unpleasant and carefully tended it; continually removing the weeds of doubt that would inevitably appear from time to time. I would use denial as my coping mechanism. So, as the human drama in the neighborhood played out, I floated above it like a phantom, taking an appropriate notice of death on the smaller scale. Dead birds.

Like their human counterpart, they would lay lifeless on the pavement. I would make attempts to breathe life back into them; and with a child's faith, I always believed I could. Y et I was continually left with the carcasses of little dead things; an inescapable reminder of the reality I so willingly averted. Was I subconsciously making atonement for my own sin? Could I breathe life back into the body of a man? I knew enough not to speak it. I had already said too much. Grandmother's doll knew what I had said. When I peered through the crack in the door, crouching in the dark, she experienced what I had seen. Cowering in the shadow of that room, still and unnoticed, only she knew that I had heard. But she would never tell, and neither would I. The chain of events that lead to that fateful outcome were completely entrusted to her. If I was not seen, was I actually there?

I decided then to relinquish the memory.

I would never speak it.

And yet, after all these years, and thousands of miles from it… it still speaks through me.

And the wound never healed.

http://www.stefanievega.com

Ellen Riingen

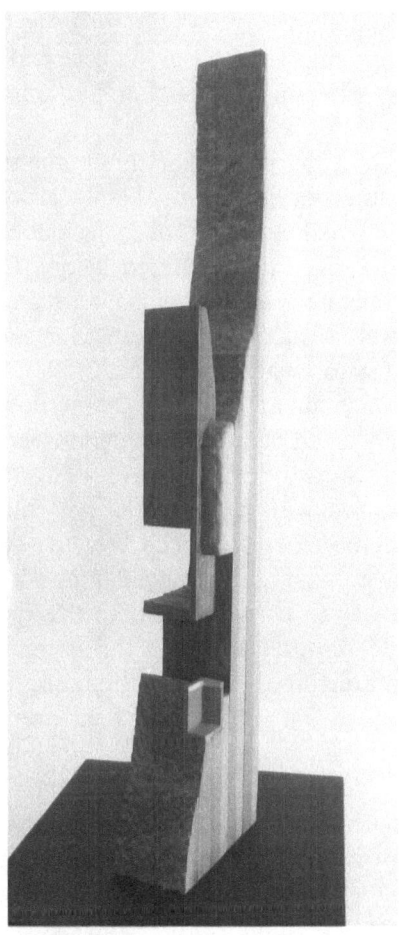

A Common Thread

I never could have imagined myself working in sunny temperate Santa Monica in Southern California just blocks from the beaches, but there I was. My seat was one of those Herman Miller Aeron chairs that probably cost more than my furniture at home combined. Two large monitors stared back at me each day as I worked for hours from project to project. My right hand was starting to become one with my computer mouse. I would fill up my coffee cup in small amounts, partly so it wouldn't get cold before I was able to drink it, but also as a reminder to get up, walk to the kitchen, and rest my eyes. Sunshine slowly became more of a beckoning siren than a warm friend.

Then one day, my co-worker threw out the thought of starting a lunchtime knitting group. Some part of me lifted my body out of the chair like a drunken jackrabbit and invited myself right in. I have never knitted before. Our group got snickers and stares at the silliness of it all in such a proper place of business. Some of the guys even wanted to start a fight club in the office just to balance out the testosterone levels. Ha! I didn't care. The silliness grew into admiration and wonder. There was always a part of me that wanted to learn how to knit, and now was the time to find out why.

I have dabbled with needlework as a child going from cross-stitch to embroidery to crocheting to sewing. Coming from a typical Navy family who moved quite a bit, needlework became a nice way to pass the time. To this day, my parents have my needle ventures adorning the house in some way. I can't go to the bathroom there without seeing toilet paper toppers that started out as potholders and went rogue when I couldn't get the increases just right. Other failed attempts became dapper derbies for my stuffed animals. It impressed others, but I knew the truth. Crocheting was not my thing.

It has only been a few months from my first knit stitch, but I have become a bit obsessed. Online tutorials, meet up groups, and on-line share communities has launched my hobby into overdrive. The variety of patterns, yarns, and needles were staggering. I love the structure and nuances of each stitch and am baffled how much can be done by knowing just two simple stitches. Twists, turns, pop outs, gaps, needles varieties, yarn science, all at my fingertips. The field of potentiality exploded in every direction.

Because of the long hours in front of a digital screen, I chose my knitting time to be unplugged, quiet, focused and meditative. I think of all of the generation of needle crafters in my family. For as long as I can remember, my mom has always sewn or crocheted. My parents grew up in the remote areas of the Philippines on the southern island of Mindanao. Mindanao is the largest of the more than 7000 islands that make up the Philippines, but it is mostly jungle areas with small villages located sporadically. Because of the geographical challenges and high expense, my parents never ventured off of the island until they were adults ready to start a new venture in the United States. Because of the remoteness and low economy, needlecraft was taught in school as a functional necessity for daily living. Much like in the States, stores sold material and threads. That was basically it. The rest was up to you.

Being a Navy wife, away from her family, friends, culture, and with three goofy kids, I can venture to say needlecrafts saved my mom's sanity, and inadvertently mine as well. There is one thing you have to be good at when being a Navy wife; it's waiting. Her needle and thread were always with her. My dad was gone for months at a time. When he was home, our family was usually moving to some new part of the country. I remember she crocheted bed covers, tablecloths, potholders, and sweater vests. She would bring me to the store to go through sewing pattern catalogs to pick out a new blouse or poncho. It was our version of mother-daughter "shopping" time. I got to pick out the material, the trim, and the buttons. Such a treat! I was sportin' an original as I strutted onto the playground. I realize now that her needle time was her outlet from isolation, her "me" time in a world of 24/7 responsibilities. It was no longer a functional pastime.

I was most fascinated with her creations in crocheting. She was meticulous when she followed the pattern in her pattern booklets that read like a completely different language. From this ball of thread emerged these intricate patterns. This generation doesn't know much about doilies, but my mom crocheted a lot of them. I suppose they can be thought of as the dust ruffles for tabletops. Her signature one had edges that folded open like wings or an origami flower. She gave them as gifts and even sold them for a steal price at the local swap meet along with her crocheted one-of-a-kind Barbie doll outfits. Her handiwork would sell within minutes. This brought her so much joy.

The interesting thing is I would never have looked back at these memories if it weren't for my new-found passion for knitting and the quiet time it has allowed me away from modern conveniences. Knitting has become much like my need to fill my coffee cup just a little at a time. It allows me that little break of time to stop, reflect, and appreciate everything that has lead up to that present moment. And it is at these times when I truly know, my mom must have looked back as well.

http://ellenriingen.com/

Joyce Lieberman

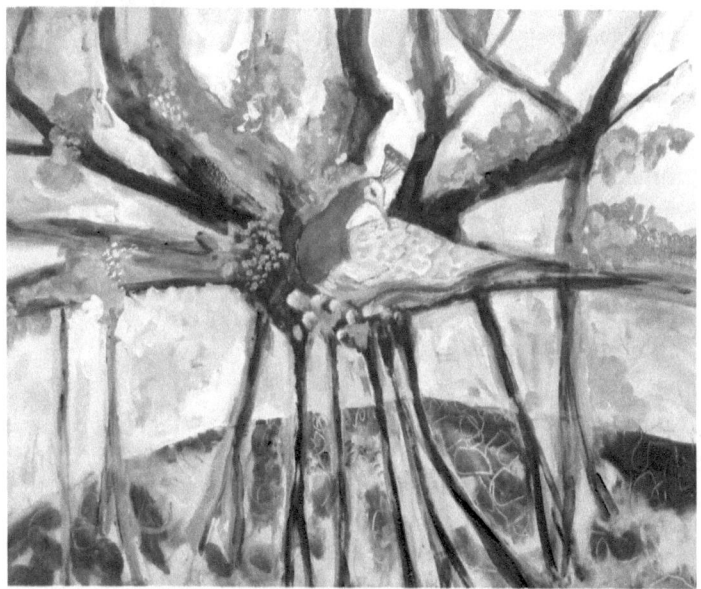

The Peacock's Tale

After 31 years in Venice, I have moved. I hung in there through a lot of changes in my rented 1911 cottage near the Sea. We went through some dangerous times there with gun fire and an especially wild gang shooting summer when they tried to "clean up" the neighborhood during President Bush Sr.'s 100 points of light, or was it 1000 points of light? Anyway, it made it a scary summer.

Even scarier was the white collar crime that came to town as greedy land speculators started seizing properties. Our landlord was defaulting on his loan with the Bank of America. He was playing 'Chicken' with them to get a better rate and he lost. My phone number was connected to the property. Greedy speculators called to yell at me about being out on the street. I had 40 years of paintings and various artworks in my home. I thought "will I have to fit them all into one shopping cart? How will I choose? How can I find homes for all of these?"

It was so out of control that I couldn't let that happen again.

Venice was the irritant that created the pearl. It was scary and I stayed home a lot and got a lot of work done. Early in our stay there in 1983, there was an old church catty corner to our house. An older neighbor guy went out to get something from the store early in the morning, without his teeth in. As he rounded the corner, thugs attacked him and beat him to the ground and stole his money. He was seriously shaken, he was a tall man and he went inside his place across the street and never came out again. He became a hoarder. The police came and took him out of the place and he died from fright in the back of the car.

We took the plunge and bought a house and moved. I found space and reorganized...I collated and re-collated my artworks. We found a 100 year old house that needed a lot of work. A lot can go wrong in a 100 year old house. Rotted floors, walls, ceilings, termites,so much needs fixing. And the learning curve on all these things is huge.

The difference between the rented 1911 Venice bungalow doomed to demolition and the 1914 airplane craftsman we bought was more than the three years.

We are bringing the place we bought back to life from serious disrepair.

In Venice, we never concerned ourselves about fixing anything until it broke.

With rent control, a hot water heater spewing in the night is your own problem, but until then, it's no ones job to maintain it. At the new 1914 house we learn to drain the sediment from the hot water heater before anything crazy like that happens. There is a big learning curve here, thanks youtube.

Cleaning is turning into my new art form. It's fun to see what can be salvaged and what needs to be new.

My old place to work was like the cockpit of a plane, everything could be reached from one seat on the floor. Now it is more spread out and I get exercise walking back and forth.

Sometimes it feels like the groove or rut, depending on your point of view, can feel like it will go on and on forever the same way...and then it doesn't. It can be abrupt. I used to get a little weepy thinking about losing my center point in Venice. Everything I knew for over 30 years started from there.

It can be exciting to rebuild a life from a new center. Planting trees and flowers is so hopeful. Focusing on new projects helps a lot. Revisiting the parade of people, young and old that have woven their lives through mine helps a lot.

My husband's band members used to call our yard in Venice, The Garden of Eden.

We have been warming the new house with friends and the gardening inland is amazing, I just grew my own broccoli for dinner. I had the last of the Japanese eggplants, and some green tomatoes left from summer with the broccoli and it's January.

A fragrant orange tree is bearing fruit abundantly in our yard.

There is life after Venice.

http://www.joycelieberman.com

Paula Goldman

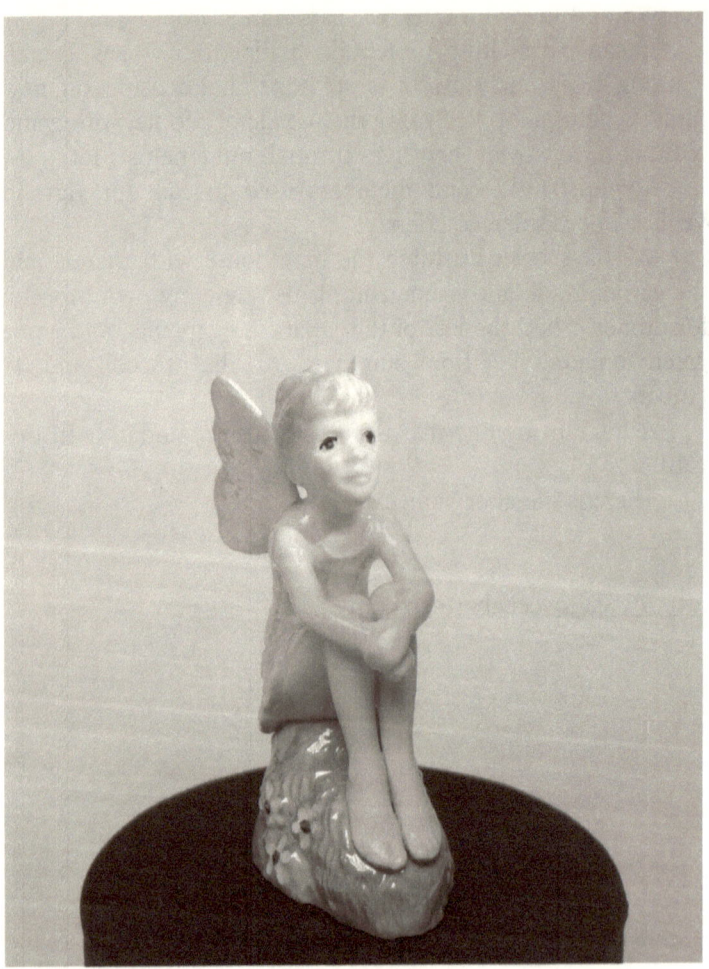

LA Story

I. Driving down my freeway, the 405, heading to an evening lecture at the groovy Pacific Design Center. In my second year of grad school, I am full of hope and promise. I exit at Sunset Boulevard, heading east. The sun has just set, the sky still feels dark blue, and the lights are beginning to come on. I round a curve and see the entire Sunset Strip in front of me. At that exact moment, the Doors' LA Woman comes on the radio. I am so happy.

II. We are walking down Main Street in Santa Monica with our one-year-old son. It is a weekend, and the sidewalk is very crowded. I notice an elderly, bent-over, homeless-looking woman rushing across the street toward us. She stops in front of our son and looks at him intently. "He might be the one," she declares. I am secretly excited.

III. I have two beautiful children. They talk a lot and make a lot of demands. I am finally up in my office behind my house trying to do some work. "Mom!" I hear my adorable two-year-old daughter yell. "Mom. Mom!" After ignoring her for a couple minutes I feel bad. I go outside to check on her and find a flock of crows in the tree, screeching. I feel bad.

IV. I am getting changed in my bedroom. My children are arguing and yelling up to me. It's beginning to sound a bit urgent so I run out of my room, in my underwear. My ten-year-old son is standing there. He looks at me and says, "I can't believe you ever got a man."

V. It is Mother's Day, and I want to look at videos of my children. They are recorded on mini cassette tapes, and I can't find the VHS adapter that allows us to view them. This is the second time it has disappeared. I drive to Best Buy to buy a third adapter. The parking lot is packed, and I pull up to wait for a car to back out. As I pull into the space, I see another car that had been waiting on the other side. The man gestures wildly and aggressively with his middle finger, and screams at me, "I'm going to fuck you up!" over and over. As I walk past his car, I see his wife and children inside, their eyes really big. I write down the license plate number.

http://www.paulagoldman.com

Bibi Davidson

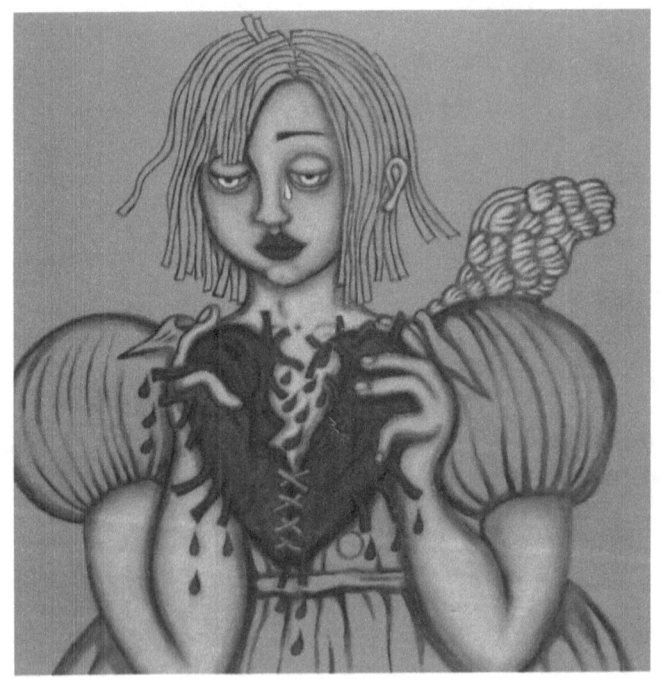

shoot me before i die1

MY FIRST PAST LIFE REGRESSION, EVENTS HAPPENED AROUND 1500 AD.

ABOUT TEN YEARS AGO, I WENT THROUGHT A FEW PAST LIFE REGRESSIONS BY A HYPNOTHERAPIST.
MY FIRST REGRESSION:

IN A MIDST OF A WIND STORM, I FOUND MYSELF HIDING BEHIND A BURNT TREE ON A HILL SCUTTERED WITH LOTS OF BURNT TREES.

APPARENTLY THERE WAS A BIG FIRE IN THAT AREA. I WAS SHIVERING, I WAS CONSUMMED BY GREAT FEAR, I

WAS BARELY 15, WITH LONG BROWN HAIR AND PREGNANT.

PEOPLE WERE LOOKING FOR ME, I COULD HEAR THEIR VOICES OVER THE WIND, I TRIED TO BE INVISIBLE, BUT THEY SAW ME AND CAME TO GET ME.

I WAS CRYING AND PLEADING THEM TO LET ME GO BUT THEY DRAGGED ME BACK TO THE VILLAGE TO BE HUNG FOR BEING UNMARRIED WITH CHILD.

THEY LOCKED ME IN A ROOM TO BE GUARDED UNTIL THEY WERE READY, I WAS SOBBING AND SCARED AND SO LONELY, MY HEART WAS ACHING, I WAS SO DESPAIRED, I HAD NOBODY TO ASK FOR COMFORT.

WHEN THE VILLAGERS CAME BACK FOR ME, THEY HAD TO CARRY ME BECAUSE MY LEGS COLLAPSED.

ABOVE THE SQUARE, ON A HILL, A MAN ON A HORSE WAS LOOKING DOWN AT ME; HE WAS THE PRINCE OF THE VILLAGE AND THE FATHER OF MY CHILD. HE WAS LOOKING AT ME FOR A FEW MINUTES AND THEN ORDERED THE MAN NEXT TO HIM IMPAITIANTLY.

THE MAN TOLD THE VILLAGERS TO LET ME GO AND SEND ME AWAY FROM THE VILLAGE. IN THOSE DAYS IT WAS ALMOST LIKE A DEATH SENTENCE.

I WAS LEAD INTO A DIRT ROAD AND WAS SENT AWAY. I WAS WALKING AND CRYING AND LOST, WALKING FOR A FEW DAYS, SLEEPING ON THE SIDE OF THE ROAD. I WAS STARVING AND THIRSTY.

ON THE FOURTHTH DAY I SAW A SMALL INN WITH A COUPLE SERVING FOOD FOR SOME TRAVELERS.

THE WOMAN SAW ME WITH MY CONDITION AND GAVE ME SOME WATER AND FOOD, I COULDN'T TALK, I WAS CRYING. I COULDN'T ANSWER HER QUESTIONS. SHE OFFERED ME TO STAY FOR A WHILE, WORKING FOR THEM FOR FOOD AND SLEEPING ARRANGMENT, IT WAS LIKE AN ACT OF MERCY FOR ME AND I AGREED.

AFTER A WHILE THE COUPLE ADOPTED ME AS A DAUGHTER AND LET ME STAY, I WORKED HARD, COOKING AND CLEANING AND SERVING, I DIDN'T MIND, I HAD A PLACE TO STAY.

THE DAY CAME WHEN I GAVE BIRTH TO MY BABY WITH THE HELP OF THAT KIND LADY, IT WAS A BOY AND HE HAD A HALO OF LIGHT RAYS AROUND HIS HEAD.

THE BOY WAS MY SUNSHINE, MY LIFE, I WASN'T ALONE ANYMORE, I HAD THIS CHILD TO TAKE CARE OF AND IT GAVE ME A PURPOSE TO LIVE, BEING HELPED BY THE KIND COUPLE.

AND SO MY LIFE AS IN A REMOTE AND THE MIDDLE OF THE ROAD BECAME MORE MEANINGFUL AND FULL OF EMOTION, WE WERE ALL LIKE A FAMILY.

AS LIFE PAST FAST, WORKING AND MOTHERING, TIME FLEW AND MY BOY GREW UP TO BE A HANDSOME YOUNG MAN. MY HEART ALMOST BURST FROM ALL THE LOVE THAT I HAD INSIDE ME.

ONE DAY WHEN MY SON TURNED 16 YEARS OLD AND THE COUPLE AND ME WERE PREPARING TO CELEBRATE HIS BIRTHDAY, SOME SOLDIERS CAME BY AND SAW HIM, IMMEDIATELY THEY RECRUTTED HIM TO THE MILITARY WITHOUT ASKING FOR ANY PERMISSION.

THEY PUT HIM ON A HORSE AND JUST RODE AWAY, I WAS TRYING TO TALK TO THEM AND CALL THEM, BUT

NONE OF THEM TURNED BACK, ONLY ONCE MY SON TURNED HIS HEAD TOWARDS ME, HIS EYES WERE FULL OF TEARS.

I DECIDED TO FOLLOW THEM BUT THEY WERE SLOWLY GETTING FURTHER AND FURTHER AWAY, UNTIL I COULD NO LONGER SEE THEM.

I ENTERED AN EMPTY TOWN WITH COBBLE STONES STREETS, THERE WAS NOBODY THERE, MY SON WAS GONE AND I COULD FEEL MY LONLINESS AND FEAR CREEPING BACK INTO MY HEART.

http://www.bibidavidson.com

Geoffery Levitt

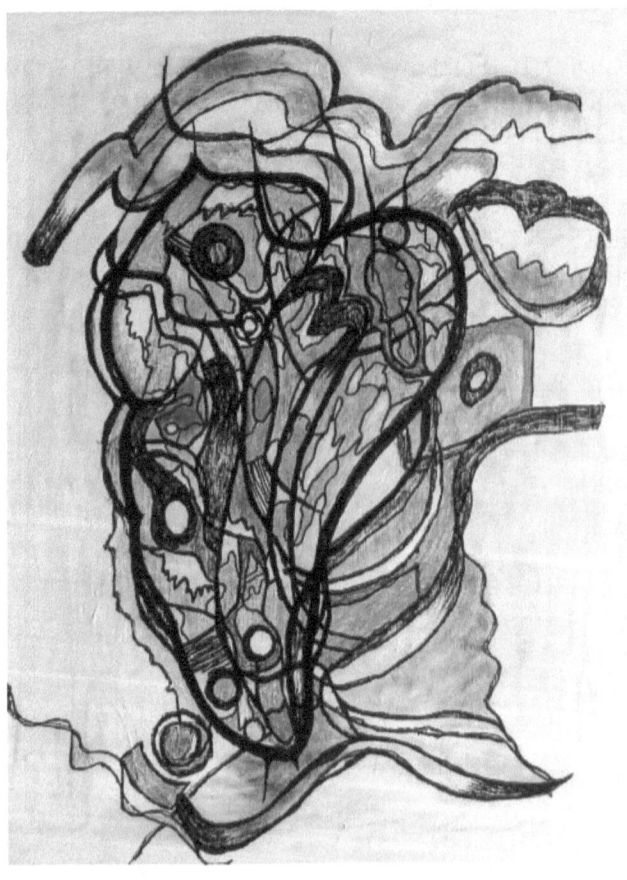

A Tale of Two Steers

My brother Dan and I grew up on a ranch in Northern Los Angeles County near Gorman. We both belonged to the Neenach 4H Club while we were in High School. My little Brother Paul was too young to belong. I was so enthusiast that I was President of our local 4H Club. Our big projects were entering the Antelope Valley Fair. I also learned how to run and maintain a tractor.

My Father took us to the Livestock Auction in Famosa. We bid on two four month old Hereford Steers and got them. They are also referred to as red white faced. Now the hard work started since this was the Fall and the Fair would be over the Labor Day weekend next year. One was named Abiyoyo after a giant in a Pete Seiger song. We were both budding musicians at the time and Pete Seiger was our Idol. I can't remember the name of the other one. All three of us boys took care of the steers with a little help from my Dad.

We had to keep track of our expenses as part of the beef project. We had to feed and water them twice a day. The first few months of their lives were spent out in pasture. The last three or four months they had to be feed very high quality food so they would fatten up. Hence they were moved into the barn. We also had to brush them every day while they were in the barn. And of course shovel out the manure from the barn. They became quite tame with all the attention. This was quite important so they could be shown at the fair and behave like civilized animals.

Although we feed them the same amount of food my brothers grew much faster. I suspected my Brother's was hogging the food or maybe mine ran around more. In any event when weigh in came at the Fair my brothers weighed almost a thousand pounds. Mine weighed 757 with minimum being 750 pounds. Seven pounds got me into the Fair with my steer. So both steers were able to be exhibited at the Fair. We brushed, groomed and washed them so they would look good for the Judges. We even used a special brush that would make their hair look wavey to attract the Judges. My whole family came to look at them. My father even brought some of his fellow artists to look at them.

It was an exciting week and a half. We had to stay over night with our animals to care for them in case there was a problem. There were generally about half a dozen of us there, some from other 4H Clubs and some from mine. We brought sleeping bags and slept on straw---like the bedding for the animals. The beef were separate from the other animals.

Dan's Steer got Reserve Grand Champion and at the Auction was bought by a local car dealership, Hunter Dodge, who shared the meat with his employees. My father bid on and got mine. The irony of this was my Father had financed this project from the beginning. My Father felt sorry for my predicament in only getting Second Prize. It went into the freezer and our family ate on it for about a year. It turned out to be the leanest most flavorful beef we ever ate. There's nothing better than homegrown meat. I had a great Dad!

http://www.GeoffreyELevitt.com

Emerald

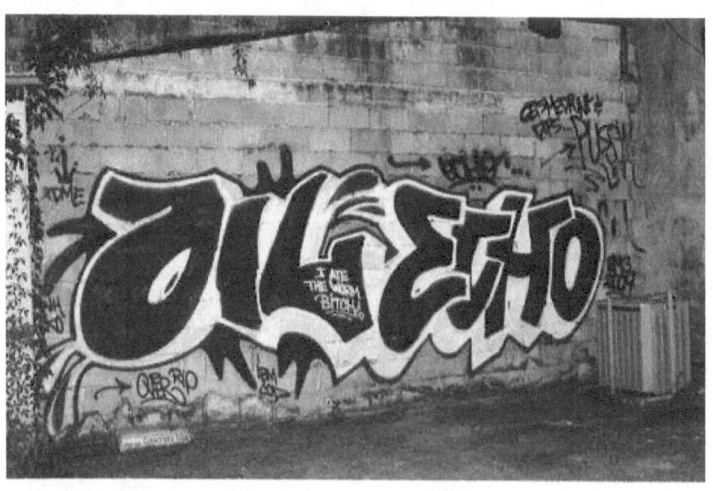

Sunday, May 9th, 2010 -12:59 pm
Happy Mother's Day

People go through life creating things they will abandon and refuse to acknowledge responsibility for.

Children are like ideas, the thought seemed great at the time but you lack the follow-through to make sure everything is carried out properly, responsibly.

Those of us, the abandoned children who've grown up into maladjusted, malfunctioning adults for whom no one will take responsibility for, we hate this day. We hate pretending you're the "#1 Mom" and lying to you about it every year.

And maybe that's why I always hate the holidays. Determined days, forcing me to tell lies to the world and those around me.

The World's Most Hypocritical, Selfish, Materialistic Mom

The World's Biggest Piece of Shit, Dead Dad

The World's Most Mentally Ill, Estranged Family

Thank you for teaching me everything I know about love. Everything I know about relationships.

Thank you for putting me here and making my existence so miserable that I was forced to retreat as far as possible in order to save myself from everything I know. If I didn't have to run so far, I would have never seen the landscape that put distance between us. I wouldn't have known how many new cliffs I could try to climb and fall down from, or how many highway walls would halt the spinning of my car as it holds the fate of my life or death in its grill.

I wouldn't have known how little I need to survive if I hadn't been able to exist for so long without anything at all.

I miss Pappy worse on days like this. Days when the abandoned children of the world are isolated in the center ring, by no one but themselves. Looking out at the warm, caring families, we turn to our sides to find others just like us avoiding eye contact with the weight that makes them feel worthless. Displaced stares meet in awkward pockets of air. We recognize our own reflection in each others eyes, and we pull closer to each others side. You have no one, and neither do I.. We'll be friends for a long time.

We're not jealous of them because they have families, we hate them because they're not alone like us. They celebrate on days we struggle to stifle sentiments. We hate them for having what we should have had, for complaining about having to leave friends for a family feast carved out by a caring dad.

We hated each other on those lonely days, for being reminders of how many people who should've cared but didn't.

I remember being trapped alone with you in that apartment in Riverside. There were no doors to close. We had no privacy to masturbate those miserable thoughts of hatred toward ourselves, so the chemicals we each held reacted to the intense chemistry of our bond. We hated ourselves so much we turned on the only other person who cared enough to be there. We brought each other so low, I was sure I had lost you and I didn't care. I left you alone. I told you I was leaving town and that the apartment was yours, not to worry if you never heard about or from me ever again.

I drove down to the St. Johns River, intending to drive right into it, but I stopped the car. I got out, intending to jump in and sink to the bottom, but I looked at the water for an hour. It was cold, the wind chopping a current into the surface.

I didn't want to die so cold, and so uncertainly. I could cut my wrists and be found bled to death in the car, or I could wait on the train tracks to meet a timely trans-continental, something more certain than jumping into a river.

I drove down Stockton street and stopped at the laundromat to use the payphone. I used one of my last two dollars to call JJ.

"Merry Christmas! Where are you?"

"I'm in Jacksonville. My phone fell in a puddle of water this morning and I have no money. I spent half my money on this phone call, but I have about half a tank of gas. What are you doing today? Do you think I could make it to Orlando on this much gas?"

"I'm at my mom's house, but you can definitely come over. Are you okay? What happened?"

"I'm fine, I've just had a really bad day. I need to get the fuck out of here, but I don't have a phone or money so I'm kind of fucked... Look, I'll call you back if I'm going to drive down there — I'm just not sure if it's a good idea or not."

I drove back to my apartment, but you weren't there. I sat in bed for hours until I heard the lock on the door begin to turn. You came in drunk, and I could tell you weren't angry with me.

"Bro, I thought you left! You can't do that shit, I thought you were long gone."

"I had no money to go anywhere. I almost drove into the St. Johns though."

"That was so wack when you left. I can't believe you just fucking left like that. You can't do that shit."

"I was going to leave you the apartment, it would have solved all the problems."

"You're nuts, bro, but I fucking love you."

"I love you too. Merry Christmas."

But now he's gone and I'm alone. A soul match suffering from sordid sanity. A close friendship that replaced an abusive family. Burned into ashes and disappearing into thin air, blowing in the wind, mining tears from the depths of my displaced stare.

http://www.emeraldartstudio.com

Jack Reilly

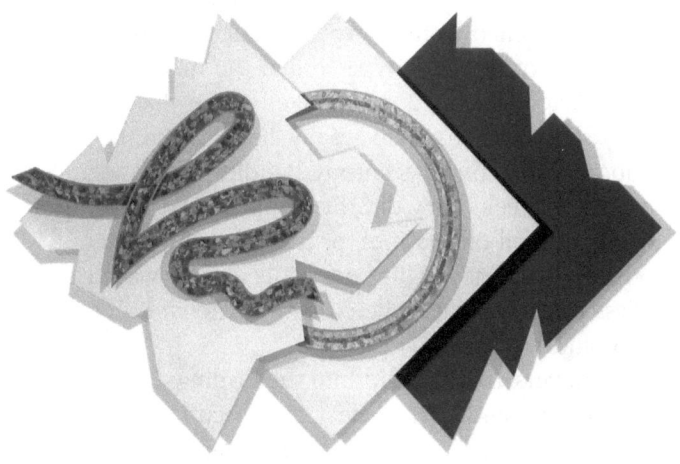

Irony of Plastic and the Color Red

At 6AM I was jarred awake from a sound like I had never heard, a kind of muted thud/splat noise. Too early to exert the effort to climb down the eight-foot makeshift ladder that led up to my loft bed, I drifted back to sleep. Back in 1980, the downtown L.A. art scene was still in its infant stages. There were no trendy boutiques or hip restaurants, but only a precious few working class eateries in the area. Rough industrial artist lofts were scattered around from Broadway to Santa Fe Ave. and beyond. My fifth-floor studio was in one of the more seedy areas on San Pedro Street, adjacent 5th, AKA Skid Row. Events I witnessed in the streets and alleys below were not what a middle class, recently educated, young man from the suburbs expected to encounter.

Later that morning I was scheduled to ship some pieces to New York. At around 8:30a.m. I finally got out of bed and shuffled over to the window and looked down to the alley. The vision I saw would linger in my mind for years to come.

Directly below my window was a man's body, twisted and contorted in the most bizarre fashion. He was lying in a vast pool of cheery-red blood. The LAPD coroner was hovering over the man, and I saw him poke a meat thermometer into the guy's stomach. I watched from above with curiosity as the coroner and a couple of detective-types rolled the man over. His face was completely flattened and looked somewhat like half of a freshly sliced tomato. Evidentially, he fell from the skid row hotel located directly adjacent my building and landed directly on his left cheek. How did this happen? Did he jump? Was he drunk and fell off the roof, or maybe even pushed off? It's doubtful I'll ever know. This poor soul's destiny was just one of countless tragic endings suffered by downtown L.A.'s wandering poor and homeless.

The movers' truck pulled into the loading dock at the rear of our building and parked next to the coroner's van. I had spent most of the previous day plastic wrapping the pieces to be shipped to New York. We exited the freight elevator, my pieces freshly wrapped in shiny, clear plastic and carefully began loading them into the truck. Simultaneously, the coroner's crew lifted the corps, which they had ever so diligently wrapped in clear plastic, into their van. I glanced at the colors showing through from behind my plastic, and then over to the starkly similar color pooling within the deceased man's wrappings.

At that moment, it occurred to me that this man and I lived in the same geographical location and time in history. I reflected on both the similarities and differences of our lives and realized that his hopes and dreams had tragically ended as mine were just beginning.

http://jackreilly.com

Chuck Feesago

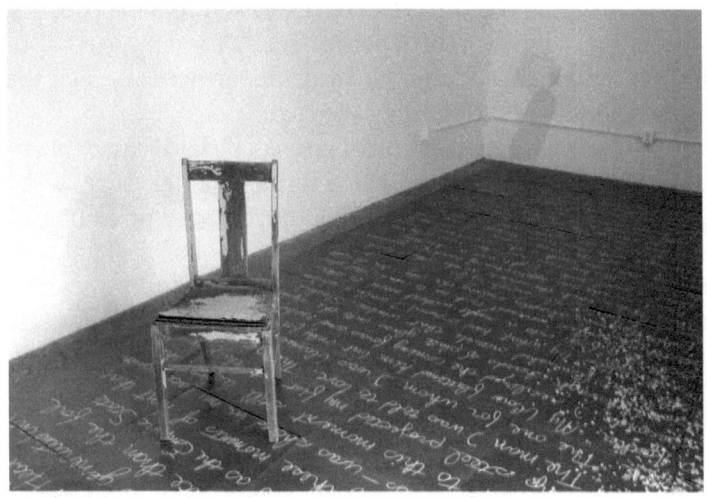

A Night Not Far Enough Away

Twisted mangled mess. The reel had been buried less than a year when this evasive mass of kinks, knots and broken ends formed and consumed the remains of normal for all. No one person — sister — mother — father — would or could extend help in any manner because of this entity's chaotic immensity. It had become my responsibility - my curse - my fault this entity existed and could not find resolution. Heat was pattern, normal and constant. It was generated over something with no more presence than the foil from a gum wrapper but presented as the Empire State Building. It was within one of these moments of heat that the entity – twisted mangled mess – was shoved in my face, igniting a reaction that to this moment still astonishes.

The glint of sharp steel projected my fist into the face of my aggressor. The man I was told to love. The person I hated to love. The one for whom I was blamed for making him a father. My blow flattened him, but only for seconds. In those seconds I realized the coming forces and hurled my body and soul through shards of plate glass into the spiny bed of thistle that flourished outside that window. Slashed, stinging and baffled by what had occurred, I walked. Walked into the cool of a fog, into a night without moon or stars. The long stretch of aimless movement took me to roads that spliced through the fields of grain abruptly ending the city.

In the midst of blackened green, officials searching for answers halted my passing. Three times, each the same as the other – harsh light in face, hands in the air, application of handcuffs, questions - something about a pool hall, a fight, and a shooting. Questions of who I was, where had I been, where was I going were answered skimming over truth with correctness. I was not that person. I was not the blame — release.

I found myself at the airport, lit bright with clean lines. Though a haze still hovered outside, a glass of water settled what was left of turmoil. Cherishing each sip, I felt I had nothing. But not the kind of nothing I had expected. It was the moment of realization that the entity was not. It was nothing. I had begun to see beyond those twisted moments, those mangled patterns, those endless afflictions of mess. The glint of steel, shards of glass and spiny needles had severed that entity, that great mass of destruction. I had something I could touch, hold in my hand and give meaning. I could feel. I had presence. I was my own.

http://feesago.com

Laura Larson

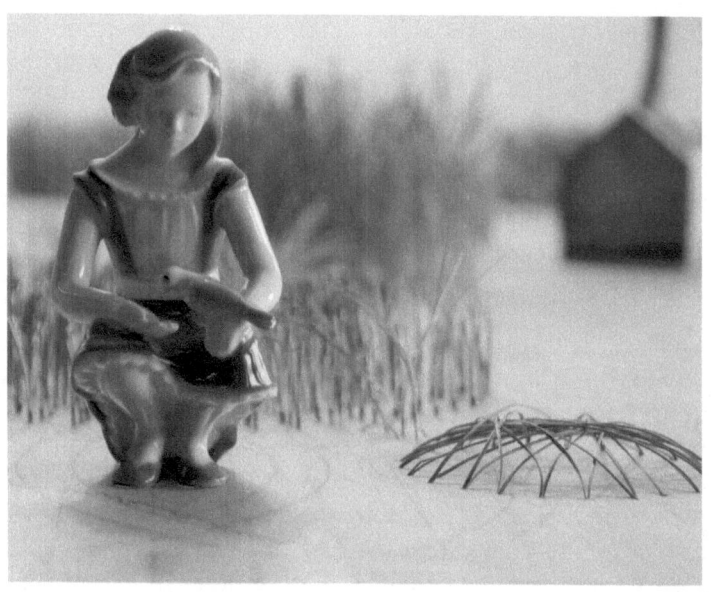

When I was in the 3rd grade living on the north side of Chicago, my parents decided to move to the suburbs. They said they wanted to have a home of their own with a backyard. It would have a garage for two cars so Mom could learn how to drive, and a basement we could make into a "rec room" for parties. Well this was pretty exciting to me. What an adventure to move out to the country. Every Sunday after church Mom, Dad, my sister Adrienne and I would pile into the Chevy and drive out to the suburbs to see our house being built. The whole housing development was called Brickman Manor. It sounded grand. They were building it on the footprint of an old farm.

There were several options for the type of house you could pick. There was a swanky split–level, and variations on the ranch house theme – 3 bedrooms, 2 bathrooms, a living room, dining room and a kitchen. We decided on the ranch house with the big picture window in the living room and bricks just half the way up the front of the house. We painted it yellow and gave it a blue roof, because those were Swedish colors and we were from Swedish stock.

The first time we drove out to see the progress on our house it was just a hole in the ground. In fact there were lots of holes in the ground – one for each home to be built. When it rained it got real muddy. But before we knew it there was a concrete foundation. The weather was changing and it started to snow and then it got really cold. One weekend my parents said my sister and I couldn't go because it was too cold. Adrienne and I were really disappointed when they told us later that the floor had been installed and they had a square dance on it. What?!

Gradually the frame went up and walls got built. Next thing I remember is that it was summer and the house was built and everything in it was brand new. I was so excited to move into this brand spanking new house. But I wasn't able to right away because I had to go to camp. No matter, I was having fun at Camp Augustana in Wisconsin, swimming in Lake Geneva, singing songs by the campfire, sleeping in the dorms on bunk beds, catching fire flies. Fun, that is until I managed to pull the cap off of my tooth with the slowpoke sucker I was eating, which exposed the nerve in the my broken tooth…Ouch. So Mom and Dad had to come and get me and take me back to the brand new house (and the dentist).

I loved the house. I loved the neighborhood. I loved riding my bike all over and exploring each new house as it was built, doing daring things like walking on planks over 10 foot drops and clambering in over windows to see all the potential of a new house, seeing how the space appeared to change as things were added. It felt like it all belonged to me – knowing secrets about the houses that the owners didn't even know, like what they looked like inside the walls.

Over where the new grade school would ultimately be built there were remnants of the old farmhouse. Adrienne, our friend Patty Rieman and I liked to play over there. Old concrete walls were angled so that it reminded us of caves – even the cartoon house that Fred Flinstone lived in. So here we were having our best time playing "Flinstones" when Paul, one of the neighbor boys came by and decided to throw rocks at us. Of course we had to defend our territory so we declared WAR on him. But we told Adrienne to get down because she was just a little girl and we wanted to protect her. The rock throwing went along fine for a while but eventually one of the rocks hit someone – ME – smack in the middle of my forehead. Apparently the head bleeds A LOT .

As we started back home Mrs. Serra, from the neighborhood saw me with my bloody face and called my Dad. WOW, I'll never forget the sight of him, all 6 foot 5 inches running fast on those spindly legs through the neighborhood's back yards (still unfenced). He grabbed me up and rushed to the car piling in with Mom driving fast to the Emergency Room to see what was what. (Adrienne didn't go – remember she was too young.) Ok, so it was just 3 stitches. I thought it felt like putting a pink roller in my hair and pulling it real tight. It was worse when they took it out…more time for anticipation and apprehension.

After the "Flinstone Incident" lawyers started showing up, just to make sure no one was going to sue I guess. I didn't play over by the old farmhouse anymore, but I still rode my bike around. Each year I went farther and farther as there were more and more houses being built, until finally there was no more room for new houses. All the land from the old farm was used up and now there was not only a "Brickman Manor" but also a "Camelot." Of course their houses were bigger.

http://www.larsonart.net

Irina Logra

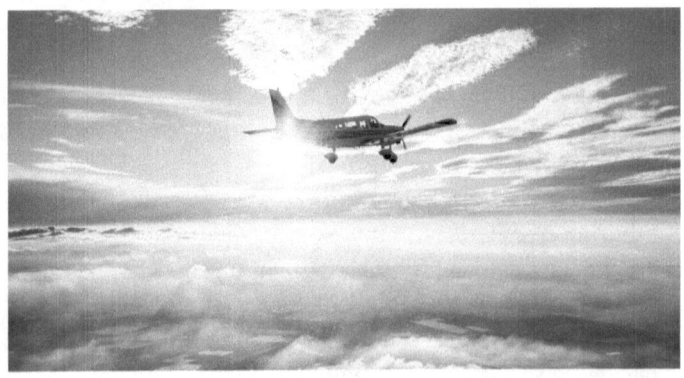

Some Americans might think that I am not very smart. During conversations, I can look very serious even while they are making brilliant jokes. Sometimes, it takes me several seconds to respond and the strong vertical sign of thinking on my forehead is not helping me to look any wiser. Do not judge my brainpower by my hilarious facial expression, let me tell you what is going on inside this head.

First of all, I'm not a native English speaker. Second, I'm lazy (but I'm trying to fight it, and have only been sporadically successful.) Depending on the topic of conversation and the presence of local slang, I can understand up to 99.9% of an English language conversation. Usually when I hear some unknown word, my brain just immediately skips it and continues listening. When the word is crucial for understanding the conversation, this is when all the fun begins. My mind grabs the word and transports it through a web of convolutions right to the place where rarely-used and thus forgotten stuff is stored. This storage is located somewhere in my deep unconscious and, with an average nerve conductance of 2 miles per second, it takes about a half of a second just to get there.

Once the word arrives to this dusty warehouse, a dilatory filing clerk takes it and, using a one finger typing method, begins to type it into a local Office Access database. The speed of the process is a bit slow. Afterall, the computer was manufactured and assembled in the 80s, when there were no Pentiums, no SSD hard drives, and no cloud storages.

Somewhere out there the conversation is still progressing, and my anxious mind begins to hasten the clerk, sometimes even using colorful phrases dotted with curse words, half Russian and half English. This old, reliable, and effective method changes the situation completely, and the results usually pop out in milliseconds.

There can be two types of results: the word is unknown, or the word is known and the definition can be found at section X, shelf Y, row Z. If the second scenario wins out, then tiny mechanic elves, well-polished shiny bugs with transparent sparkling wings, immediately fly to the listed destination and bring the word's definition to the reception table. It takes approximately seven elves to deliver ten letters of explanation and the whole process usually lasts about another half a second.

The way back to the surface of the conscious is usually ten times quicker, as my mind has lost the narrative line completely by this point and resides in the severe panic. It uses all emergency tools to accelerate the speed, including Nitrous Oxide Systems and nuclear reaction.

With all these scientific achievements, the whole process usually lasts about 2 5 seconds. Several tortuous shameful seconds during which my brain works faster than the speed of light and more selflessly than a Japanese kamikaze, but even then I still may not be able to understand you completely. Does it mean that I am not intelligent? I think it means that I haven't read enough English books and haven't watched enough TV shows yet. So I'm out for the day with my Kindle and Netflix. Please, do not call me slow. My shiny mechanic elves are tiny and sensitive creatures.

http://lographoto.com

Karen Kinney

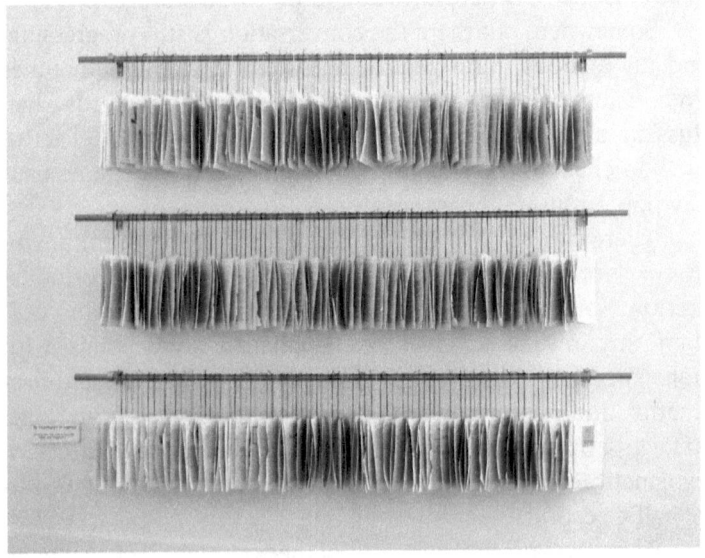

Ah. This morning my whole body is sore. Like, sore in places I didn't even know could be sore. The reason for this is an exercise class I took with a friend yesterday evening. A "core fusion" class. I figured, hey, strengthening the core can't be bad, right? But first, you need to understand something about exercise classes in LA. Sure, you get some normal people showing up. But you also get the "I will never age, I am super-human-woman who will continue to sculpt my body religiously until I'm in a wheelchair" kind of person. This is so not me. I mean, sure, I'm all for trying to be in decent shape. But sculpted perfection has never been on my radar, ever. I think I'm just too lazy for that kind of quest. And I'm also not into wearing the accompanying super skimpy workout outfit that will be sure to show everyone how awesome my body is.

But anyway, knowing this reality about LA and exercise, I still went, thinking maybe it would be something I'd be able to get into, that I'd develop some strength in the process and get a bit more in shape. And wow, this class was probably the hardest, most excruciating class I have been to in a really long time. I kept looking at the clock hoping it would end soon, because I couldn't remember if it was an hour or an hour and a half. Mercifully, it ended up being "just" an hour. Unfortunately though, my friend and I were positioned right in front of the instructor, which meant extra inspection of our form. This is the worst part for me of any class. Please, please do not inspect my form. I am fully aware it is not up to par. My muscles are almost non-existent. That's why I'm in this class. If I could really stretch my leg the way you're telling me to, I would. Trust me. All these thoughts swirled through my head as the instructor inched towards me, looking at me slightly disapprovingly, "encouraging" me to try "harder." I wanted to say, look, I am seriously trying as hard as I can and am probably about to pass out. Instead, I looked at her with a bit of fear in my eyes as I ignored my body's protests and attempted to make it do things it never knew it could do. Perhaps I tried a little too hard, which is why I can barely move it this morning.

So, the question now is whether I will return to this form of torture. Perhaps I will just lie here in bed and ponder it for a while. Maybe I will go eat a croissant or two and then go find a latte somewhere. I don't want to overly tax myself in any way today. I'm good at relaxation. Why can't there be a "how to relax" class in LA? I'd sign up for that. I'd even teach it. Let's just try to be as comfortable as possible...now there's a quest I can fully support.

http://www.karenkinney.com

Rob Grad

The End of the World, Lunchtime

The second time in my life I thought I might die, I was in Hawaii.

Hawaii is beautiful. Except when you're drowning. Technically, I guess it's still beautiful, but at that moment, you tend to be too busy to notice.

My girlfriend wasn't feeling well, so she stayed back to rest while my friend Jerry, our host for the week, took me to the beach for a swim. Jerry had a nice house and red hair.

Outside of Oahu being a visual slice of paradise, there was nothing special about the beach that day. The waves weren't big. There were no warnings. No flags or lifeguards with signs. No incoming storms. The water wasn't particularly choppy. It was just inviting and delicious. I saw a big rock a short way out near the wave breaks and I decided to swim over to check it out.

Usually the ocean is too cold for my skinny little chicken frame of a body, but in the tropical waters of Hawaii, I was fine. I figured I'd hang out on the rock for a few minutes and then swim back to the beach.

Sitting on that rock alone, I pondered heady thoughts about my life, where I had been, and where it all led from there. I took in my amazing surroundings and my dumb luck/good fortune to be in love and on this incredible vacation with my new girlfriend, considering I was totally broke, and the recent implosion of my once promising career as a young budding rock star.

After some interesting thoughts, but no conclusions about the state of the universe, I decided it was time to head back. I jumped in the water and started to swim. The sets of waves were crashing close together, but they weren't big and I didn't have far to go. I swam for a bit and came up to see where I was.

Nowhere.

I had drifted too far to get back to the rock, and I was no closer to the shore. I could feel my energy dwindling as I was treading water. Determined, I put my head down and swam some more. If I could just rest for a minute and catch my breath, I thought, I could easily make it back to shore. But the waves were coming in too fast. I kept trying. Nothing.

I started to get nervous, which quickly morphed into panic. I screamed out to Jerry on the shore to let him know I was in trouble. I saw him take his shirt off and dive into the water to come get me, but I knew he would be too late. He was too far away.

I looked up at the next wave bearing down and realized this was it. I wasn't going to have enough air in my lungs to stay under while it passed. And I'd get crushed if I tried to stay above the water. My aching legs were slowing down, heart thumping out of my chest. I was about to start swallowing water.

Then a thought crossed my mind.

I might drown now.

It was a calm, matter-of-fact thought. Simple and concise, with no fanfare or panic. An unemotional statement of fact. The scariest part was the buildup. Imagining what would happen, and afraid of how much I'd suffer. But with that one flash realization, it all disappeared.

In my moment of truth, I was okay to die. It was surprising.

Resigned to my fate, my body started to sink. Right then I felt the tip of my big toe scrape across something. I didn't know what it was, but I swung my leg back around to try to find it again. It was solid. Could it be?

Arching my head back to keep my mouth out of the water, I balanced the very tip of my toe on the top corner of the rock. It wasn't much to stand on, and the current kept trying to throw me off, but it was just enough for me to stop treading water and breathe. I could finally rest. Oxygenated blood flowed back through my limbs and everything relaxed.

After regaining a little strength, I took a deep breath, went back under and was able to propel myself through the current. When it was shallow enough for me to stand, I stopped swimming. My legs felt like tree trunks and could barely bend, but I managed to walk the rest of the way in. I'd had enough swimming for one day.

That trip to Hawaii was during one of the best periods of my life. Right before one of the worst. Which was right before another one of the best.

Life is a mess. I can make all the plans, check the tides, take every precaution and try to think of every outcome. Still, anything can happen. And usually does.

Things I remember about my trip to Hawaii:

1) The picture my girlfriend secretly took of my back while I sat on the porch staring at the landscape, holding a cup of coffee.

2) My friend and girlfriend's silence after watching the movie "Naked Lunch" at my suggestion when I said "Wasn't that amazing?"

3) Being in love.

4) Almost drowning.

5) Learning that it's possible when my time really does come, I might not mind.

http://www.robgrad.com

Susan Lizotte

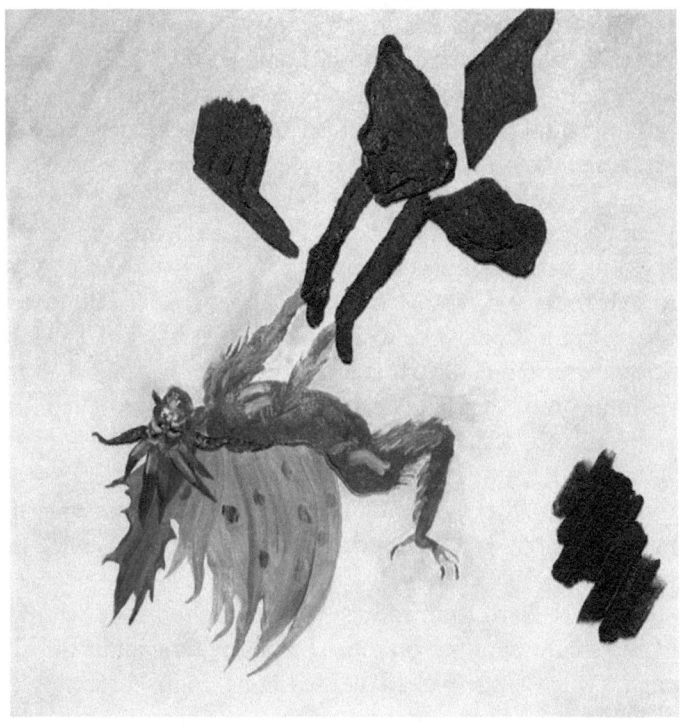

When my third daughter was 9 months old I was applying to preschool for her and on all of the forms was the question "what is your family health history". I was adopted as a baby and this question was really, really bothering me. My biological parents were 20 and 21 years old when I was born so I was fairly certain that they would be alive and I decided to find them and have all of the answers to my own personal questions. The facility where I was born had supplied "non identifying" information about my birth parents and it quickly became apparent to me that this was like putting a puzzle together. I was able to get most of the puzzle by myself, and after a visit to the actual facility I got the name and phone number of a woman who helps people like myself find their parents. I told her my story, even telling her how I was so tired of hearing my adopted mother tell anyone (and everyone) what a terrible baby I was. According to my adopted mother I was dressed in the finest baby clothes and walked daily in some beautiful stroller. The moment anyone looked into my stroller I would cry and scream uncontrollably. I've heard this story so many times and as I recounted it to the angelic woman helping me, she simply said "of course you cried, you were in mourning for your mother. Any face that peered into your stroller was the wrong person." I was struck by how wise she was and she also told me that this story meant that after I was born my real mother held me. She said "when you find her, ask her if she did hold you and I'm certain that she will say yes!" She called me back one hour later and she had my birth mother's phone number. She told me everything that had been written on my original birth certificate, which of course I had never seen. So now I had the names of my parents, addresses and my mother's number. I summoned all of my courage and called her that evening.

It was so hard to introduce yourself to someone who left you and might hang up on me. The phone rang and I heard a woman's voice as she picked up the phone. I introduced myself and told her where I was born. There was silence for several seconds, which felt like an eternity. When she spoke she said that she had been waiting for this call her entire life. I started crying, she started crying. She apologized and tried to explain why she had left me, why things were the way they were. There was so much to say. I asked if I could come and see her. She replied absolutely. I asked if she had held me after I was born, and she said yes and that I was taken away from her fairly quickly. So it was true, wow!

I flew to Green Bay two weeks later and she greeted me at the airport. I met her son and two daughters. My mother had brown eyes and brown hair and a very round face. Each one of my new siblings looked like a carbon copy of her. I however have green eyes and brown/blond hair and an oval face. My mother kept saying "you need to meet your father." I nodded, feeling pretty overwhelmed by so much sudden family.

My Mom drove me over to my real father's house after calling him at three o'clock in the morning to tell him that I was actually HERE in Green Bay. He took it in stride and as I got out of my mom's car I was immediately struck by the fact that I felt as though I saw myself in a mirror, only as a man version of me if that makes any sense at all. He had the same eyes, same hair coloring, same face shape and his thumbs even bent funny the way mine do. He smiled deeply and said "Jacqueline Marie I've been waiting so long to meet you."

http://www.susanlizotte.com

Debbi Green

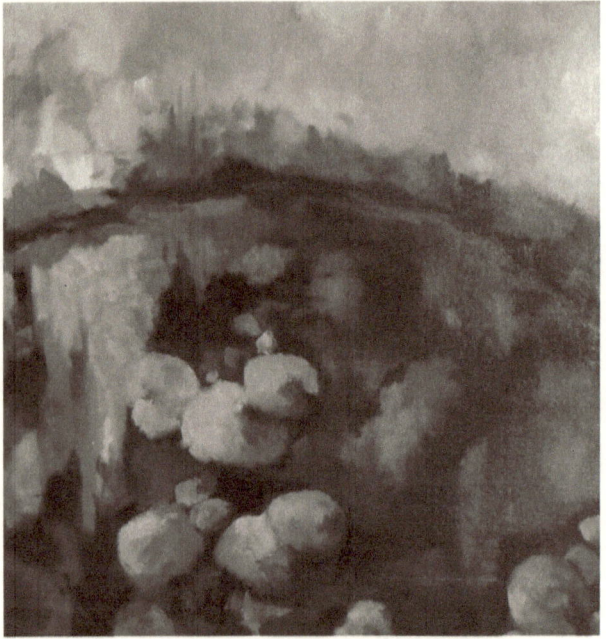

Earth Day; 24x24, oil

Debbi Green in 1969.

I am on a ship, about to go around the world for a year and get a year's worth of college credit.

I hadn't taken the time to meet a lot of the girls in my quarters. I was trying to get a handle on studying with so many distractions and not be pissed off that I left my lifetime friends home in Los Angeles.

Our first port was London. All the conversations were about shopping and going to Harrod's. I wanted to meet the locals and experience new adventures.

The first day was all about sight-seeing, Big Ben, the Square, etc. I knew the next day I would jump on a train and find something to write about in my journal. As I peered through the windows at each stop, I would know where to get off. A saw an old cemetery! Rye, a fourteenth century town! I was in. Or off the train in a flash.

The hillsides, the homes with thatched roofs, smiling people! As evening came, I found a tavern crowded with locals. I told them my story and we shared pints of ale. A couple of men kept asking me if I had a place to stay. Of course, I thought they were trying to pick me up, so I said I had a place. Suddenly, the place was empty. Everything closed up. 10 o'clock curfew…wish I had known.

I rang the bell on a few Inn's but no answer. I did feel safe but now it's starting to rain and I needed some shelter. Ah! I big red phone booth. I was settled in and then a giant spider came down on his thread and landed on my forehead. I was out of there! I walked a bit and found a grocery store front with an awning. I figured when the milkman delivered his wares in the morning, he would wake me and I would continue my journey.

Nope! Two Bobbies came walking down the cobblestone street. They questioned me and suggested I go with them. I thought I was being arrested and kepting saying "No, I would be fine." They finally convinced me that I could stay at the jailhouse and go on my way in the morning.

They gave me their umbrella and we walked to my first night in a jail cell. Each gentleman brought something to make me more comfortable….a bigger blanket and a cup of tea.

I woke the next morning to a bright shining day. Folded my blanket and brought it to the main office. The room was filled with men/Bobbies! They all stood as I sat down at the table. In the center were locally made pastries and hot tea! They all had questions and we had a good laugh about how I thought I was being arrested. I hugged each one of them and said I would learn the rules as I traveled through Europe and the world.

When I returned to the ship, everyone was showing off what they had bought so I didn't share my story with anyone. I could wait. My friends back home would love this story.

http://www.debbigreen.com

Gary Lloyd

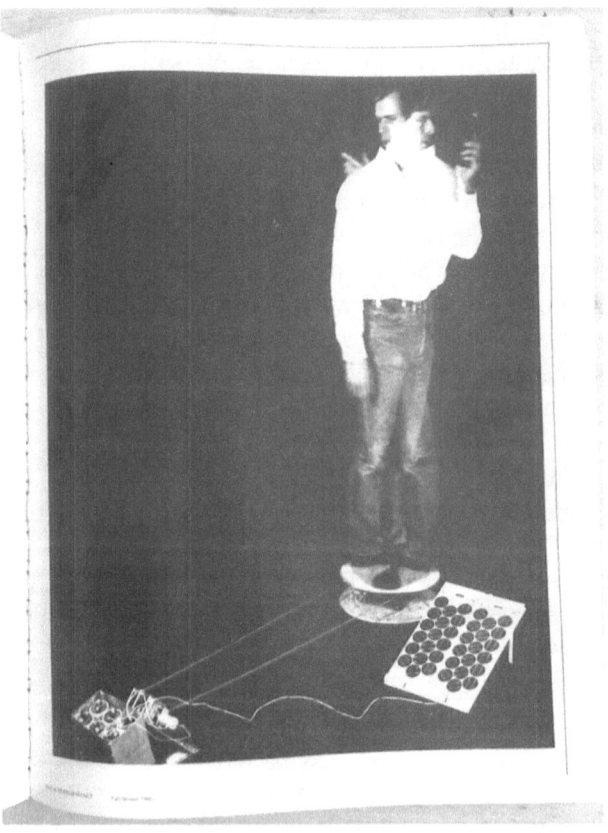

Me standing and spinning on the circular platform driven by a pulley, belt and electric motor and transmission powered by the first commercially available photovoltaic cells while using an early cell phone. Photo by Wenden Baldwin 1979

"No longer an outsider"

It is late January 1998 in Chacon, New Mexico and the snow is 32" deep on the vega by my home, the temperature is 11 degrees, no wind, there is a full moon with no clouds. My neighbor, Elizardo Romero, knocks on my door at 8pm very anxious with his two blue healer dogs prowling around him like wolves in heat!

"Dad didn't come home tonight and I'm really worried because he left on his horse at two to find his prized bull Felix in your upper vega and his tracks lead up the mountain and disappeared right after that!"

Having known Elizardo for many years we've become brothers and share everything so this is clearly an emergency. I saddle up my Morgan I've named Trails and and follow him on his saddle bred mare up the road on my land bundled up for the cold night with snow shoes, rope, GPS and an early cell phone, jerky, whisky, a gallon of water and fire starter, water-proof tarps, my 45, bear spray and a mini Med pack from the search and rescue team we both belong to. I make a quick call to Peter Vigil 4 miles away and tell him were headed out to my ridge to find Frank, Elizardo's dad, and Felix.

The moon thankfully lights our way as we carefully plod crunching the hard packed snow on my road that leads to the 9,578' ridge. At 8,500' Elizardo's horse won't continue and Elizardo's recently broken ribs won't let him travel another step further....he's beat after searching for two hours alone. We stop, make a fire and a covered triage teepee next to it so he can get warm while I search further on snow shoes since the snow is impossibly unsafe to plod through at 40" deep. We can hear wolves howling, not a good sign! I've packed bear spray and my service issue 1911 as well as a few flares and set my GPS to help me return to our triage station so I feel somewhat confident. I check my cell phone and have no signal so onward I go into the now colder night looking for Frank, Felix and snow shoe towards the sound of the moaning and yapping wolves. After a mile or so I finally see a faint light and call out to Frank. No response at all but the wolves suddenly stop which is not good! As I make my way into an old makeshift corral at the ridge I finally see Frank Romero curled up next to his horse with his faint flashlight glowing in the corner of the corral, unconscious with a badly broken left femur nearly protruding through his quadricep! Frank's breathing is shallow and he's way too cold. I count at least 6 pairs of eyes in the brightly moon lit night. They are prowling around about 30' from us so I light a flare and set it into a standing dead tree's fuzzy broken limb and set it on fire! This seems to cause the wolves some concern and partially diverts their attention away from the four of us. As I'm felling four aspens to make a travois I see that Frank's Bull is backed up against a big rock face defending himself. I put a lead on Felix and coax him away from his Boulder. After an arduous hour I've been able to construct a strong travois and attach it to Frank's horse. Loading Frank on to it takes another hour. All this time the wolves keep prowling around us occasionally testing me by closely running by me nipping at my Carhartt coveralls. The bear spray is totally ineffective and I finally have to resort to my 1911 and kill one! I hate killing any animal unless I'm going to eat it but this is survival so it's done and I haul the alpha male over to the area his pack has retreated to and hang him up on an aspen by his tail. Sadly I return to Frank on the travois behind his horse with the wolves whimpering and growling much further behind and snow shoe down the mountain totally exhausted. Suddenly I get one bar on my cell phone and dial my neighbor Peter Vigil who miraculously answers at 11:46pm. I give Peter our GPS position. He automatically calls two other search and rescue neighbors and the CHRISTUS St Vincent Regional Medical Center in Santa Fe, New Mexico. I continue down the mountain another 300 yards to our triage where Elizardo waits with a booming and very welcome fire that has by now attracted three neighbors who've just made it up the mountain to him. We drink whiskey and Frank murmurs something in Spanish that my neighbors laugh at uproariously but Frank's breathing is very shallow by now and his left ear is frozen solid along with most of his left hand turning that frostbite blue no one wants to see. Within 50 minutes we hear the chopper from Santa Fe near by and set many flares in circle an open vega near us where they land and evacuate Frank with Elizardo back to Santa Fe while the rest of us retrieve Felix, our gear and horses and return to my home where at least 25 men, women and my boys are waiting with hot chili verde, atole' and whiskey. In a few hours Elizardo calls to say that Frank is ok with a set leg, and amputated left ear and two left fingers. The patron of Chacon, Elias Trujillo, takes me aside and says, "Until now amigo you have been an outsider but now you will always be one of us. You will never lack for support whenever you need it my brother!"

It is the highest honor I've every received.

(no website available, please do an internet search for information on the artist.)

Sierra Pecheur

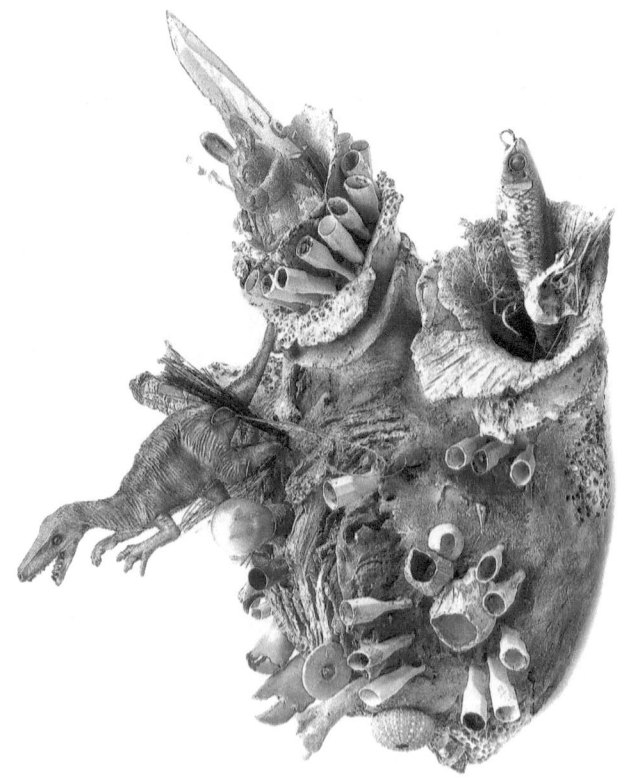

Oncoming Headlights

The sweet whiff of decay, so slim it might be a mouse or a slightly feathered baby bird, is almost as homey as a sliver of skunk roadkill, momentarily breathed in through the car window.

The child's perfect parental conflict story: on a road trip there is a dead rabbit by the side of the road; maybe they even see the rabbit hit. Mom bursts into tears and dad chants, "See the dead bunny, clap hands, clap hands."

I remember mists on summer beaches, the only footprints my brothers and mine. We kick the mist like dry ice smoke and do whatever crosses our minds–slide ice plant slopes on card board boxes, squat and hold our noses to examine dead seagulls, fish, or seals. This is before the time when there had to be a point or even before the pure desolation or sheer freedom of no point at all.

I find comfort in the sweet fat sound of gum cracking, mouth closed, the interior pop. I can't whistle through my fingers, snap them, or wink with that "You're the one. It's okay, we're in this together." Quite possibly, I think, my step mother wants to break my spirit but she can't. However, I damn near did it myself later on. Or maybe memory is a lie and I am creating mythology. In defeat we leave foot prints for those behind to use, the mistakes, without which, I am blind.

Last week I saw "My Life In Plastic." A young, penniless actor, unable to find work or pay the rent, signs up for Tupperware sales training. He completes the course, sure that this is one more humiliating actor's test. His Mum leaves a message on his machine, "Listen, Jeff, sell Tupperware as one of your characters. Why not Ceil?" Jeff Sumner, a consummate, comedic story teller says, "I can't do that. Ceil would never sell Tupperware." Then, as he fixes supper, non-stick frying pan in one hand, non-stick spray in the other, he finds the words PAM TEFLON. Maybe Pam could sell Tupperware. She has a blond wig with bangs and bob, a cross between geisha and thatched hut. She is fearless, brazen, no constraints.

Pam loves Tupperware, loves Tupperware history–Mr. Tupper patented the "burping seal," distinguishing it from competitors. She loves Tupper's "Wonderlier Bowl." She loves Tupperware events, parties at peoples houses, and business. Two men, whose girlfriends dragged them to one of Pam's parties and had no intention of buying anything so ridiculous, bought and bought big. Pam seduced them with her hard, charismatic, and hilarious sell.

Pam takes over his life. Jeff goes into therapy. Pam is the one who gets the phone calls. All the messages on his machine are for her. He's losing himself as Pam performs fearlessly, ecstatically, as Pam becomes the Pacific Region Sales Champion. He was right. Ceil would never sell Tupperware.

But Pam is brilliant. He has entered the theatrical world. He sits on a little stool, hands clasped between his knees and swings himself from side to side. Excruciatingly, he flings himself into the traffic of opinion, just as the fawn that ran towards my car years ago on a Pennsylvania country road as I raced for the Trenton train station and work in New York. It ghosted up out of a mirage, frail legs flying like the tassels on Omar Sharif's camel in "Lawrence Of Arabia." The fawn stuck in the middle of the road, head up, eyes popped wide, unable to change course. I stopped, got out, and steered it into a field of baby corn. I just made the train.

Now I make different runs to work. I take Kato, the dog, for a walk. Kato, part Chow, gun-metal grey like a werewolf with little, grizzled cheeks. I've known him for nine years, since he was two. He could barely swallow and was starving. The vet said he was a walking dead dog. I cooked chicken with rice, and garlic, and fat–lots of fat so the food would slide down. I saved his life. He does silly little paw tricks, reaching out as I come up the walk. Calling him Flower Poosh, and Snerk Katerk, I am fearless in my love for him.

The fearlessness Jeff Sumner dares in public, is the risky gift we have to give at any age. Before we become unidentifiable human remains in the inexorable move from toddler to kid, to youth, to adult, to middle age, to creaking ancient, our lives thread into the tapestry, each one a warp or woof of the time we were the knots, woven and unwoven. All of it exists, out in the universe, floating into our minds and hearts. The brilliance we don't know we have, the sadness, joy, fear, intelligence, the leap of abandon, fawn legs flying.

On my way home a blind man crosses Barrington holding his cup of 7-Eleven coffee, tapping with his red-tipped stick–fearlessness again. At home there is star jasmine, rosemary, lavender, mint, roses, and three times a year lime blooms. I sniff in the early morning cool. Usually, I have to yell at my cat Portley to stop clawing the wing backed chair. It goes like this: I wake, I lie in bed and run cobalt light, like gumball spirals, around the people I love, I yell at Portley, I get up, open the front door, stand behind the screen and sniff. Like childhood mornings of footprints, and mist, and dead things, and ice plant slides, I am pleased for no particular reason.

http://www.sierrapecheur.com

Linda Zigman Kosoff

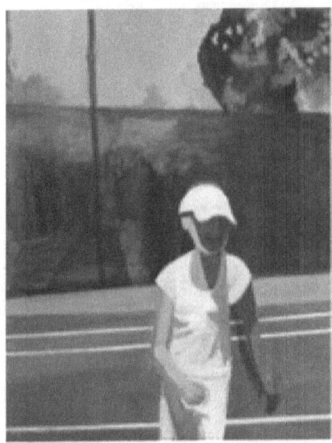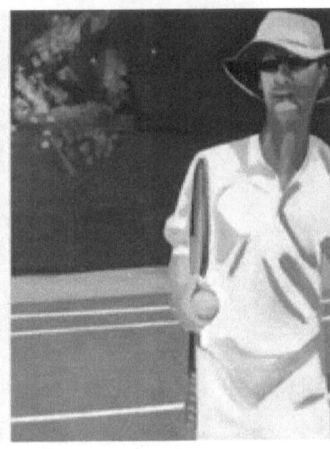

Growing up on Walden Street in Newton, Massachusetts, I had always been shown old photographs of myself, my older sister, and my younger sister, in our other home; our first home. My parents' first house was quite a step up from where they had grown up. They were able to buy a single-family house in Avon, MA, in a new development, in the suburbs of Boston, with other young families. They were able to get away from the small, three-family house in which they were raised. I lived in their first house until I was three years old. Then we moved to a more desirable city where the school system was highly regarded. With my dad working as a draftsman at Raytheon Corp. and my mom working as an elementary school teacher in the Boston Public School system, they were able to afford a two-story Colonial-style home on West Newton Hill in Newton.

I was shown so many photos of myself at the Avon house that I don't know if I have actual memories from that time, or if I think I have memories because of all those photos. Many pictures are of us kids in the knotty-pine basement. My dad fixed up the basement all by himself and was always very proud of it. As the years went on, he became very sentimental about his knotty-pine basement. He would tell everyone the story about how he never had done anything like that before, and how his neighbors showed him what to do and so he went for it.

I remember photos from our birthday parties and visits with our cousins down in that basement. I remember photos of my younger sister, my younger cousin and I on a couch and my sister always falling sideways. She was barely a year old and could not hold herself upright yet. My dad would always point out the knotty-pine panels that he put up over the unfinished basement. Knotty-pine was the 'in' thing in the early 60s and the fact that he did it himself gave him a lot of pride. No doubt he wanted to impress his wife, his mother-in-law, and his parents. Later in life when he reminisced, he wanted to impress his daughters. And he did.

When my dad was eighty three years old he was diagnosed with a glioblastoma that was terminal. My mom had passed away two years before from Pancreatic cancer.

I had been living in Los Angeles for the past thirty plus years and visited my dad every month since his diagnosis. I don't know who had the idea to go to visit the old house in Avon, but we decided to go and visit. As my dad would say, why not? When we drove up Packard St. my dad became happy and was naming all the people that had lived in the houses; our old neighbors. They all sounded so familiar since I had heard about them all of my young life. We came to our old house and we both just stared at it from the car. My dad seemed happy to see it. He wanted to get out of the car and see if anyone was home. He was noticing the new garage that was added onto the side of the house. We rang the door bell but no one was home. He wanted to show me more so he boldly walked around the other side of the house and showed me where the basement entrance was--where he had painted a big letter 'Z' (for Zigman) on the outside door that led down into it. The 'Z' was no longer there.

The owners arrived home soon after and my dad had no problem introducing himself as the first owner of their house. He told them the whole story and mentioned the knotty-pine basement. They asked us to come in and see the house. It was all so strange. I felt like I knew the place because of all the photos I had seen and been in. But when I was in the house, I remembered nothing. It was so small. They showed us the downstairs where the basement was. The knotty-pine had been updated with sheet rock and painted white walls. They said there had been a big water leak years ago and their son, who was in construction, fixed it for them. My dad said it looked great, but I knew he was sad that his pine panelling did not exist any longer in the home, in our other home; in his first home.

http://www.lindakosoff.com

Diane Pirie Cockerill

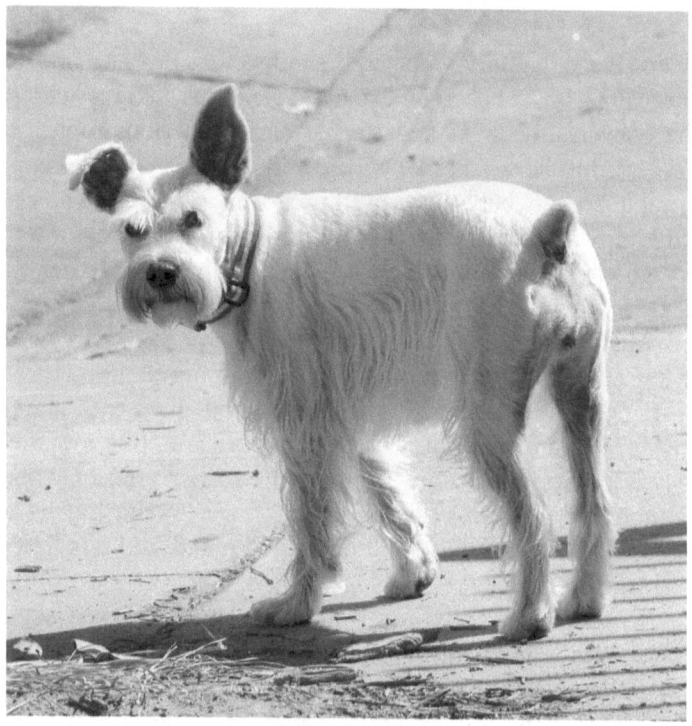

Camp

Through carefully orchestrated conversations and determined avoidance, a friend kept me in the dark about her life for close to forty years, but it was one afternoon three years ago when I finally heard her story, giving me a glimpse of a life well lived but filled with shadows of historic proportions.

Years ago, I answered an ad in a local newspaper placed by an advertising company manager, looking for a paste-up artist and offering a fair salary plus the magic words, "Will Train."

I interviewed, got the job and stayed for three wonderful years. My boss, a sharp, no-nonsense yet quite personable woman named Neko, ran a tight ship. We all adored her.

An offer from another ad agency prompted my resignation but Neko and I parted ways on wonderful terms with promises to keep in touch.

I kept this promise and met for lunch, once a year, for 36 years. Every January we shared sandwiches, desserts and tea and caught up on each other's lives. Neko insisted on keeping the conversation light and steered clear of serious topics, so I deferred to her wishes. She lived with her husband in a comfortable home where they raised their three children, who also led happy and productive lives. After a couple of hours, we'd say goodbye, hug, and look forward to our get-together the next year.

Fast forward a couple of decades and we were once again sitting at Neko's dining room table, reminiscing about our years of friendship, and her retirement years now filled with grand- and great-grandchildren, and teaching origami. She inherited the skill of origami from her mother and her creations were extraordinary. During this particular lunch, Neko looked at me, looked away then took a deep breath and said "It's time I told you my story."

Neko's father and grandfather came to the United States from Japan around 1920, leaving wives and family behind while they got the lay of the land. After settling in Phoenix, they sent for the mother and grandmother and established a vegetable farm to begin their American saga. Born in 1926, Neko and her family lived in a tiny house that had no electricity until she was in the 8th grade. The family managed to grow many varieties of vegetables on their small farm. The grammar school was conveniently located down a dirt path but high school presented a problem as it was many miles away and her family could not afford a car. A kind teacher offered to pick them up every day so Neko and her siblings were afforded a junior and high school education. Students who earned straight As would receive 15 cents a week, enough for a 10 cent hamburger and 5 cent Coke. Neko received the 15 cents almost every week. During her 9th and 10th grade years, she was a model student, her family thrived and life was relatively uneventful.

But, they were Japanese.

It was the 1940s with the world at war. One day, Neko didn't show up for school and her classmates did not know why. Her family had been given only two days to pack what they could carry. There was no room for anything personal, only clothes and shoes. The truck came to take them away, and with dignity and grace, the family boarded the bus for Camp. As the truck pulled away from their family home, Neko looked out the back window to see her dog frantically running down the dirt road chasing after them. I cleared my throat, dried my eyes and her story continued.

Camp. An odd word. Stuck in the middle of the Arizona desert, barrack-type buildings were built with no heat or air-conditioning – just dust, wind, confusion and faces of desperate people longing for the American lives they'd left behind. Neko's father, who had never cooked a meal in his life, was told he would be a cook and, fortunately, was allowed to bring any leftovers back to his family. Her mother was a waitress and seamstress, who sewed kimonos. Neko graduated after her two final high school years then worked as a seamstress, too. No books were provided and she said she missed this activity the most. What a harsh reality, watching her parents work so hard and listening to all the other campmates complain. Years of the desert's blistering heat, cold and wind left many of her family and friends weak but always hopeful.

The nightmare ended abruptly, four years after her family arrived at Camp. Buses came to take families back to Phoenix. Shortly, Neko moved to Los Angeles in the Little Tokyo neighborhood to live with other Japanese girls. She sewed all day, to make money to send back to her parents and kept some for herself so she could start her own American life. She met a very nice man on a blind date, married him, and had three children. They managed to buy a house in Culver City, California in a neighborhood bordering celery fields. It was a neighborhood where Japanese were allowed to live but three blocks north were still off limits. When her children were older, Neko went to work in the advertising company where we met.

This lovely woman related her story without a hint of bitterness. She ended our long lunch by giving me of one of her origami creations and thanked me for listening to her! I was speechless, moved, angry and struggling to understand all I had heard. To this day, I have Neko's origami creation on my desk to remind me of her profound story of strength, determination and acceptance

http://www.dianecockerill.com

Linda Sue Price

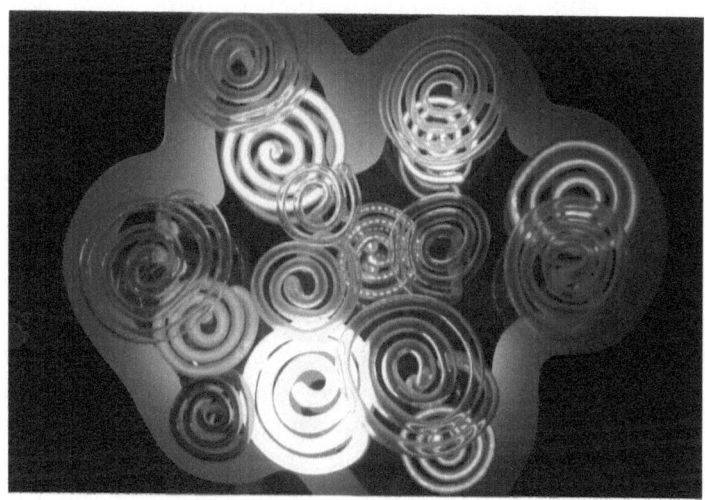

Focus on the Light

About fifteen years ago I was feeling funky—really stressed and arthritic. I didn't like what was going on so I decided to restart my yoga practice. I committed to doing one yoga class a week for a year. After class I was so relaxed I thought I would fall asleep driving home. I found that for each hour I did yoga I got two extra hours of energy. After three months I began doing two classes a week and eventually three. I was doing it for the physical energy I was getting. Then after about a year the benefits of meditation started to kick in. I would drive to my yoga class upset about one thing or another. By the end of class, my mindset changed. The things that were upsetting no longer bothered me. I don't think of myself as a meditator but as I learned yoga was developed as an aid to facilitate the meditation process.

As the meditation effects deepened I discovered what I call the 'pause button.' One day I was having a confrontation with a co-worker. Normally, my emotions would escalate but this time was different. I had an out of body experience where I began watching the two of us. I wasn't responding to my co-workers emotions but instead I was observing them. The changed dynamics caused my co-worker to calm down. I was amazed. A few months later it happened again with another co-worker. This co-worker seemed to like to provoke in order to get attention. Something happened that upset me. Normally I would have charged into that person's office and had a confrontation. This time I considered my options and decided that a confrontation would take more time than I was willing to give because whenever you had a conflict with this person it wasn't a simple conversation. It would become a discussion that lasted for days. My choice to not confront changed the dynamics in this relationship. Eventually the provoking behavior stopped.

After this second incident I realized something had changed in me. It seemed that when I found myself in a stressful situation instead of reacting, I would pause, think and then choose my reaction. I wondered how this had happened and then I overheard someone in my yoga talking to the instructor about how her mental space had changed. She had been doing yoga for about eighteen months—just like me. When she described her new mental space it could have been me talking. That is when I realized I was experiencing the meditation effects of yoga. Since then I have learned that I can say almost anything to anyone if I stay calm.

The next thing I discovered was learning how to stay in the moment. I went through several traumatic events in the ensuing years that gave me huge opportunities to develop this practice. And unfortunately, it is a practice. Even though I've been doing it for over ten years, if I take more than a week off the old behaviors start to creep back in and I start edging towards funky again. So I continue my yoga practice now not only for the physical benefits but also the mental benefits and I value both.

http://www.lindasueprice.com

Carolyn Campbell

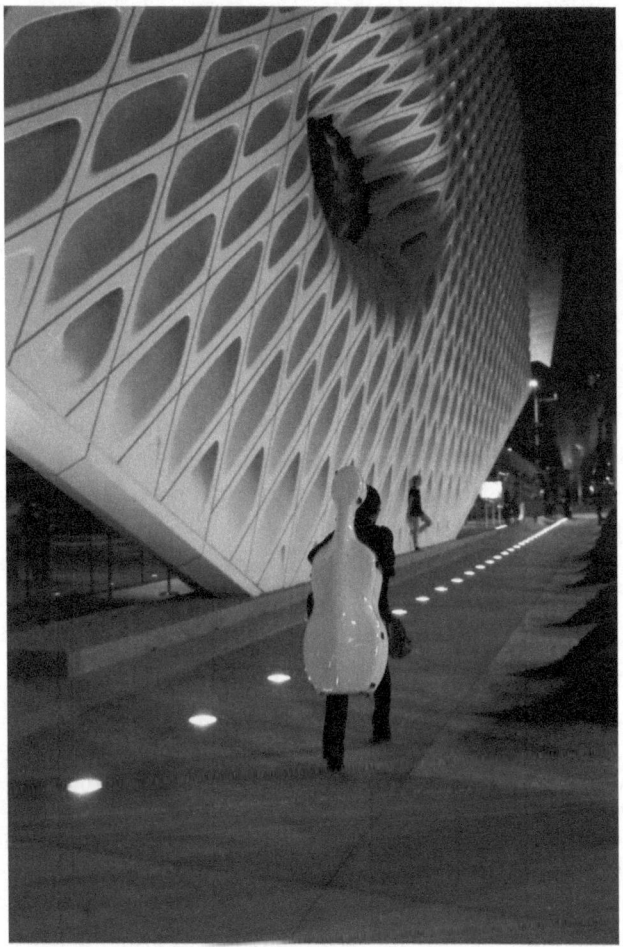

Champagne and Chicken Blood

A child of the sixties, I kept up a reckless pace well into the seventies, yet had no apparent consequences until the fateful day Robert, my travel agent called, "Carolyn, someone just cancelled their flight to Paris and I have a cheap ticket. Want to go?" I told my boss I needed a break and booked the trip.

That night I ran into a dear friend at a party and announced I was traveling to Paris for the first time. He said, "You must go to Père Lachaise Cemetery. It is home to more creative souls than any place on earth."

"Really, like who?"

"Well, your idol, Oscar Wilde, for one." I now had my first Parisian destination.

Over drinks the following night, I told, Jerome, a tall handsome grad student from Lagos with a sexy British accent I had been dating that I was off to the City of Light in a week. We both shared a passion for travel and he asked me, "Why Paris?"

"I'm going to visit Balzac and Colette. Many of my heroes are in a famous cemetery there."

He didn't share my excitement. Instead, Jerome lowered his head; he shot me a look of concern. "You must be very careful. There are a lot of unsettled spirits in a graveyard. You need safeguarding."

"You're kidding," I exclaimed, incredulously, "From what?"

He described a strange ritual that he wanted to perform on me. "It will give you a cloak of protection. Not all souls rest in peace."

At first, I declined. "I'm a big girl. I can take care of myself."

"Listen to me, Carolyn, seriously, you have to do this." I knew he meant it, so I agreed.

He launched into a list of what we needed: "A live chicken. We can go to Central Market tomorrow." I promptly volunteered to keep it on my back porch. What was I saying? Jerome continued: "Please get a roll of dimes from the bank and I will purchase bottles of champagne." He was adamant that we do this right away seeing as I was leaving soon.

The next day at my apartment, he asked for a knife and a bowl and explained he'd be drawing on me in blood. By the way, I needed to take my clothes off. My eyes rolled. What a convoluted ploy to see me naked.

After wringing the chicken's neck, he made a deep slice in its chest and squeezed a stream of blood into the bowl. I then heard the glub-glubbing of champagne being poured in the bathtub, followed by the plinking of dimes into the frothy mix. Dipping his fingers in the scarlet ooze he smeared my forehead, shoulders and arms with symbols. His touch was warm but the goo was sticky and revolting, not spiritual in the least. "Now please sit in the tub."

As I stepped into the tingly concoction, he poured champagne on my head and dropped coins over me, while reciting an incantation. The mood got serious when I closed my eyes and an electric sensation shot through my body. Jerome then abruptly announced, "We are finished. Please do not shower until this evening."

Ceremony done, we promised to keep in touch and he gave me a farewell hug.

Five days later, I arrived at Paris's Orly airport and headed to my hotel. Early the next morning, I picked up some flowers from a newsstand to leave as a memento at Oscar Wilde's grave and took the Metro to Père Lachaise. Inside the entrance gate, bordered by rows of stately granite crypts, I exchanged greetings with the guard.

So far, no signs of negativity, in fact, the entire cemetery appeared sweetly benign. The scent of floral wreaths and rich loamy earth filled the air. Edith Piaf's tomb was buried under a mountain of tributes. Similarly, Chopin's crypt was draped in ribbons of the French tricolor and lit with votives. Everywhere I looked there were sculptures symbolizing grief; female mourning figures, bats and skulls embellishing doorways to the afterlife. It was eerie, yet beautiful.

I found Oscar Wilde's tomb, a towering winged sphinx, and while reading the epitaph in his own words incised on the back, I heard the whisper of an Irish brogue in my ear:
"And alien tears will fill for him
Pity's long-broken urn
For his mourners will be outcast men
And outcasts always mourn."

Startled, I look around for the source, frighteningly, no one was there.

Toward dusk, I left the cemetery. Riding the automated people mover in between subway stations I leaned against the illuminated sidewall. Suddenly, I heard a loud crash. The fluorescent panel began to flicker. "Was it a power outage?" Within seconds, I heard loud male voices arguing and the treadmill began shaking under my feet. There was a young couple about 50' away. The man took a protective stance in front of the woman. I then saw three figures striding toward us.

I felt incredibly vulnerable; traveling alone at night with valuables in my purse. "What an idiot," I thought. Why hadn't I taken a cab?

A trio of skinheads: one sporting a Mohawk, another with shaved head and neck tattoos, the third in a greasy ponytail and skull earrings began shoving, then punching the young man. There were no police in sight.

The couple crumpled to their knees; the girl sobbing. The men laughed loudly then careened in my direction.

I steeled myself for the worst; imagined being battered, robbed and left to die in the underground. Who would identify my body? My breathing was shallow. I willed myself to disappear. The heavy steps of the men's boots made the flooring sway violently yet, I was oddly motionless. They were now alongside me; I felt their menacing energy and could smell their musky odor. Then, remarkably, their dark presence flew right past me.

Champagne and chicken blood. I had protection.

http:www.carolyncampbell.me

Martin Cox

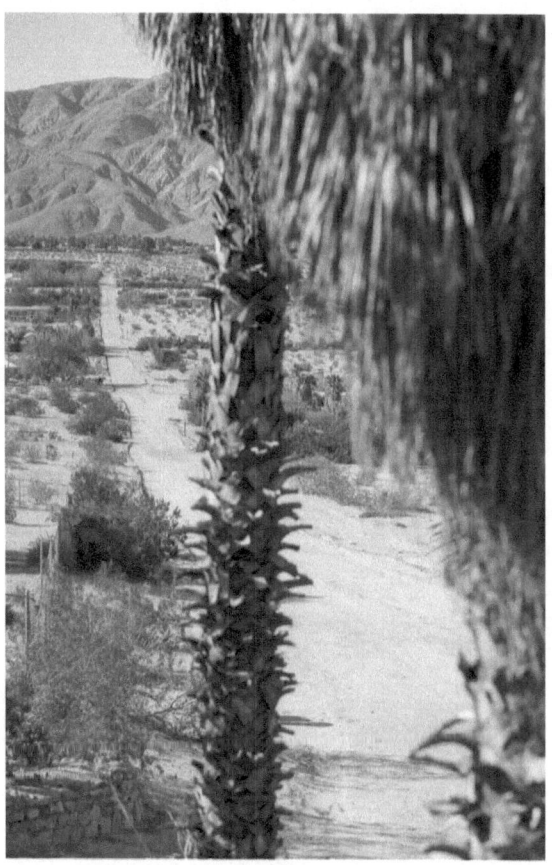

4:21AM in the Anthropocene

I read a review in the Los Angeles Times about a new book called *The Next Species: the future of evolution in the aftermath of man.*

    I bought a copy to take with me to read in the desert. I had been offered a house in Sky Valley while its owners were in the Britain.

I jumped at the idea of a mini residency, alone with my thoughts. My plans for the week were to explore, to take photographs, spend time in silence and catch up on some reading and drawing.

In the book, science journalist Michael Tennesen describes what life on earth could look like after the next mass extinction.

The house was located very close to the San Andreas fault, on the very edge of the North American plate where it rubs up against the Pacific plate. The home is perched on the side of a hill at the end of a very straight unmade road.

I read my book in the evenings after I had taken walks, photographed the landscape and drawn some pictures. The writer had interviewed a number of scientists who agree we are headed toward a mass extinction, perhaps in as little as 300 years.

The house had few neighbors and offered a long view far down the valley towards an oasis marked by hundreds of palm trees, a result of a geological faulting in the bedrock allowed water to rise to the surface.

In Los Angeles I live in a dense hilly neighborhood with noise and traffic, helicopters, music, people shouting and police sirens. Here, alone in Sky Valley there was an unfamiliar silence.

I read on… "Already there have been five mass extinctions in the last 600 million years".

"We can see some of the warning signs of another extinction event coming, as our oceans lose both fish and oxygen. In *The Next Species*, Tennesen questions what life might be like after it happens."

A coyote shrieked.

Before nightfall I had explored the oasis, noticing the stark contrast just outside the ring of trees and then the wild abundance under the palms where it was cool and damp, where birds, insects and reptiles lived and died. Even an incredibly rare lizard lives there, in fact it only lives at this oasis and nowhere else on the planet.

The book discusses the future of nature and whether humans will make it through the bottleneck of extinction. Could the conquest of Mars lead to another form of human?

Later that night, I was awoken by something shifting. An odd diamond shape appeared on the ceiling, it warped, vanished then reappeared. Stripes of light and dark slid across my view. My heart was beating fast in the silence.

Then a sound. What was it?

A humming, whooshing, and more shapes now climbing down the walls. I sat up.

The whole ceiling now stripped and gyrating in light patterns.

Suddenly I realized that the light was coming from outside the house. Terror grabbed me. I sat forward to see the source of the light from outside the bedroom.

It was a car. It was the headlights of a car.

A car was coming up the incredibly straight dirt road, the road that leads nowhere but to this house. I looked at the clock as if it would offer an explanation of the driver's origin or intentions. 4:21am it read blankly, in red numerals.

What to do? Hide? Get a weapon?

The engine revved as the vehicle made the grade up to the house. They were here now. I stood against the wall next to the window out of sight.

Just below the house, a car door opened, headlights still glowing. A figure was throwing something. A thud at the door. They had thrown something that hit the door. I remained motionless. I thought about extinction, of canyons, craters and deserts, of living on Mars, I thought of the lonely lizard, of living on the edge of the San Andreas fault, of humans living at the end of their era.

Suddenly the car was backing away, it turned, kicking up dust, reversing its direction, now red lights were moving away. Rapidly.

I stood at the window, looking out on the dark night, the two tiny red lights retreating towards the precipitous escarpments of the little San Bernardino mountains formed from sediment accumulated during the Paleozoic Era. The outline of deeply eroded mountains peaks made visible silhouetted by stars, the milky way arching upward from behind the horizon.

I opened the front door slowly. Palms rustled softly in the warm breeze; there on the step was a copy of todays Los Angeles Times.

http://www.martincox.com

Emily Halpern

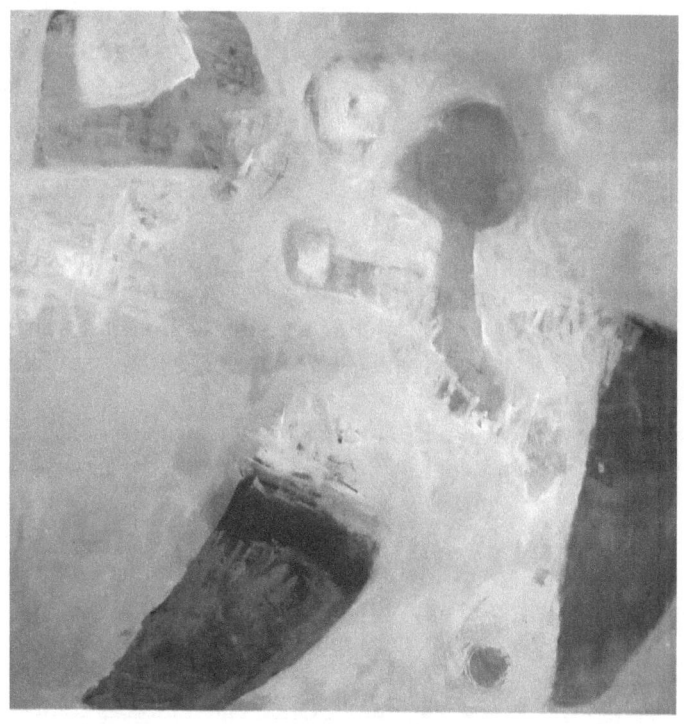

I've always been a curious observer of the world around me. One of my first memories in life was being in the seat on the back of my mother's bicycle at night. I noticed that as we moved, the moon did too- as if we were being followed by a large flashlight in the sky. And in observing things, it's not just the big things, but the little things that I like to examine. My Dad and I once went for a walk and knelt down to watch an ant hauling a dead insect many times its size. Another ant came along and tried to take the insect and in retaliation, the ant with the insect hurled what would be the equivalent of a log at the other ant. We were fascinated at the little drama taking part beneath us. The more you look, the more you see.

Now and then unexplainable happens- and these sorts of things happen to me when I'm in a relaxed state of mind, where images and thoughts appear and disappear in my mind. It can be little or it can be larger. I was once walking along a road, daydreaming, walking, daydreaming, walking and in my mind's eye, saw my eyeglass lens pop out- which then it inexplicably did at that very second. Another time I was waiting at a bus stop as a teenager. In my mind, I saw a car full of boys pull up and ask me if I wanted a ride- and in my mind I said yes- and then had the vague notion that something bad would then happen to me. I thought to myself- why on earth would you get into the car with them?! Say no! And at that very moment a car full of boys pulled up and asked me if I wanted a ride- and I shook my head no in shock. The latest thing to happen to me was being in a restaurant beside a family with about a fifteen year old daughter with Down's Syndrome. I thought to myself, wouldn't it be neat if another family with a teenage girl the same age with Down's Syndrome came along and sat down beside them and they didn't know each other? And that's exactly what happened. I wish I could heighten my intuitive senses and have more of these odd little instances.

I'm envious of friends of mine who have forms of synesthesia. I consider these friends slightly magical. For some, they see colors when they play music. Others taste food as colors or colors make sounds to them. My friend Dawn says some numbers are unfriendly and sharp to her while others are cheerful- they also have colors. She says the number seven is yellow and slightly aggressive while three is cuddly and blue. Other, slightly magical friends of mine can see calendars in their minds. My friend Roberto can tell me what day we first met eleven years ago and where and what I was wearing and can accurately recall every date since then that we met. He can recall dates without effort. Even if I don't have synesthesia or see calendars myself, having friends with these capabilities is an interesting window into a different world.

I'm also interested in what Freud called: Eros and Thanatos: the desire to live and the desire to die. Thanatos is a curious thing. It tells me to throw my purse off a ferry or jump off a bridge. Thanatos tells me to pull the person's hair in front of me at a movie theatre or jump up on the stage during a Broadway play and create havoc. Thanatos is a mischievous rascal alright. I don't do any of these things of course- but it's interesting to observe these little thoughts flowing in and out of my mind.

I rarely mention any of these things I've talked about to anyone except close friends. When I have talked about these things, people have misunderstood me and made me upset by calling me weird or dangerous- of which I'm neither. I'm just an observer in this world, trying to get a little closer to the strangeness and the mystery.

http://www.EmilyEHalpern.com

Greg Andrade

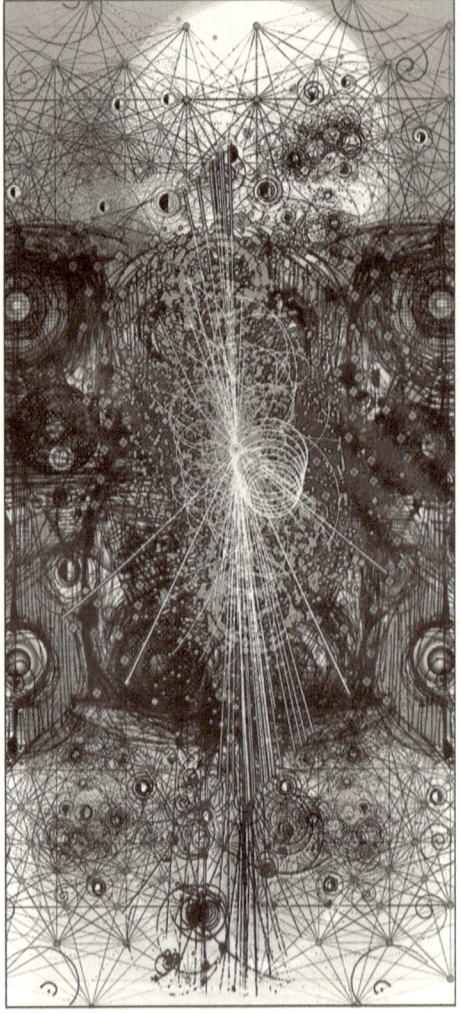

GOD PARTICLE

The brush clears and then you're left with
… Now what?
She left for the forest with her razor-sharp tongue in hand, flip-

ping and flapping and lashing. That very tongue has clear-cut many of the tallest, toughest of forest tree stands. So I leave as well, with my heart in hand still pumping though it seems a bit bland. I'm the type who always understands—creature comforts—but I was slowly becoming a creature of the meat-eating variety that began chewing up days one upon another. Maneaters whip as you toe the line until soon there goes the money and you're giving it away one piece at a time. My mojo had left the building and I ran screaming down the alley. No more playtime or fun with Dick and Sally. She broke me, or did we work together to make it happen? I wondered: Do I knock myself out to make it better? Should I be reaching deep into the abyss to find myself headed to Japan where niceness is like a disease, where a language barrier doesn't even matter?

Then came the car crash and I became completely or somewhat rested by the virtue of hospitalization—yes surely blessed, (Dude, I use to put it away without even getting rested) but the rile is faulty and slowly turned my life into bile—a loss of my best friend's life was in the balance and sniffer-snuffering around life's more rickety old dusty shelves only revealed more dust. I became one viewing all the other more mature adults trying to find themselves as I turn to the sad-ass reality that hits like bricks on the interior of the mind—I'd lost a friend and the fault was mine. There was no formula for success and I found it completely and utterly inferior to look to an upper typologically-advanced respected superior for relief—for guidance—so I suffered though the wretched wreckage of a mess that was mine. I realized this autonomy, too, held guilty secret hidden truths; no mentorship opportunities existed for one such a louse. There ain't no famous lives of brilliance left in homeland insecurities and there's no clairvoyance that was going to give way to some type of spinning top buoyancy. I had to balance the books myself and it took over twelve months to resurface. I found that nothing supersedes more notorious notions of erotic spanakopita over the shitty ingredients of the GMO whopper, beastly burger I had created for myself. There was no going home—ever. It would never be the same. I guess I'll have to book way up in cold ass Antarctica, I thought to myself. I'll chew whale fat up for supper, uncooked, like sushi-style hungry bear and I'll be out running down the street clad in only hole-ridden underwear while it's raining pain and agony up and inside and out over there. Nothing was clear but fearful, wet, soggy thoughts of the dowsing hell of loss and guilt.

I was pushing hard and feverishly fast on the panic ringer button bell with no one there to help—of course no one answered the phone anymore. I just had to fend for myself to open passion's door in order to live again. Plotting pushing punching growling demanding reality bears never ceased their demands and they scratched up all the fucking chairs. They didn't allow time to stop—no time and nowhere to sit, no resting allotted—no, not for even a fraction of a little bit. Eventually, I felt better and knew that I had better get going; got piles and piles and piles of stuff to do. I forgave myself, no time trying won't do, fading away ain't on the list of options. Today the days are forever always a bit poisoned, like a snake that has deadly fangs of serum that includes an antidote all at the same time. It's all hidden down in the pit of my throat and mentioned only once in a long while.

http://www.andradestudio.com

J.J. L'Heureux

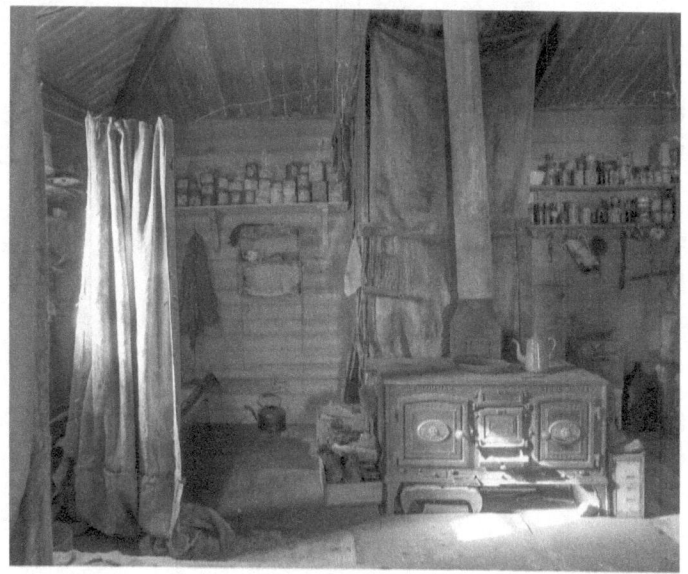

Sir Ernest Shackleton's Stove, inside Shackleton's Hut, Cape Royds, Antarctica

Expedition to Shackleton's Hut, Antarctica

I have an enthusiasm for the Southern Ocean and Antarctica. Many Antarctic summers I have the opportunity to be on an expedition to different regions and seas surrounding the continent. Except for the sounds of the rookeries and the wind, there is a complete absence of industrial sound or any suggestion of it. It is as if each scene has been encapsulated and frozen in crystal pure ice.

Visiting Emperor Penguin rookeries with crèches full of active grey chicks, watching Weddell Seals give birth on a beach surrounded by hungry Skuas and standing back while giant Elephant Seals battle over a harem are my early memories of Antarctica. I watch from the ship's bridge for the first iceberg to appear on each expedition while the Albatross glide past me.

Expeditions not only contain animals that are special to the continent but the history. With every visit I become aware of a story and another person from the age of exploration. An island, grave, whaling station and the historic huts where the men stayed during their expeditions introduce me to a piece of history I might have missed.

The Ross Sea has been my current focus for the past few years. It was named for the British Explorer James Ross who visited this location in the early 1800's. In the west of the Ross Sea is Ross Island where both Sir Ernest Shackleton and Robert Falcon Scott built their huts. Mt. Erebus volcano is also located in the area and the Ross Ice Shelf. Roald Amundsen started his South Pole expedition from the Bay of Whales and there are many research stations in the Ross Sea including the U.S. McMurdo Station.

To succeed in getting to such places as Shackleton's Hut, Cape Royds, involve a long and difficult sea voyage as well as the high probability that one will not be able to land due to conditions such as sea ice or terrible weather. I have experienced this at a number of places I had looked forward to seeing. Once having landed, often on an ice shelf, there is a long, uphill climb in icy and windy conditions past a huge Adelie Penguin colony. The small-unpainted hut is at the end of this struggle as it was for Shackleton and the men who lived there for more than a year.

Entering the hut and getting out of the constant wind and cold brought me a sense of accomplishment. After my glasses became adjusted to this new environment I saw a large stove in light from the window. The stove was the sole generator of warmth, the center of social as well as physical survival for the men and here I stood.

http://www. jjLHeureux.com

Mara Thompson

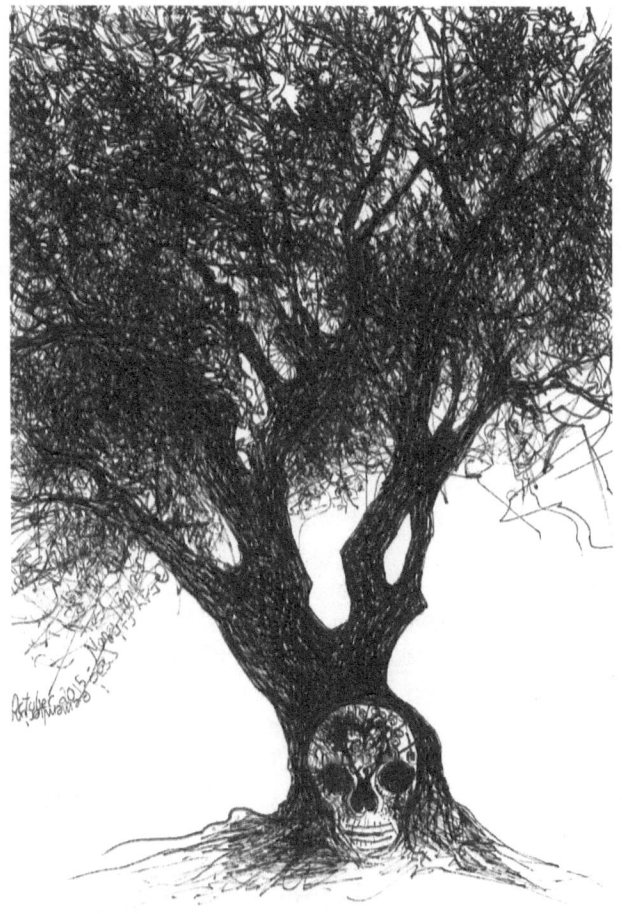

Day of the Dead

On the Ridge

When in my twenties, for a few years, I lived alone in a house by the river. Well, my little girl was there too except when she was in daycare or visiting her Dad. It sat three miles out from town, and was reached by a dirt road that followed the river. As so many places in that area did the house abutted a National

Forest. It was quite magical.

When I was not splitting logs for the wood stove I used in the winter or working in town I would go off to explore the area. I would drive down logging roads, comb freshly plowed fields after a rain to find arrowheads or hike.

On a crisp fall day I went up the slope behind the house, keeping to a moderate pace. About half way up I rounded a clump of Inkberry, a sort of Holly, and came face to face with a deer. She was about six feet away. She had brown eyes and lashes. Our hearts beat twice before she turned tail and ran back up the deer trail. I thought, "This an auspicious start to a hike."

At the top of the ridge I sat on a stump to catch my breath and soak in the quiet. After a time the silence was accented by shrill calls from a Sparrow Hawk. They like to sit on high places to scan for the next meal.

Being outdoors always increases my feel good endorphins, which may explain why I was moved to carve the words "Little Queenie" into the stump before moving on. Yeah, "Little Queenie" is also a classic song.

On I went. The woods in the fall are wide, I had a sense of no boundaries, no direction was impeded by obstacles. Further down the river however, was an area of caves. Among the woods are areas of exposed and ancient rock formations. Caves are common in the Ozarks which formed from water seeping into soluble carbonate rocks such as limestone. It is said that outlaws loved the area because they could hide in the caves and likely had relatives nearby I reckon. Once I found an old wooden trunk in that area, the wood nearly gone but the hinges and clasps were still there. I like to think it was heisted by bandits and dumped there.

On I went into new territory. Slowly I realized I did not recognize where I was. I stopped walking.

Of course, being twenty-something I did not have a compass with me, though I did own one.

I looked for moss on the trees as the northern side with the least sunlight encourages moss growth. Climbing a bit higher on this new ridge I heard a rushing sound. Not the rushing of water though. Immediately after hearing the sound I saw passing not far above me a formation of ducks winging their way in a generally southern direction, I assumed. Oh happy day! Two directions, north and south, sort of confirmed, confirmed enough I'd say. Slowly I turned around in a full circle taking in the woods once again. Off in one direction I could see a substantial break in the trees. It must be either the town or the river because everywhere else was heavily wooded.

Being my best bet to find my way out I stuck out towards the clearing, and yes, I passed my "Little Queenie" stump and was home free.

Eventually I was forced to move from the river house, this wonderful place, after I finally figured out that all the men were either married or crazy, or possibly both.

Always I will hold the Ozarks as a magic place in my heart. However, next time I'll tell you about the terrors of the summer bugs and how we bested them.

http://www.mythmara.com

Joanne Julian

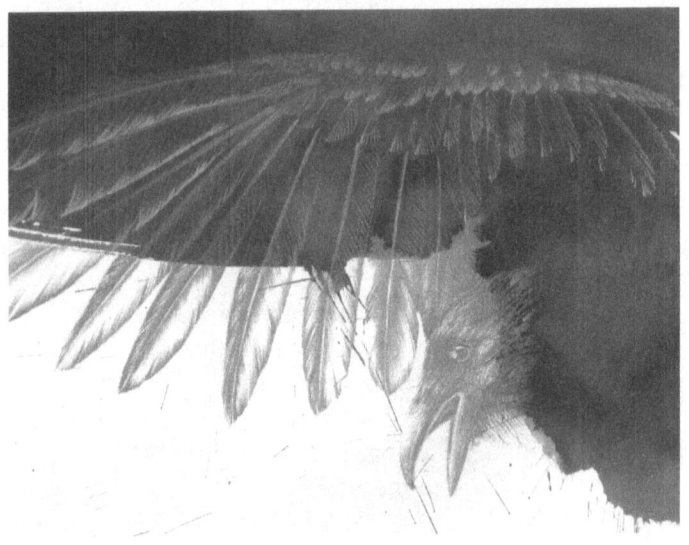

My story is one of gratitude. It is about my colleagues at College of the Canyons as well as dear, life-long friends, and how they assisted me when I was diagnosed with cancer almost 25 years ago.

Four of my pals at the College were organizing team members. On Monday mornings every two weeks, Patti, Administrative Assistant in Student Activities, called faculty, staff, and friends to request and schedule patient-friendly, healthy meals and their deliveries. Marilyn, the College Registered Nurse, received the food deliveries in her office freezer until I could pick them up every other Thursday evening. At that time, she would walk me to the faculty parking lot with the meals loaded on an audio visual cart; she helped me get them in my car, so I could get them home and stock my own freezer.

Beth, Financial Aid Officer, and Lori, Duplication Center Director, made calls too, to many of the same people in an effort to organize volunteers to drive and assist me to and from the hospital. Not only did these pals transport me, they sat with me and kept me company while I was waiting for my radiation treatment or while I was being infused with chemotherapy – a major time commitment. After they brought me home, they stayed with me until my daughter, Suzi, then ten years old, was brought home from school. In addition, they made sure I drank the two gallons of bottled water which they were instructed to bring with them, so I could flush out the chemo within the next 24 hours.

During this time, amazingly, I continued teaching full-time at COC where I was also Dean of Fine Arts and Humanities and part-time at California State University, Northridge. I was allowed to have a two-day schedule. Tuesdays and Thursdays were very long days, but this allowed me to get my treatment on Fridays and recover on Saturday, Sunday and Monday before teaching again on Tuesday. This routine went on for the first seven months of my treatment. During that time, I did not have to go to a market, shop for groceries, cook a meal, or drive myself to the hospital as all this was provided for Suzi, and myself by these angels.

Before we ate a single bite, Suzi and I would sit at our kitchen counter, and as I would unwrap and store the packages of food, she would make a list of who gave which meals, so we could write our thank you notes. About the second month in, we got the idea that in spite of chemo's effects, our food was so mindfully prepared and delicious that we decided to collect the recipes and publish a cookbook to document not just the healthy and tasty ingredients, but the love and good will that went into preparing them. Again, my friends came through and provided their recipes, and Jan, our Dean of Instructional Resources, oversaw the publishing of the cookbook right on the Campus.

A month after my treatment was completed, and I was on the mend, I had a thank you party in my home and studio for all those that loved us, supported us, cooked for us, and transported me. That totaled 198 people! My gratitude party was catered by our local Armenian market. My dear life drawing students dressed up in black trousers and white dress shirts and served the luscious trays of gourmet delights and bottles of champagne. That very night, sitting at my drafting table, Suzi and two of her friends from grammar school sold The Angel Cookbook back to those same 198 people who assisted us and were in attendance. Yes, they bought back their own recipes, and the proceeds from the cookbook still benefit a disabled student through the College of the Canyons Foundation with an "Angel's Scholarship" every year.

Mindful of providing the proper amount of information for a child of 10 years, I thought it appropriate for her to accompany me once to visit each of the three doctors on my team: my surgeon, my chemo oncologist and finally my radiation oncologist whom we saw together for my initial visit. We saw too many patients to count while we waited to be called for our turns in the treatment room. From toddlers to the elderly, most were bald or close to it, and this had an effect on her. When we were walking back to our car after my appointment that first day, she simply announced that when she grew up, she "wanted to do something to treat and cure cancer."

This year she will be 35. For ten years she has been a medical physicist creating radiation treatment for all types of cancer. She is practicing at the Barnhart Cancer Center at Sharp Hospital in San Diego County. How lucky can I get?

http://www.joannejulian.com

Elijah Richard

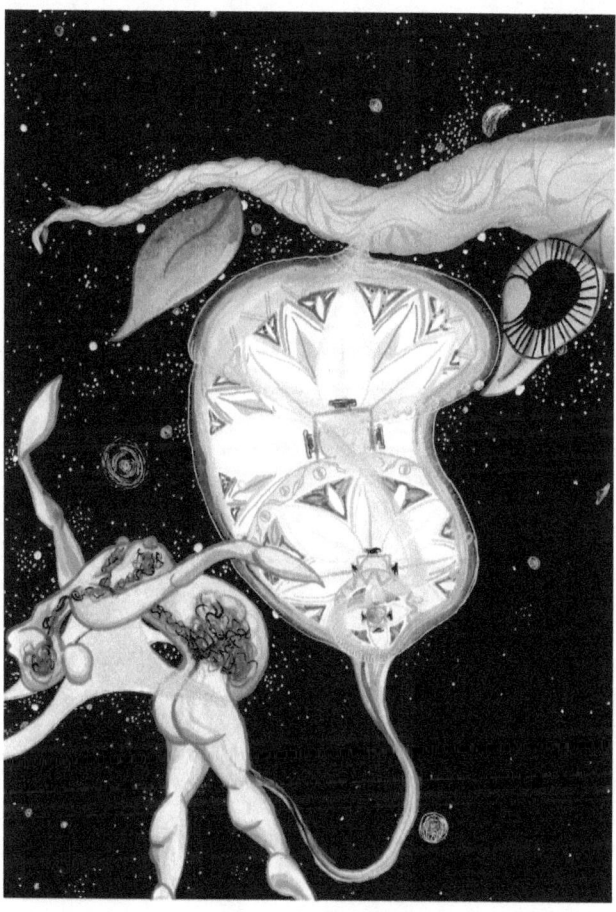

I asked my three mint plants once "what's wrong with people?" Within my minds meditation the word acquaintance peaked-alone from the silence. I pontificated i pondered what could these young mint plants mean by this simple word. So i did a quick scan of my whole life reencountering every conversation meeting and interaction with people that made me feel one way or another. I then weighed situations on the scales one side where i've gained acquaintance and the other side when

I didn't feel a bond of familiarity or lacked a genuine growth of knowledge for this individual. I could see when we as people can't make that connection via empathy humor love or reflection of ideals it gets gunky if it gets anything. We create fear for no reason well no legit reason just a dust like film that coats most people we encounter and the task of "dusting" gets tedious and most of us just fail. Let's say if you like cute cuddly tiny bow on their bangs yorkies and dislike powerful no b.s. clipped ear spiked collar pitbulls you might be under the illusion of visuals. The pitbulls have more virtues as personality and abilities go they are great with protection and loving with human babies while yorkies simply desire attention and make you as an owner feel like you are important. Same goes for hue-men, people, strangers etc. Being expressive without the feeling of being exposed is the key that the plants shared. These plants live on earth getting to know you all about you about each other themselves. This might be kind of farfetched for those who won't see the perspective of a being who resembles them. Yeah i might be a bit hood also a bit deku and kinda dolo but none of those oppose the ability to seek see and seep wisdom. If all knowledge is self knowledge do we all have something everyone needs to know? I hope you can digest the meaning of my Words but people can even twist the shortest poem to mean some other shit beyond reflection eternal. "Me we" kid safe n beast approved. #thotcreations

@thotcreations

Karen Frimkess Wolff

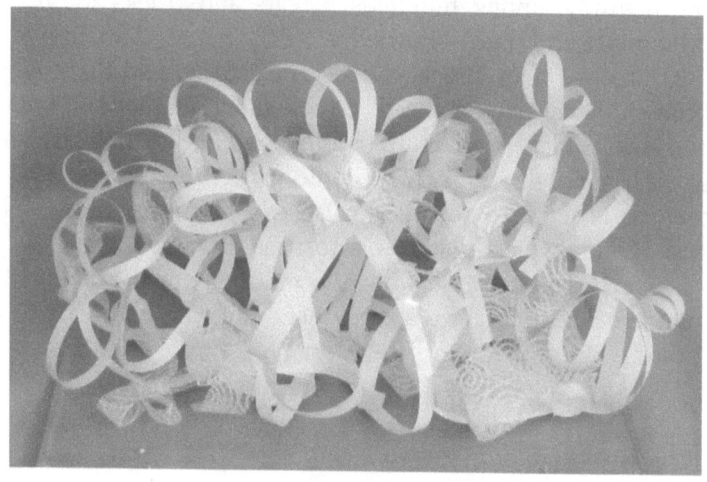

LINEAR THOUGHT (2015) Paper, Mylar, 13"(h) x 22"(w) x 13"(d)

On the last weekend of October, 2015, my friend Dori Atlantis, and I had gone up to a Sequoia Resort in the Tulare County Foothills, about 5 hours from our homes in Los Angeles.

On our way home, driving south on Highway 99, we stopped in Bakersfield to eat salads at Wendy's, use the restroom and fill our gas tank.

There was an Exxon Mobil gas station right next to the highway as we got off and I have an Exxon Mobil credit card. We went to a Wendy's half a block down the road first and then to the gas station. The pump rejected my credit card twice so I went into the station's snack shop/store to find out why The clerk said they didn't accept their own cards there—no reason.

So we left and drove to another gas station across the road but they were just putting yellow tape around their pumps and not selling any more gas. On the opposite corner we found an ARCO station and finally got the gas we needed to continue our trip home.

We got back on Highway 99. Filling our gas tank had cost us an extra 15 minutes.

Back on the highway, within about 10 minutes the traffic slowed and finally came to a complete stop. We sat still on the highway among hundreds of cars and trucks for over 30 minutes and didn't know why.

Finally a man in a large truck next to us said there had been a 10 care pile-up ahead. It took about another half hour and slowly a lane opened up and the long line of traffic began to clear through. Later, back home in L.A., we learned that there had been a 20 care pile-up caused by a sudden, powerful gust of wind which blew dust across the highway.

We had been saved from the massive wreck by our 15 minute delay and the gas station that didn't take its own credit card.

http://www.karenfrimkesswolff.com.

Karma Henry

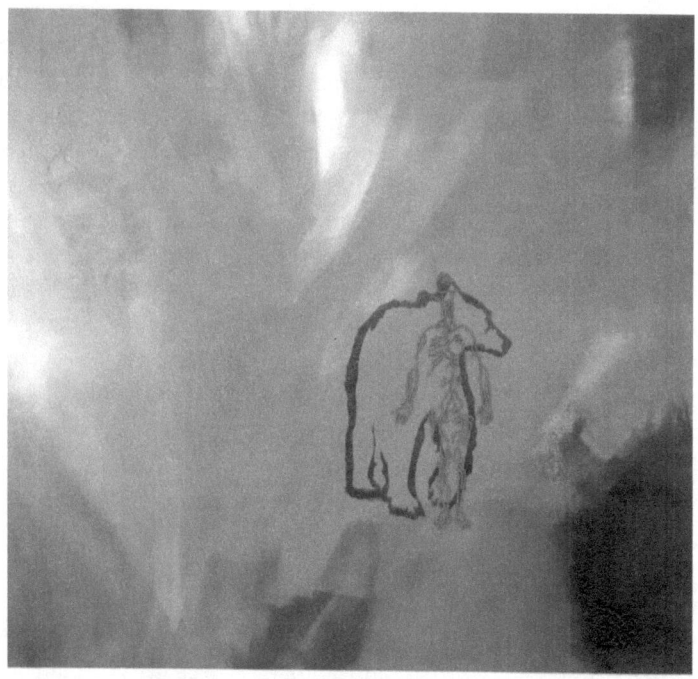

We had worked a double shift that Friday. Three of us sat around my coffee table devouring Chinese food. It was amazingly hot and fogged up my glasses as I opened each box. Fragrant spicy Kung Pao Chicken wafted into the air.

We were tired. Adrenaline soon took care of that as our pagers went off, loudly, one by one. Before the last one went off we were running out the door, back to the hospital. Jumping in our respective cars, we maneuvered out of the driveway and caravanned, at about 65, to the hospital. All we knew was "gunshot wound". By the time we parked and ran through the back door, our nursing supervisor was waiting for us. She yelled as we entered the double doors, "NO time! They're coming NOW!"

The turquoise scrubs were heavy and scratchy as I pulled them on. Soon I was running down the hall of the operating room on autopilot. Before the room was ready, a gurney carrying the patient, 3 ER staff and the rest of tonight's OR crew, was practically flying down the hall and into the room with me. I tore open supplies quickly while the nurses were moving the patient onto the table. I ran to the main sinks and to soap up and scrub my chapped hands. I could taste my dinner still, the garlic from the spicy chicken permeating my nostrils under my mask. I was already perspiring and clenching my jaw from the tension. I could her him screaming from outside the door. I saw him grab my nurses arm and look into her face pleading, "Don't let me die!" I noticed this because he wore several huge silver rings and they glinted under the OR lights when he grabbed her. The pleading was to all of us, and we took it to heart, and then packed it away so we could do our jobs.

He was bleeding profusely from a large wound in his torso. The paramedics had plopped some pads and lap sponges onto his wounds to soak up the blood. I was amazed he was conscious at all. He was just a teenager. His face so pale, almost translucent. His freckles seemed suspended on top of his skin, contrasted from his dark curly hair and blue eyes, which were wide with terror. He was crying now. The padding was removed unceremoniously and it made a wet heavy splatting sound landing in the kick bucket under the table.

It's amazing how fast you can organize a pile of stainless steel and cotton gauze into something worthy of a Michael Crichton novel. I was silently counting my instruments and I looked back over to see that my nurse was pouring Betadine over his exposed torso. I could still see the ring marks he left on her forearm where he grabbed her. My gleaming mayo stand stood ready as he was put to sleep. I had my scalpel and assorted clamps lined up and waiting for action.

The surgeon on call began an exploratory laparotomy to assess the damage. We were in the abdomen within 3 minutes of his arrival to the OR suite. Our arms were awash in blood, bile and stool as we tried to stop the bleeding. Anesthesia kept ordering and pumping more blood into the boy. It was a lesson in defeat to keep clamping off veins and arteries and staunch the flow of blood. We worked furiously for a half an hour. The damage was too great. I was told he was shot point blank in the chest with a shotgun. The room was unusually quiet barring the noises of machinery and the occasional phone call from the blood bank.

Our surgeon looked up at all of us. "Suggestions?", she said flatly. We all shook our heads No. "There's nothing here we can save. I don't want him dying on this table. We need to pack him and get him to ICU. His family needs to see him before we let him go". With that comment we packed as many sponges in as we could for compression, placed surgical bolsters on his incision to keep the wound closed, and wiped off his head and neck and arms and hands, trying to make him presentable for his family knowing they would be saying goodbye in just a few minutes. As soon as we had a surgical dressing on his abdomen we transferred him to the gurney and ran to the dimly lit ICU. The family was waiting at the nurse's station. Hysteria soon followed and I was grateful that I needed to return to the OR to tidy up.

I walked back into the OR suite to gather my instruments. I think I walked maybe five steps into the room and it suddenly got blurry. My cheeks flushed and I realized I was crying. Later, my nurse walked back into the room with her head down, shoulders slumped forward, and she began to tell me about the scene in ICU. He lasted 15 minutes after we got him to ICU. I heard the devastation in her voice. The two of us spent the better part of an hour cleaning up and doing paperwork. We were now going on our 20th hour of work for the day. Beyond tired, we finished up and turned off the lights. Changing clothes and shoes we headed home.

When we got there, we kicked off our shoes and sat on the couch, minds numb. On the coffee table sat all of our take out boxes, tipped over, empty. We looked over and there on the floor was a tiny black mutt of a dog snoring. In our haste we had forgotten to put the food in the fridge. Too tired to cook, we fell asleep, upright, feet on the coffee table and pagers in our hands.

http://www.KarmaHenry.com

Leah C. Dixon

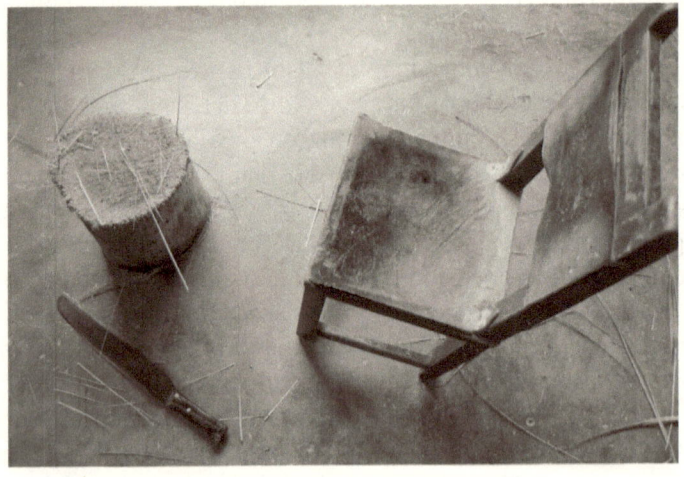

"Chair, Stump, Machete". December 2015 at a weavers factory near Trinidad, Cuba.

Attitude as a Defensive Weapon

Once when I lived in Brooklyn, I was coming back late at night on the L train from Manhattan. I had gone to see some live music with a friend. It was well after midnight on Saint Patrick's Day, amateur night at all the bars around town, which still had several more hours before the 4am last call. Nights like that I was glad for the subway home, as it didn't subject me to the drunk drivers. But there was still the walk from the subway station to my apartment. Normally, it would only be a two block walk, but after 11PM the near gate is locked. So I had to take the longer route, as did everyone else who got off at that stop. I reach the street level and start walking home through the snow.

As I'm walking away from the subway exit, down Wyckoff towards Troutman St., a guy in a truck passes me by and honks, shouts something out the window, something witty like "Heyyy, baybeee!". I turn my face away and push my hand palm outward in the universal 'back off' gesture, and quickly turn to walk down Troutman. This is a narrowish one way street with parking on both sides. I'm walking on the left side. I look behind me to where the driver had passed that intersection and see him put his truck in reverse, back up, come back through the intersection, and turn to come down the street I'm walking on, right towards me. I'm completely alone at this point, no subway passengers around. In a dark warehouse block with very little lighting and no activity on the street other than me and my new admirer. He pulls past me again and shouts some more stuff out the window at me. At this point I'm getting concerned because I still have a good 700 feet or more to cover before I make it onto my own residential block. Unable to comprehend my lack of interest in his charms, he begins to pull his truck over to the left-hand parking spots, the side closest to where I'm walking. Adrenalin is beginning to pump in my body at this point and I am ready to move fast and slam the car door back on him if it even opens a crack. I've been studying at a karate dojo in the neighborhood, and while I'm by no means a badass either then or now, but I knew enough to plan some possible reactions if it escalated. But I REALLY didn't want it to go that far. Not sure how I thought of this at the moment, in that instant as his car came to a stop, but I found myself shouting in my meanest, loudest, most stern voice I could muster: "IF YOU STEP OUT OF THAT CAR, I WILL FEED YOU YOUR BALLS."

He paused for a moment.

I stop walking with my back to the wall of the building behind me, not wanting to put him behind me again.

I listen to the thrum of the engine idling in the cold Brooklyn night.

Then, without any further ado, he pulls his truck away from the curb, back to the middle of the street, forward to the stoplight, and turns down Irving St., presumably to find an easier target for his advances.

http://www.illuminoidalarts.com

Michael McCall

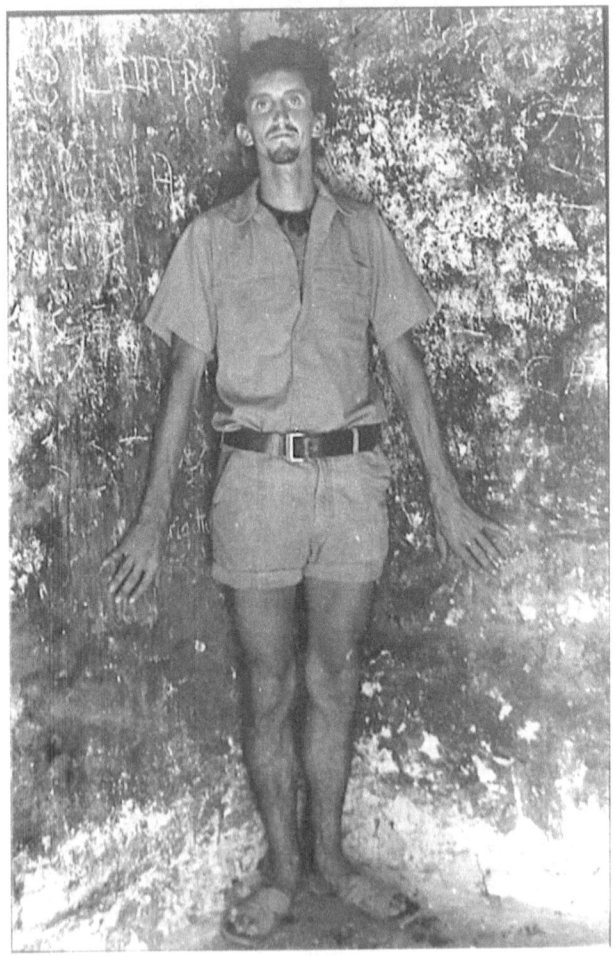

May 6, 1977   Chichicastenago, Guatemala

The trip from Huehuetanago had been a steep incline in a crowded bus, past tall pine forests, strange rock formations, on a road that followed the edge of the cliff. The bus driver seemed careless as he sped around each curve, moving the young Indian girls herding goats to the side of the road with a short blast of his horn. I had heard of busses taking flight off the cliff roads in Guatemala, and I could see how. At that point you just have to relax and let it happen, believing in your guardian angel and having faith it's not your time yet to die.

We got to Chichicastenango safely. After finishing up the rum from the day before, the sleep at Pasada Juliana was deep and generous. Standing on the balcony the next morning, looking over the shingled roofs of the village, the Church of Santo Thomas prevailed over the city. Built in 1545 A.D., on the ruins of a Mayan Temple, the colonialists left the 18 steps leading up to the church from the street. These steps represented the months of the Mayan calendar year. As we walked through the arched wooden doors into the main sanctuary, the copal incense so thick you could barely see, much less breathe. The light shown through the upper windows, a heavenly, majestic light bathed over the colorful clothing of the K'iche Mayan Indians there worshipping. Later, after reading a bit about the church, I discovered the front doors were only to be used by the Native Mayans, and our entrance had been on the side. Oh, well.

http://www.michaelmccall.org

Ann Phong

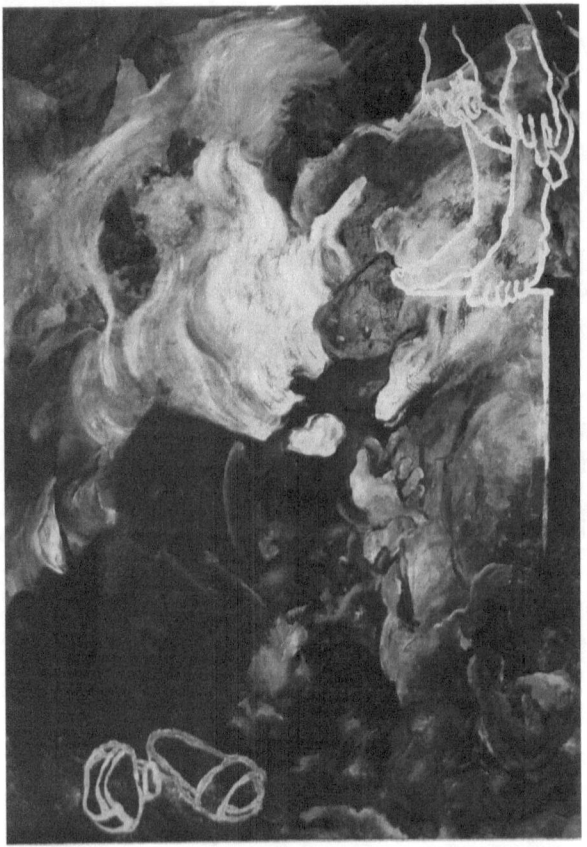

Jump, 96x60, acrylic

It was 1975. In my senior year of high school, the North Vietnamese Communist took over the South where I lived. Everybody's lives became tougher mentally and materially. We had to write our family biography report almost every week to give to our local government. Everywhere we went, we had to go to the police station to ask for an approval stamp on our paperwork.

I thought I could take it—until the time I finished high school and I tried to enter the only university for my major in Saigon. But I faced a harsh reality: I was rejected 3 years in a row.

Living like there was no hope for tomorrow, I used to ride my bike around the city to look at people whose property were confiscated and who had to live on the street as a result. Those scenes of homelessness reminded me that I was not the only one who lived at the bottom of the barrel.

Later, I changed direction and went to take exams to enter into teaching for high school. I was accepted. Many of the old regime teachers were in the concentration camp at that time, so there was a need for new teachers.

Then, one of my junior high school students asked me to go with her family to escape the country by boat. It was during the stormy season on a night without a moon. Our leader said that the police wouldn't expect anyone to take that risk. So we made our bid for freedom and fled to the shores of Malaysia—safely.

As dangerous as it was to make the journey in rough waters, those who traveled over more calm waters were often captured, killed or raped.

During the time that we lived in the refugee camp, I saw many people who had lost their wives, their children, or their siblings during the escape. These people often wandered to the ocean shores of the refugee camp to mourn the passing of their loved ones. They let their lives pass this way; days and months were spent with their underwater memories, even as they breathed the air of freedom on land.

The camp was always full of Southeast Asian refugees. Walking around the camp, seeing them cry, laugh, talk, and shake each other's hands, this all made me felt like I was living among both the living and the dead.

My refugee story is decades old. I am living in Southern California now where I can go to the beaches anytime. Looking at the Pacific Ocean from California, my feelings are carried—all the way from the other side to the seashore where I now stand. I can imagine how Vietnam lives at the end of the horizon line. I still have flashbacks, many memories of the past, that stay with me in the present.

Today, when I read articles about the refugees who flee their country to look for sanctuary, I empathize with their desperation. Painful human tragedies keep repeating itself on every corner of the earth. It only needs one dictator or one group of power hungry people to ruin whole countries and the lives of their citizens.

http://www.annphongart.com

Jon Measures

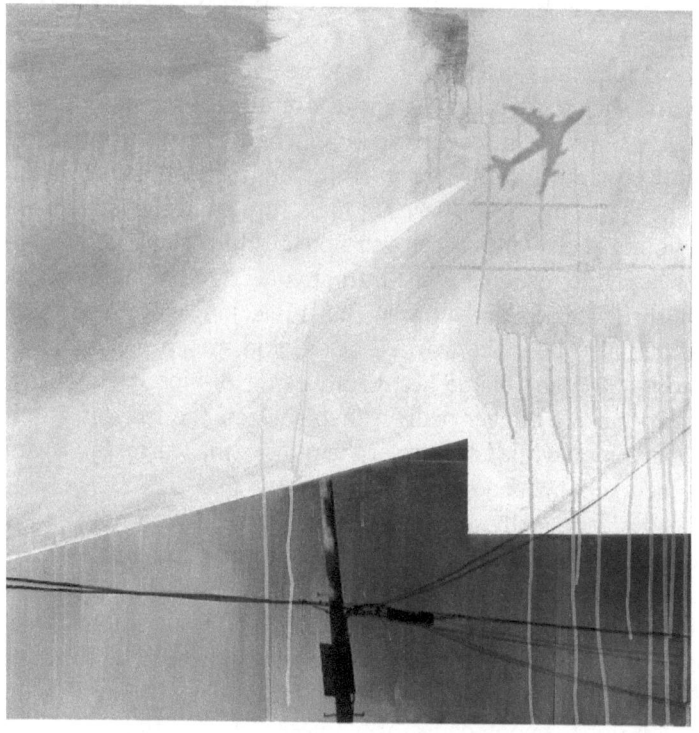

As Tears Flow Down; acrylic, and collage on wood panel.

I'm Quite a Happy Man

What's my name?...I haven't the foggiest. Some of them call me Dad or Granddad. Sometimes she says, "come on, be a good lad". I don't know her name either; I can't find the word, it's a short one, like a jab. Once in a while her name pops out, usually when I'm not thinking about it: when that happens she smiles with her whole face, rosy cheeks and all. She's the one that takes care of me. She does everything for me: she feeds me, cleans me, does the shaving soap, washes my teeth, and has me go for a wee. She gets a little stroppy from time-to-time when I won't get out of the bed. I think, ooh it's so warm and cozy and if I do get up I'm not going to do anything anyway because I'm a lazy lad these days. I think I used to be quite busy doing this and that but not anymore, I like to sit on the couch or lie in bed.

I remember nothing. I know me and her are glued, lots of years, she's the best one, she's always there. I see little films in my head of her from time to time when she was young, she's smiling at me and saying something but the words float off into a giggle. In my head there are little clips of her when she was a young pretty one, short and not too thin. Her face was like a soft gentle rose that won't hurt anyone. So, that's why we had the bridesmaids and flowers that time, long, long ago. Now, sometimes she looks worried or sad and sometimes even a bit cross but I can't blame her; I start being all bloody shoo, shoo and a bit of a bugger really. When she gets the face on, I want to hide for a while, stay under the quilt in the warm, I just want to be like a hedgehog in a ball.

I'm not really writing this of course, I lost how to use words, not that I was ever much for reading and writing but if push came to shove I did used to be able to read something or write a letter. When I look at words these days, it might as well be Chinese. I was a country boy, in the fields and the river and I always liked pictures more than words.

I don't know dates or names anymore but I can see pictures and I have the taste of memories in my head but they get muddled and they're quickly fading away. Sometimes I hear a song and I can picture a scene from long ago, it comes back for a moment and then it's gone again.

There are some others around. The young girls, not too young now but they were my little girls. There's the blonde one that always comes around helping me, she's a real good one, always on the go and she's very patient and likes to rib me about things. Then there's the shorter one that has a little red car, she laughs loud and goes, "hurry up Dad, come on". There's the lad too, with a beard that comes sometimes. I think he lives far away, maybe in another country, on a plane. He calls me Dad and takes me for rides in the nice new one. I can see him when he was a little boy, old faded photos. He looks like me, chip off the old block. I like going for a drive in the country, always did. I don't drive these days but I can just sit and watch the world go whizzing by while he's behind the wheel. I do seem to be quite good at knowing which way to turn, one trick that I've hung on to. The same lad also helps me do some painting. He says to just do abstract ones that way no one can really tell if it's any good. I painted some wobbly lines that I wanted to be straight and he seemed to like them. I'm not sure myself but I don't much mind. Painting pictures was always one of my favorite things; you can lose yourself when painting.

I'm in the last stage of life, I'm not sad though. I can't tell you much because my head is like scrambled egg, but my life was a good one, now I love everything. I love the two doggies that come around my feet; the little one is a bit of trouble and then the big soft one, older and gentler. They don't speak and don't want anything but a bit of biscuit and a pat on the head, very nice, lovely little things they are.

There are good things in getting old. Me and her can sit on a bench in a park for lots of ticks and it's alright, no need to worry. So, now I sit and I sit some more and if someone is kind enough to turn it on, I'll watch the goggle box in the corner with people laughing, telling jokes or singing songs. There are times when it's all too much but there are times when I can be a very happy camper just being me. Now, thanks to Mr. Alzheimer, whoever he is, I don't have anything that bothers me too much all my wants and problems, they're all gone. I'm still here though, smiling as much as I can. So, you don't need to feel sorry for me because I'm quite a happy man.

http://www.jonmeasures.com

Preston M. Smith

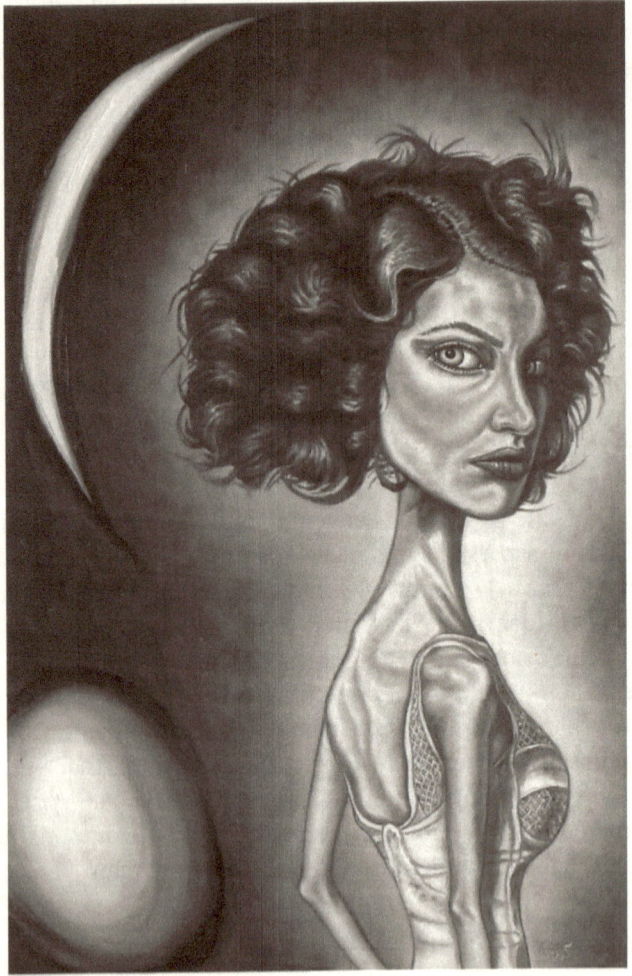

I was about five years old and living in Laramie, Wyoming. My family had moved around a lot, but at the time we were living in a big house at the top of Indian Hill on Mill Street. Our house was situated at the top of the hill on the right-hand corner of the cul-de-sac.

I had a good friend named Judy that lived across the way from our house and we used to play together all of the time, alternating back and forth between houses. That particular day we were at my house in the basement. The house was large and you had to wind down the staircase, past my parents bedroom from the main floor and all the way down to the bottom level in order to get to the basement. The basement was a huge space, littered with boxes and junk, a spooky place to be, with ample hiding space for playing hide-and-seek. There was little light down there, so I never ventured down alone. That day we were together, so it was okay.

There was a television down there and our old couch was facing it, leaving the rest of the huge space sprawling out behind it. To the left of the couch was a bathroom with a Jacuzzi, but my parents kept this locked as to protect us kids from getting hurt. Judy and I were playing around on the couch, when she suddenly had to use the bathroom. I told her that the door was locked and that she would have to go upstairs to use another one. She skipped up the stairs and out of sight.

I was alone, eating a plate of grapes on the couch. I remember every detail so clearly. The television was turned off as I was popped grapes into my mouth. I remember building myself up in my mind, telling myself that I was not scared. I was trying to act like a big kid. I was only five years old and I remember this plain as day, rationalizing my emotions like I would do now.

Suddenly, I had the strongest feeling that something was standing behind me as I sat. I was terrified. It seemed inevitable. I sat there for a few seconds, but of course could not control the urge to look behind me. I mean if something was there, I could not let it sneak up behind me without knowing. I stood up and turned around slowly, rationalizing, as time slowed. I would like to tell you that nothing was there and that it had simply been my imagination, but I can't do that. Something was there, and it was staring at me. It was doing more than that. It was grinning, but it was the type of grin that said, "I know something you do not." It had huge eyes, a creepy smile, and it was hunched over, with its hands out front, walking towards me slowly as if it was hunting me.

I stood frozen in my place. I did not expect to see anything. I mean you look a million times in your life, but nothing is ever there. Not this time. This thing that did not seem to be alive (but might have been at some point in time) was moving towards me slowly. It was smiling a sinister smile the whole way and its eyes pierced right through me. When it reached about ten feet in front of me I finally couldn't take anymore. I passed out on the floor. At least I think I did, because everything else is blackness.

I was too young to understand what it was at the time, but looking back, I know that it was an Indian. It fit the bill perfectly. I know it sounds corny seeing as we lived on Indian Hill, but my house was cut deep into the ground right near an ominous man-made rock formation. Plus, I had no idea what an Indian looked like at that age, so I could not have made it up.

I always wondered what happened after I fainted. Did it come up to me? Did it stand over me and peer down? Did it try to reach out to touch me? It terrifies me to even think about it. I told many people in my life this story, and most of them have believed me, I think because of my conviction. There were however certain people who did not. I was always afraid to tell my older brother, but I did tell my parents one time. They were amused, but brushed it aside, chalking it up to my active imagination as a child.

It was not until my parents, my brother, and I were having dinner one night at a restaurant as grown ups, that things changed. We were in the middle of our main course when my parents launched into it.

"Tell you brother about what happened at our house on Mill Street when you where a kid," my father spouted. He and my mom were smiling at this.

"No. I don't want to," I responded.

"Seriously. It's a good story. Tell him."

My brother looked at me, waiting. I don't know why, but I eventually consented. "All right, but don't laugh."

"I won't," he said with conviction.

I launched into the story, but about a minute in, he stopped me. His eyes had grown large and he had a look on his face that sent a chill up my spine.

"I saw it too," he said staring at me.

"What?" I was shocked.

"An Indian right?"

"Holy shit."

I couldn't believe it.

I had not even gotten to the grapes, yet he proceeded to describe the figure exactly the way I had seen it. He had witnessed it in another part of the house however. We sat locked in conversation for the next half an hour.

My parents stopped smiling and watched in disbelief.

http://www.pmsartwork.com

Michelle D. Ferrera

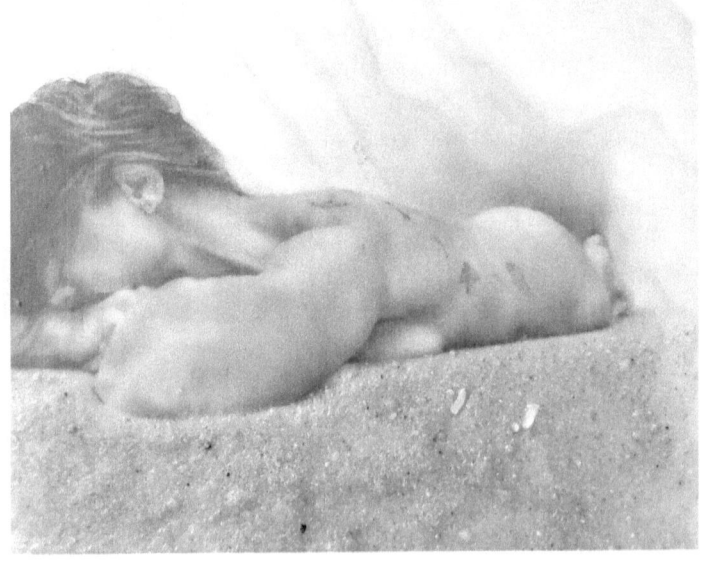

I used to say and tell people that I'm an "adrenaline junkie" which would mean I was on the prowl for my next fix, a rush of adrenaline full of risk, ways to surely test life's limit. Ah, ignorant innocence. I refuse to punish myself for stating this claim, rather feeling blessed I didn't push the limits too hard to miss what I'm experiencing now. I'm an adventure lover, seeking out life's unexpected gifts that will enhance my life. The best gift I could ever imagine is having a second chance at life, a life out west, which allowed me to meet "him" and send us on a journey that will last, as we like to say, a "thousand years" or more.

My husband and I experienced our honeymoon in Italy, an adventure that only existed in my dreams. With my lover true and through, ready for the unexpected in a place so romantic, so full of cloud and haze, lost in each other, we soaked it all in with no distractions for three weeks. We had nothing planned, just our flight back. The in between, our oyster! The plan, the destination. We've already found each other, so the rest is just details and added color.

Sorrento - Amalfi Coast, 2014: Sunset on my face, no one around but chirping birds, my lover swimming back and forth in this infinite pool that leads to the sun hiding behind the horizon, motorcycles and scooters buzzing like insects in the distance, the slight trickle of the piscina to soothe the soreness of my feet from an uphill journey from Port to mountain top, where our hotel home rests our full hearts. So this is what it's like to really feel relaxed, responsibilities so far away, just decisions of what boat to Capri we shall take. Each day a new adventure, no expectations just sparkly dreams checked off and ideas to refresh each mornings carb loaded breakfast. So many colors and sounds soaked in already and still due settimana to go! Mio marito, mio sesso, intelligente, bello, marito. He is working so hard learning this language, the roots of my blood, integrating his and mine, weaving our love together, insieme, as we make our way to Patti, Sicily. To have nothing but acceptance of my past, my failures and the moments that led me here, makes it so easy to give so much more love than I ever thought I had to the man sitting across from me. His European sunglasses shining through the glass of the bus, tapping his ring finger on his thigh. My guess, he's listening to some Rock! My lovely Lubin husband. So handsome in every way I dreamed a man should, could be, wanted to be. To quote True Romance, "he's so cool!" And yet modest, warm with that Sparkle in his eye, always glowing and making me smile so hard my eyes water and welt up. Can I be this happy? Damn right! I found my lover. I never met a man quite like him. A man that makes me feel so WILD.

http://www.MDFerrera.com

John Eden

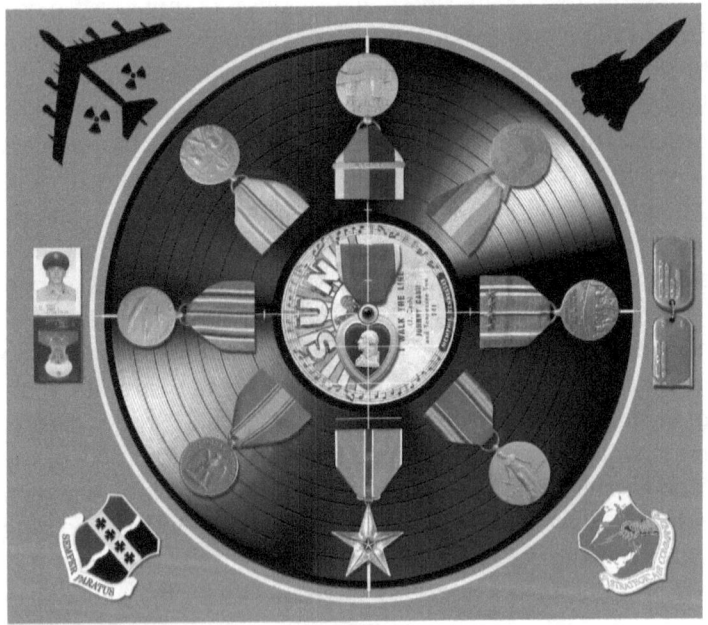

"I Walk The Line"

Walk On

At the end of WWII, my father accompanied the first group of American scientists into Hiroshima just days after the atomic bomb blast to measure that city's unimaginable devastation, seeing firsthand, the burn victims and the phantom human forms that were seared onto its city walls. Similar to what I saw displayed secondhand, thirty-five years later when I visited Hiroshima's Peace Museum at ground zero.

Like 'Saving Private Ryan,' my mother's oldest brother waded onto France's bloodstained Omaha Beach during the Normandy invasion as a 'replacement soldier' and then fought his way throughout Western Europe. He said that he walked all the way to Germany with a M-1 rifle in his hand. He's gone now, but every time he tried to talk about those horrific experiences (the smells & images), he would choke up and say something like 'I'm no hero, I was lucky, and that's all. The ones who didn't make it are the real heroes and I can't get those ghosts out of my head. I just tried to stay alive.' He believed his success in staying alive grew out of his boyhood hunting experiences that might appear counter-intuitive. His Oklahoma country-boy father taught him to always target the animals that were bunched together, because the odds of 'bagging your dinner' were mathematically higher. He figured that German soldier would have learned the same basic hunting skills, so his thoughts were always to 'stay apart and not to bunch up.'

To Examine Critically: Stay Apart, Don't Bunch Up and Question Everything

To observe, to live inside oneself, apart and separate; it's what I believe writers and artists need to do, and that has been my calling for as long as I can remember.

I grew up in a small Southern California town that skirts the extreme northern fringes of the San Fernando Valley, just north of where the Interstates 5 and 14 meet. The Newhall-Saugus area has now been eclipsed by major development projects within the Santa Clarita Valley and the art world knows it as the unlikely location for Cal Arts. It had been a quiet farming community until the never-ending real estate boom that started there in earnest in the mid '40s, but during my early childhood it was still mostly open farmland surrounded by hills that were riddled with mining caves dug by Chinese migrants searching for their American dream.

Escape, Escape, Escape

Up until the age of 16, most of my weekends were spent exploring our valley's arid surrounds, but with a driver's license, wheels and a few bucks for gas my life changed forever. Roads out to the city and the beach became El Camino Real, points of teenage interests connected together by circuitous routes washed down, first with bland AM radio that soon gave way to Madman Muntz's audio tape cartridge players that poured out more dangerous FM album sounds by The Animals, Bob Dylan, the Rolling Stones at will, and like Kerouac, I was 'On The Road,' moving forward and yet compulsively glancing backwards too.

<u>If I were asked what defining moments in my formative years put me on the road less-traveled, I would have to say it was the archery accident that took place when I was twelve and my time spent in the U. S. Air Force during the Vietnam war.</u>

I had been given an archery set for Christmas and during the following holiday weeks I would spend most of my time traipsing 'Indian-style' around a nearby dry riverbed that snaked its way through our valley mostly shooting at imaginary targets. My mother's family connection with Eastern Oklahoma's Choctaw tribe has instilled a lifelong interest in Native American culture and at age twelve I was all about being Ishi, 'the last wild Indian' in America. On one occasion an older neighbor boy came along hoping to try archery for the first time. Early on, he suggested we play a game where the boy holding the bow would yell 'look out' and the other boy would duck down to let the shooter fire the arrow over his head at an imaginary bad guy. The major problem with that suggestion, besides just being a really bad idea, was that neither one of us were skilled enough with the bow to perform the maneuverer safely. It was my bow; therefore I went first, after yelling the warning he ducked as planned, so I pulled back the arrow to release, but the arrow's tip fell off my bow hand. I had to reset the arrow and go again. In the confusion, he must have thought that I had already released the arrow, because he stood up just as I let go of the shaft, it thrusting point blank into his eye. His doctor said later that he was 'lucky to be alive,' but having lost one eye, he would go through life visually impaired, with no depth perception.

From that moment on, I carried the hidden indelible stain of that boy holding his bloody hand over his punctured eye, permanently etched into my mind's eye and all the gut-wrenching anguish associated with doing such a terrible thing. There was nothing I could do or say that would undo the pain and damage that I had caused him and his family. Looking back, I'm sure we both suffered from PTSD syndrome, but at the time, therapy for such things were nonexistent. This traumatic experience made me a natural pacifist, not wanting any more virulent images in my head, like the ones I knew my uncles and father brought back from World War II. Perhaps, they were heroes —I knew, I was not.

Will we be heroes of our own lives, or will we merely be swept along by our own particular circumstances?

That to me is the primary question that I had to come to terms with. We can't control what life throws at us, but we can control how we respond to those adversities. During the Vietnam War, all young men of draft age had to register with the Selective Service for possible military duty selection. Some made the decision to evade the draft and others were granted various deferments thereby avoiding military service all together. Shortly after graduating high school, my father suggested I join the Air Force to avoid being drafted into the Army or Marines, which certainly meant fighting in Vietnam. Having taken an Aviation Science class in school that stoked my interest in flight, I mistakenly assumed that by enlisting in the Air Force proactively, I would be trained in a non-combative air support role with skills that could be used later in civilian life. But like my 'Auld Da,' Murphy's Law mandated that my initial duty was to be a Military Air Policeman. My first stateside assignment was to guard SR-71 Spy Planes and the B52 Strategic Air Command long-range bombers. These B52 aircraft were somewhere in the air over the United States 24/7, armed with nuclear bombs and were missioned to destroy whole cities in the case of a nuclear war. This policy was known as Mutually Assured Destruction (or M.A.D.). Before being cross-trained into my final job as a base photographer, I walked a mosquito-ridden flight line in the rice-paddies of Northern California as an M-16 toting "AP" waiting to be cycled on through to Vietnam while guarding those deceptively beautiful nuclear-armed aircraft, all when the end of the world seemed so palpable and real.

Breakdown And Conversion

Working the nightshift on the flight line was grueling; exposure to the elements for 8-hour shifts took their toll, especially on cold winter nights. I kept wondering about which city the aircraft I was guarding was designated to target. I was haunted by what the devastation might look like and if I was in any way culpable. On one hand, I was not a fan of anti-democratic hegemonies around the world, but conversely, I really hated how our politicians and their military counterparts allowed so many of our young soldiers to die without any long-term goals or endgame plans in mind. It all seemed so unconscionable. My fear of becoming part of some dark historical event was looming large and my psyche was compelled to push back by way of exhibiting extremely erratic behavior on the flight line in a nuclear weapon zone. The behavior was noticed, a breakdown really, and I was sent to a hospital for psychiatric evaluation. Truly, I could have just gone along with the program, but I sensed it would have been the end of me, as I was. I was diagnosed with manic-depressive tendencies, but not severe enough to be discharged. It was then, that I was cross-trained into photography and my future path was clear. I think I had learned from my archery accident a micro truth: if something feels wrong, don't give into the impulse to go along just to get along. More recently, a macro truism has presented itself: one generation's truths do not necessarily transfer on to the next.

Mi perogrullada no es necesariamente tu verdad.

http://www.johneden.org

Dori Atlantis

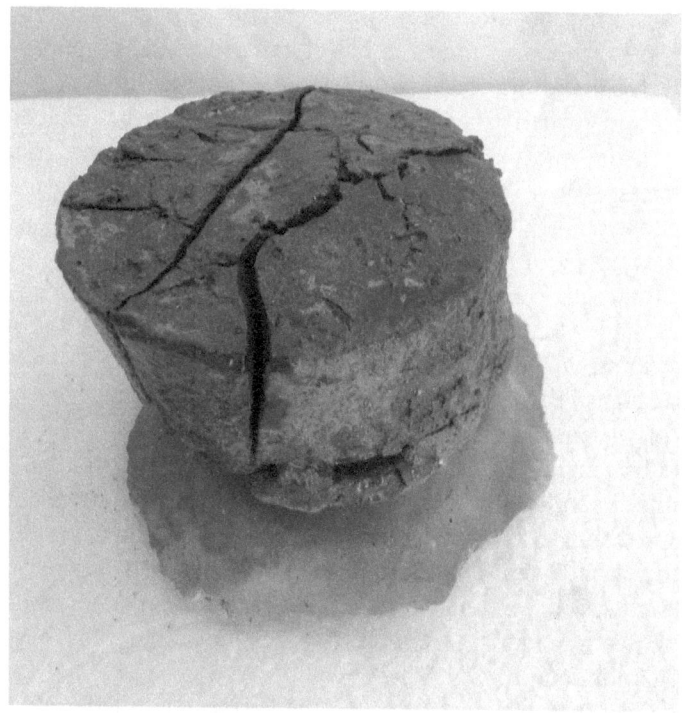

Tripping Home from Badger, CA

After a long art weekend in Badger, California, Karen Frimkess Wolff and I decided to visit another location further up the mountain. Karen's truck was fully packed with our disassembled piece. Everything was strapped down to not fly off. Our clothes, water and food were stuffed behind the seat. We got directions from our friends, and drove up the long winding road.

We spent an hour at the other place, beautifully situated in the Sierra Mountains. After our visit, and wanting to get to L.A. before the rain/snow started, we were given these directions: "stay on Dunlap Road until it dead ends, turn left, follow that road, passing Ruth Wells Road, until you reach the 180. Turn left again and stay on that road until you get to the 63, turn left again and take that to Visalia."

We had no GPS or cell phone reception to fall back on.

With Karen behind the wheel and me as the co-pilot we began driving down Dunlap Road. We came to the first dead end and turned left. The road was paved with a white line down the middle. With the road winding tightly and going very slowly, we were able to see wild turkeys. Then the road narrowed and the white line down the middle of the road disappeared. We took a turn and came on a billy goat eating grass on the road. He reluctantly moved out of our way. We began looking for any road signs. What was the name of this road??? We came on horses, llamas and dogs but could not find any road signs. Fences along the way had No Trespassing signs, No Hunting signs, Do Not Enter.

The asphalt road became gravel. We were starting to panic. Karen saw the Ruth Wells Road sign. This must be the right road. No cars passed us as we continued down the very curvy road. There were no houses next to the road. No people in sight. Next we went over a cattle guard into an area with no fences at all, animals roaming freely. Should we go back? No, we continued on.

We came to a sign signaling the entrance to a federal correction facility along with many scary precautions. We drove through and briefly thought about asking for directions at the prison's visitors' center. I saw a huge man in an orange prison suit being frisked by a guard. We didn't stop. We drove through the prison. We realized that we hadn't locked our doors after we were a safe distance from the prison. We debated about turning around and heading back. We kept going.

Karen pulled to the side of the road after seeing a boarded up store with a decrepit sign "Sleepy Hollow". We thought perhaps we could get our GPS or cell phones to work. I tried to find the road on a map we had printed off the computer. No luck. A dog barking at us from behind a chain link fence drew an older man to come investigate. I told him we were lost and trying to get to Visalia. He said "go down Dunlap Road until it dead ends, then turn left , follow that road until you reach the

180. Turn left again and stay on that road until you get to the 63, turn left again and take that to Visalia."

We did that and finally made it to Visalia where we had lunch at Denny's.

http://www.doriatlantis.com

Cathy Weiss

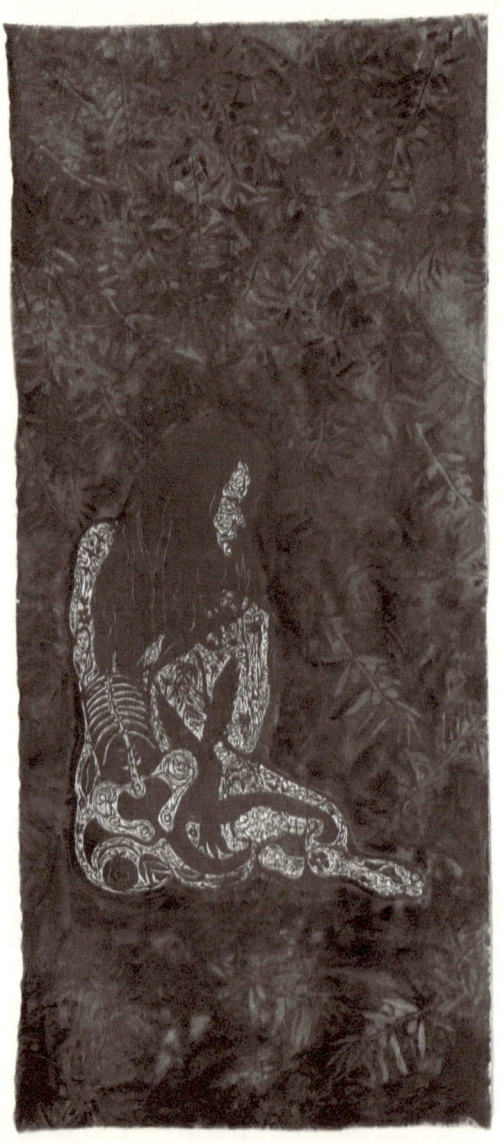

Ten Days Apart:

It was a typical afternoon and everyone was home. I remember I was sitting on the staircase talking to my husband when the phone rang. My husband picked it up and said, " It's for you." I said hello, the voice on the other side said, "Hi this is some-one from your past," I knew who it was. I said, "Is it Marcy?" She couldn't believe I knew it was her. I had only really heard about her from my parents, I was always curious about her, what she looked like, more specifically did I look like her? I had two beautiful children and a great life. I felt no anger or longing just curiosity and a need for questions to be answered. We talked and made a plan to meet. She was in town visiting her daughter. I asked her how she found me and she said she had always had my parents phone number from many years ago and so she called and spoke to my mom. She lied and said she was an old friend. This didn't sit well with me but I had questions and needed to have closure. So we met. It was a sunny day. We met in front of a restaurant on Melrose. I brought my family. For better or worse I have kept no secrets from them. I can't stand secrets and lies. She told me I had a sister who was waiting to meet me. We all drove over to her home. I can still see her smile and warmth when she opened the door for us.

Ten days later the phone rang. On the other end was a voice, "Hello, this is your birth father. Your dad gave me your number. I'm in town and would love to meet you."

It was pure coincidence that 10 days apart I would hear from both of them. We met at my dad's restaurant and the three of us had a lovely dinner. I learned of a sister and two more brothers. I learned many more things. Years earlier my birth parents ran into to each other and my birth mother let him know my dad's name was Milton Weiss. Every time he came to greater Los Angeles he would look my dad up in the hotel's phonebook but but to no avail until he finally landed in Beverly Hills and found him.

My biggest worry was how my sister and brother would accept my new reality. I knew my mother couldn't. I understood, but her fears were unfounded. My father was always about love and acceptance.

There was always a hole in me, a place where pain would always find its way in. Having this closure changed my life. I understand how lucky I am, to have my family, who I love more than life, to know who I am and where I came from. Most people take this for granted. I live in gratitude and love. It turns out I was the lucky one.

http://www.cathyweissink.com

Sidney Tuggerson Jr

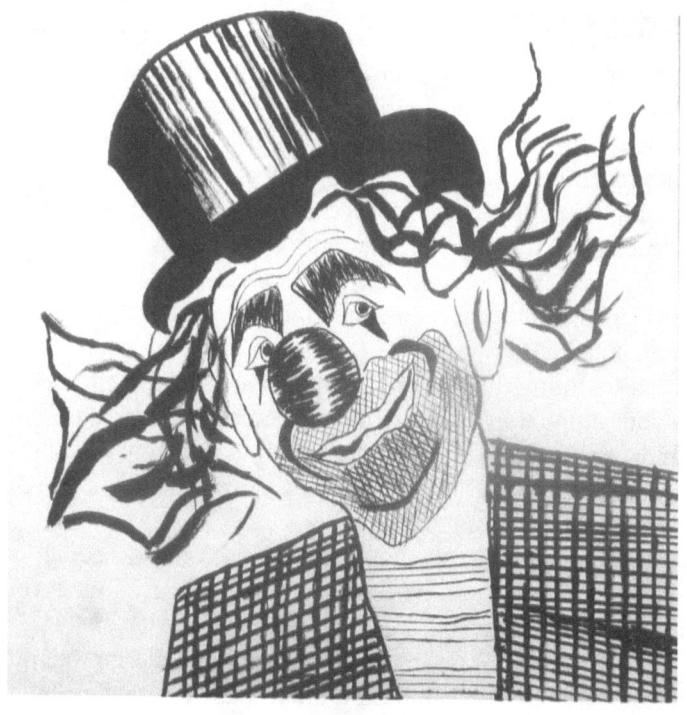

Clown

I was born in Reddick, Florida. Marion County to a family of six kids, five sisters and myself, as the middle child. siblings, we were taught to love one another and respect the right of other, my mother and father didn't have a high school education. But they made sure we got one. Raised on a Ranch type farm with plenty horse and cows my grandfather was very instrumental in my upbringing as a young man. He was a bull-dogger only stood 4'ft. 9" he taught me how to respect the animals, growing up as a little boy I got the chance to ride the horse and wrestle the cow. My sister and I use to go to the barn where there was a trap door where we drop bail of hay to the horses in the corral then we would jump on their backs some of them try biting you to get you off. my sisters and I used to get into the pasture and take my grandfather red kerchief and wave at the bulls acting as matadors. growing up as a child my siblings and me, we have had wonderful times together.

My intention was to go to college, by the end of my senior year after graduation. I found myself inducted into the service. So I volunteer for the Marine Corp. August 1966 since the Marine, known for their fighting skill. I thought my chance were much better for my survivor in Viet-Nam. although I was fighting for right here in America, the good old U.S.A. that didn't recognize that caused. they just demand you service your country. which I did, knowing that I would come back here in the U.S.A. endure the same pain and suffering for the right to be an equal citizen.

It's a funny thing when you in a war, no matter what race or your ethnicity you are, and you became one. because your life depended on your survived, no grip or hostility was shown to your fellow man, but soon as you return home you go your separate ways. nothing change

When will society accept you as a black man as equal, not under distress or war or disaster? that's the only time your color doesn't matter.

To this day, my sibling and I remain the bond between us, and our kids and their kids and grandkids. not too shabby for a farm boy

(Please do a search for artist iniformation)

Linda Parnell

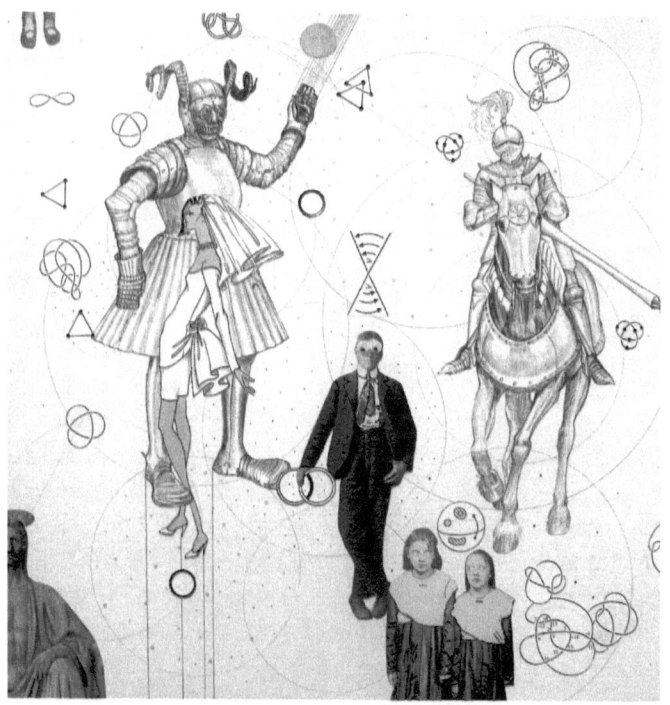

bride and her bachelors

20 things about me

—robert wyatt and i became real blood brothers in 6th grade. many years later he became a black panther. robert, if you're reading this, BRING BACK THAT LITTLE KNIFE YOU STOLE FROM ME!

—wondering what i'm doing in other dimensions; when are we waves and when are we particles?

—i could walk when i was 8 1/2 months old and could run at 9 months.

—i was very small and used to hide and get lost a lot. people would tell my mom she needed a harness for me but she refused and said I seemed much to much like a little monkey already and she was certainly not a circus character!

—wish i could talk with max planck.

—i have a dear friend who lays in her bathtub for hours saying she's completely free of all laws since only maritime applies.

—certain colors vibrate my teeth and other colors stir melodies in my head.

—-almost got my mom and dad arrested while on vacation when i was about 7. parents were driving along, talking, not paying any attention so i started looking through my dad's fishing box and got out the fishing line. had a little knife in my pocket (the one Robert wyatt stole) that i cut the fishing line with and then tied some socks to the end of it. slowly let it out the car window like a kite. the sock was behind the car about 30 feet when it hit the window of a cop car.

—can read minds.

—always oriented to compass directions

—read voraciously yet i'm the worlds worst speller. once, almost wrote a check for 'ate' dollars.

—when i was very little i thought i was subnormal; was given some sort of IQ tests in 6th grade and my life changed for the worst as everyone wanted me to do school work! so i ran away, checked into a hotel with a check from my mom's checkbook; the hotel dude let me get into the room and then he called my parents. had planned pretty well for the escape — brought along wheat thin crackers and orange juice. when my parents got there all they wanted to know was where was i going? I was heading up to newfoundland where there are no schools, getting a dog, and become a fisherman.

—have trophies from winning racquetball tournaments.

—during meditation (or was it medication?) i once got to a place where i couldn't tell if I was a plant or a mineral or animal or what!

—when listening to music i focus on the outer parts rather than the main section.

—alter ego is zelda biaggi

—always trying to open the front door with the car clicker. never works.

—favorite vacation is to go to another country and not have any destination or plans...just head out to see what adventures come!

http://www.artslant.com/global/artists/show/27283-linda-par-nell

Peter Hess

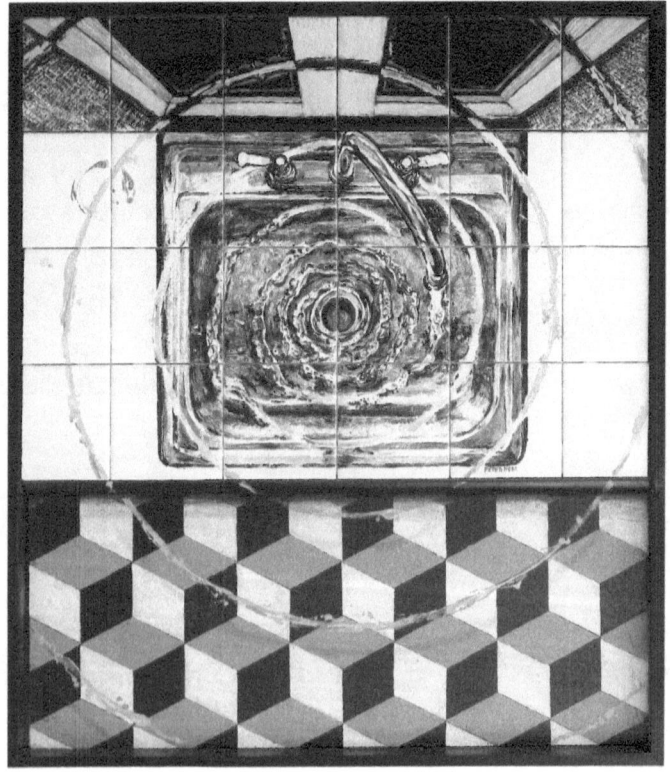

The Kitchen Sink

Dear Mr K

I address you as Mr. K rather than by the given name with which I called you when we were children because, having not laid eyes on you (to my knowledge) for nearly 40 years and, presuming that you are still among the living, you are a grown man of advancing years as I am myself. I have no right to address you as a friend would since I never treated you in the way that friends ought to treat one another. In fact, I would characterize my behavior toward you as harassment bordering on torment.

Only by this letter would you know it, but it is now you who torment me.

I write to you today with some urgency since I learned that another individual deserving of redress is no longer living. That would be Mr. G. When I was gripped with remorse recently, I Googled him and discovered that he had passed away very, very recently. To drive the point home, I was able to view his cemetery marker on Find A Grave. A black engraved slab of standard shape and size, unremarkable, and I have no idea what or whom killed him in the prime of midlife. For a moment it occurred to me that maybe he took his own life, and that my harangues were a pebble in the foundation of his despair.

You may or may not have known Mr. G, but you had things in common. Those things made you my target, even as I myself was a target for those crueler and stronger than me. Both of you were rotund and far from handsome, both of you were shunned by hot girls and jocks, both of you had only a small circle of friends and both of you seemed to have above average intelligence. You were in F Troop in PhysEd. You belonged to strange after school clubs. You were rarely without your books. Most of those descriptors could have been applied to me, but to a slightly lesser degree. And therein lies the difference. That is why I taunted you, and shamed you, and name-called you. Both of you. Because I was like you, only not quite as much.

And there were others on whom I inflicted pain. The one with the twitch, whom I trailed through the supermarket aisles and whose gestures I lampooned, even while his mother yelled at me to please, please stop. And there was the one with the twisted hand. And the poor one with the old clothes who was so easy to beat up. And that one on the nice bicycle who flew to the pavement when I stuck a broomstick through the spokes. Tearing the wings off butterflies. Pitting red ants against black ants in a coffee can to watch them fight. And the vandalism, and the shoplifting, and the lying. I still wince when I think about the things I did as a boy. Recounting them, I must seem like a monster. Are all children so cruel and indifferent? Impossible. Children are innocent.

http://www.PeterHessArt.com

Cindy Rinne

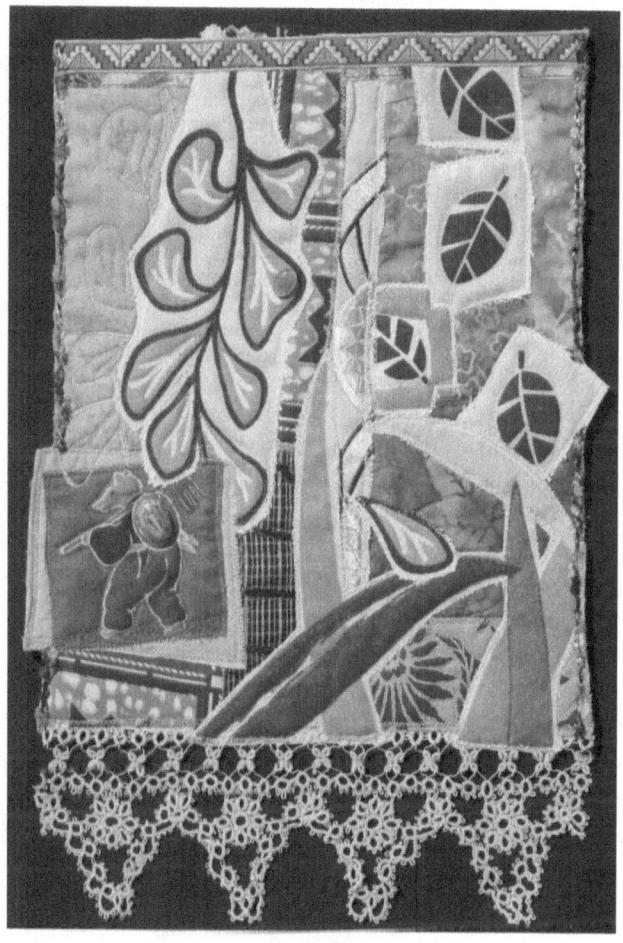

Fox's Journey. 15x10" Fiber Art 2014

Of Earth & Water

Some say Turtle created the world. Certainly impacted mine. One summer Grandpa in Cicero came from Illinois to visit my family in Kansas City, Missouri. He was thin, and wore wire rim glasses. Two of his fingers were missing from a work-related accident. Grandpa in Cicero was a factory work-er. His two wives passed away by the time my father was 16. I roller skated on the back patio. The patio was a small circle with a metal pole to hold up the green fiberglass covering. I used the pole to spin around on my metal, four-wheel skates. As I was skating, Grandpa in Cicero tried to get my four-year-old brother to taste beer. My brother wasn't too sure about this strange smelling brew. My mother kept telling Grandpa to stop, but to no avail. My brother tried a sip. Pulled his head back into his shell.

Grandpa took me on a mile hike to Indian Creek. My family didn't tend to take walks. This was extra special because I got to be alone with my grandpa. I usually gazed at this creek from the car. The large dip in the road where the creek ran would flood with spring rains. That left one main road to get home. I jumped from rock to rock and slipped at the edge of the rushing water. Grandpa grabbed my arm to steady me. I enjoyed the sounds and looked for fish. Climbing up the hill on the return walk, we found a turtle in the road. It was unusu-al to see a turtle in the suburbs. Can we keep him? Grandpa carried the turtle home. I have a pet. Mom placed the turtle in the bathtub with some lettuce until we let it go. Grandpa from Cicero died when I was ten. I missed going to his house every other summer and eating Chicago pizza.

FAST FORWARD. My son thought he was Michelangelo from the "Teenage Mutant Ninja Turtles." This was when these characters first came out. He would talk to them in the sewer on our street. Guess what he was for Halloween. My daughter didn't identify with characters or pretend in this way, so this was new to me.

The idea of being a turtle was so real to him that he joined the local turtle club. We attended monthly meeting at the San Bernardino County Museum. He listened to the speaker and checked out children's books from their library. We learned a lot. A couple of members saw how serious he was and gave him two box turtles. The club members were particular about who adopted their turtles. Sunny and Sparky lived in our garden content to eat snails which helped make the herbs bountiful.

They knew the sound of our voices and would turn their heads to greet us. Sunny and Sparky were good listeners. Their eyes held wisdom. One day, my son took them out of the garden and fed them strawberries on the patio. Sunny decided he was a water turtle and leapt into the pool. He didn't know how to swim. I fished him out to safety. Some say Turtle is Earth Mother.

http://www.fiberverse.com

Andrea Bogdan

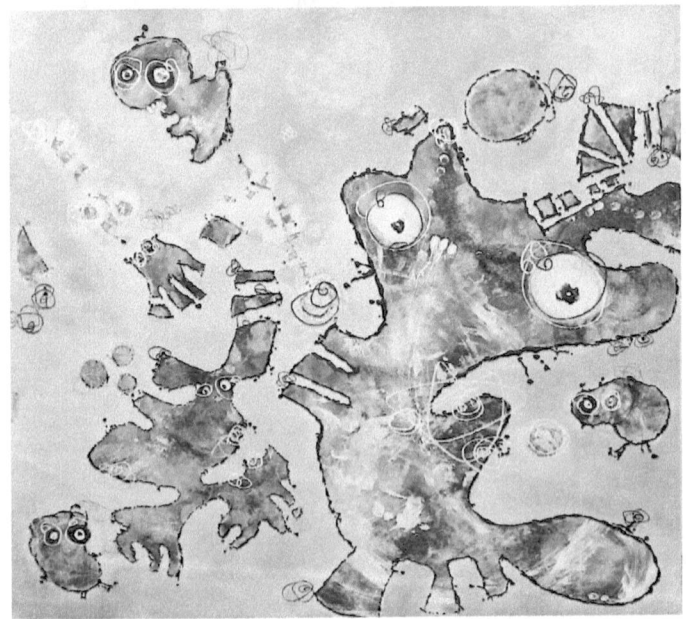

The Rebel

Agonal Breathing

I passed the violet-colored pick-up at the Pacoima on-ramp same as every other workday. Our trucks were identical, twin smiles of brotherhood that know the value of a sturdy ride.

It was Monday, and perfect in every way. My appetite for invention was finally tempered by the systems, rules, and fear that had closed my throat enough to make me grateful for the morning air. The fire in my belly still smoldered, but it was no longer a destructive, self-immolating flame. As long as the right forms were filled out and turned in on time, all was well. And on this day I was content because my committee would meet on a project I understood and believed in.

In the cafe I teased the cook about his perfect omelets and chatted with the cashier about her daughter's art. Joining the

CIO at a table, her meeting notes spread out like a fan, we agreed to start a new project together. Usually these talks ended with instruction about process, but today it was easy and light.

Only months before I was on both knees, head on my chair, sobbing. It was a ridiculous pose. It was late evening and the building was empty. I had lost three key people, and was unable to fill a new position. In the morning my remaining unhappy staff would return and I had no solutions to our problems. So to have an easy interaction about something that mattered was a major victory.

Back in the office, walls covered in post-it notes, I shuttled between projects, moving easily from one to the other, as my checklist dictated. This type of efficiency made me happy. The ad agency arrived early for the "meeting before the meeting" and I squinted at cost estimates and budgets, signing where there was a match and editing where there wasn't. This meant work would get done, and plans would be followed. By now my beloved efficiency meter was quivering at optimal output.

It was a very good day.

We set up the room with vigor. This was "my" meeting, and I sweated every detail, from the temperature to the lighting. I was pleased to see three executives arrive. Can you hear me? Can you see the slides? Which parts surprise you? What should we do next? The sun was seeping through the blinds and I closed them to protect our eyes.

Scanning the room for reactions, I glimpsed my boss typing on his phone, another V.P. checking the time. That's ok, I told myself. It's late. People are tired. This isn't everybody's priority. Just yours.

Adjourning, I gathered notes for my assistant so decisions could be documented. As my boss slipped past he prompted me to meet him down the hall in HR. Excellent! The four unfilled positions had been vacant too long and I welcomed this intervention. "Wait in my office," I told the agency. Help was on the way.

When I got to M's door, it was closed. And locked. Darn. I must have heard wrong. Where did they go? I heard the familiar creak of his chair as he rose to let me in. My boss is at the guest table. I'm offered the opposite seat. I sit sideways, trying, impossibly, to face them both because M has returned to his desk.

The words rolled over the table like a low, distant thunder. "Today is your last day," my boss said. He laid a large, mustard-colored envelope in the center of the table. A tangle of words followed. Loyalty. Thank you. It would be easier if you resign. He exits.

M slid over to the seat next to me. "I'll get D to take you through this," he offered.

"No, M, I've known you a long, long, time, and I'd rather you do it."

In fact, I had known M for 15 years, and my boss for almost 20.

"Can I say goodbye to my staff?"

"What will you tell them?"

"That I'm going on a great adventure."

Back in my department the hall was silent. The doors were closed. My assistant looked shocked to see me, but said nothing. I found the other two huddled in an office. One was sobbing, and the other, in character, blurted, "What the f#k??!!"

Driving home I looked for the violet-colored pick-up so I could wave from my sturdy, predictable ride.

http://www.andreabogdan.com

Dakota Noot

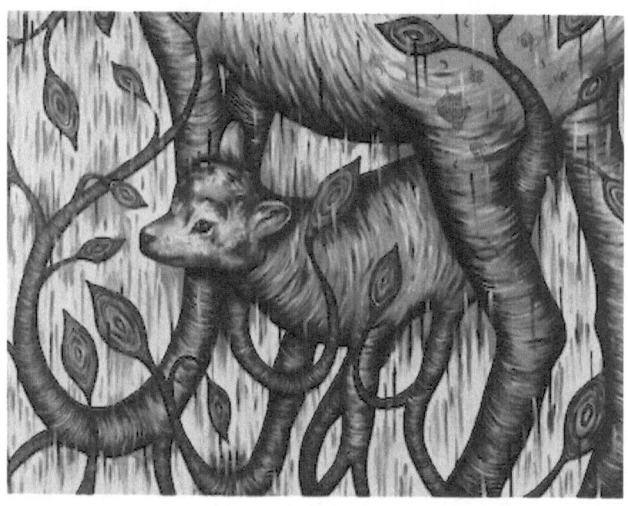

Nature exists in California. I was not prepared for that fact, but it sprung forth like a flower between the concrete. I knew nothing of the Etiwanda Preserve before going there. I barely even knew how to get there. I had to rely on technology to find the place, but after several missed turns and screaming matches with my phone, I arrived.

I thanked my car for survival as if it were a steel god. It sadly didn't respond. I gaped at everything around me, not caring that I looked less like my usual self and more like an escaped asylum inmate taking in the outdoors for the first time. I simply breathed.

It wasn't too hot that day. The sun lazily glided in the sky: a rarity of calming warmth in the summer. I saw my friend waiting for me. He stood by scattered rocks, each covered with graffiti. Even in nature, man persisted or at least bored teenagers did.

We greeted each other, taking time to observe our surroundings. I saw mountains in the distance, but my friend said they were barely that. Coming from the flat prairies of North Dakota, anything taller than a two-story building seemed like a mountain.

I wanted to see mountains, experience them, and drink them in. Even now, I am not accustomed to seeing mountains. It's bizarre. I hoped that hiking up the path would feel like traveling into a television set. The images I had only seen on a screen could turn real.

My daydreams didn't account for the actual walk.

We started hiking, awkwardly making our way through paths of jagged rocks. An ocean of sagebrush was all around us. If the slightest wind would hit, the plants would move like a gentle wave. I must have been suffering from heat exhaustion to think that. Maybe it was hotter out than I thought.

After several stops and fights over the water bottle, which I won, we arrived in creek on the preserve. We had moved from the desert into an oasis of trees. It was beautiful. It seemed like an illusion.

The trees welcomed us into their shade. I would live to get skin cancer another day. We kept walking, watching a stream of water run over the rocks. There was no one else here. I had found tranquility away from traffic.

I was surprised that California had untouched pockets of nature like this, but it was still California. Instead of a babbling brook, the steam ran like a clogged faucet. The drought persisted, but I still stood in awe.

We found a large rock to sit on, giving us room to unload our backpacks. Under the leaves of Etiwanda, we shared sweet oranges, freshly picked from my friend's home.

I was raised in a far colder place than California. It was in this trip that I realized how beautiful California is. I could never have imagined hiking into anything taller than a bunny hill. Even eating a fresh orange was odd to me. I had never eaten a better orange. It burst with juice. California was a hot, dry place, but filled with intensely beautiful moments like sharing an orange with my new friend. The land burst with flavor.

I had found my new home. I would then get lost finding my apartment on the way back.

(Please do an internet search for how to contact this artist.)

Ron Therrio

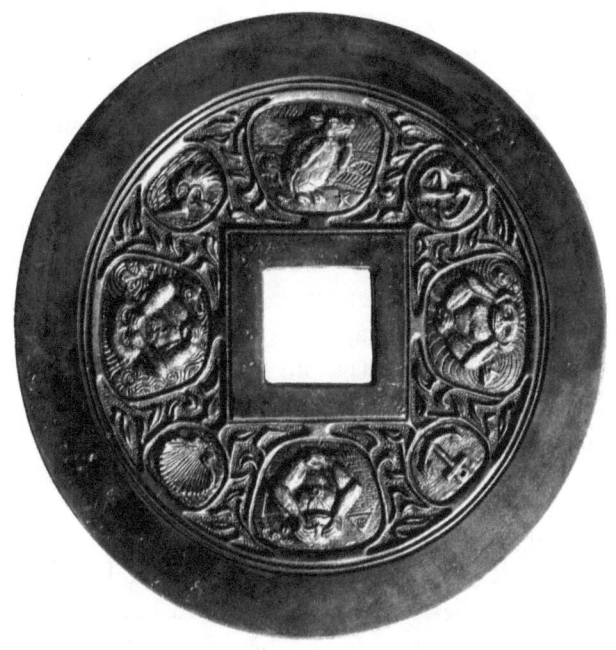

München 72

I remember a few days earlier I was sitting in a record shop of sorts, choosing a few and sitting at a turntable booth with headphones listening to J. Geils Band's first release tracks 4 and 5 off of side one, Big Brother's Summertime and Ball & Chain, and a bit of Hot Tuna and V.U. I was 17 years old and the date was August 31, 1972. I was in Munich Germany.

The day was bright and the shop was in the center of the athlete's Olympic Village universe. I was wearing an official Olympic warm-up jacket I had liberated from my brother or one of the other Olympic Cyclists that I knew. I also had gleaned an Official ID badge of dubious authenticity. My brother was on the Olympic Cycling Team. The year before he had won the US National Championships in the junior division for both the road

& track events -- very impressive due to the fact that one event required stamina and endurance, and the other required explosive strength and tactical sprinting abilities. I do not think it had ever been done before, nor has it been done since.

Although I kept it a well guarded secret, I was enjoying Munich. We were staying at my Opa's home in Lohhof, just outside of Munich. He was soft spoken and kind and had a pleasant, gentle nature; yet you could sense an inner strength and dignity, not one to be trifled with. The train was a short walk from his home with a bakery and a market that sold Gitanes nearby. Also a 3rd cousin whom I believe was living in Northern France had driven down in his early 1960's Citroen 2CV. He stayed for a few days. He too was a very pleasant soul. German was my first language, my mother was German. When I was about four years old, she switched to speaking only English with my brother and me when our cousins came to live with us. Even so, at this point in my life I still understood quite a bit and could speak enough to get around.

The following day I went over to the medieval town of Dachau. I wanted to visit the memorial to the lives that had perished under the Nazis. When I arrived I stood out front, unwilling to enter. I was repulsed that so many had died in that place, and yet people all around it just went about there business as they do anywhere else. It was a beautiful summer day- -empty darkness was all I could feel inside. I walked down the road and came upon what appeared to be a hippie/gypsy camp site. A few of them were close at hand. They greeted me, and invited me to have a visit. I accepted the friendly invitation and they shared a joint with me. It was potent, and I started thinking how cool it would be to just stay and travel with them. Shortly thereafter a few grey clouds started rolling in from the west. I then asked myself why choose to camp so close to "that" place? It was at this point my thoughts started racing around and turned darker. I thanked them for their hospitality and abruptly excused myself, awkwardly moving on, eventually making my way back to Lohhof.

I spent the next few days going to the cycling events, acquiring any and all of the "comp" tickets I could get my hands on, and selling them at a reduced price outside the events to the Anglo touristy types. This coupled with a few trips to the Marienplatz and visits to the Hofbrauhaus to spend the fruits of my labors. My brother was the youngest cyclist on the U.S. team. His event was the Tandem Match Sprint. He and his partner did not fare so well. The first match was with the Russian team. The Russians won the match and went on to win the gold medal. Their second and sudden death match was with the East Germans (GDR) and, well, the GDR won the silver medal. It was time to get back to the Hofbrauhaus.

The next morning, I woke up to find that the terrible darkness had descended once again. I felt a knot in my stomach as I heard slivers of news about what had happened the previous night in the Olympic village. The rumors were of the Israeli athletes being taken as hostages by a group of Palestinian terrorists. We knew very little, and throughout the day only little tiny bits of news filtered in. The brief conversations amongst us all ended on an optimistically hopeful note, but the mood was somber. We had the use of a VW bus and my father, mother, uncle, my brother's girlfriend and I loaded up the van, collected my brother from the Olympic Village and drove into the Bavarian Alps for a few days. Although this trip was in the original plan, it seemed as if we were running away. We were escaping to avoid the harsh reality that life so often serves up. Ironically, we ended up in the Neuschwanstien Castle, known as the Fairy Tale Castle, built by King Ludwig II as a private retreat and homage to Richard Wagner. Understandably, it was an inspiration for Walt Disney's Magic Castle. It was hard to fathom in such a setting, the horribly news; how the events in Munich had finally unfolded.

The painful truth and overwhelming surrealism made it difficult to feel anything but numb.

http://www.Rontherrio.com

Barbara Kerwin

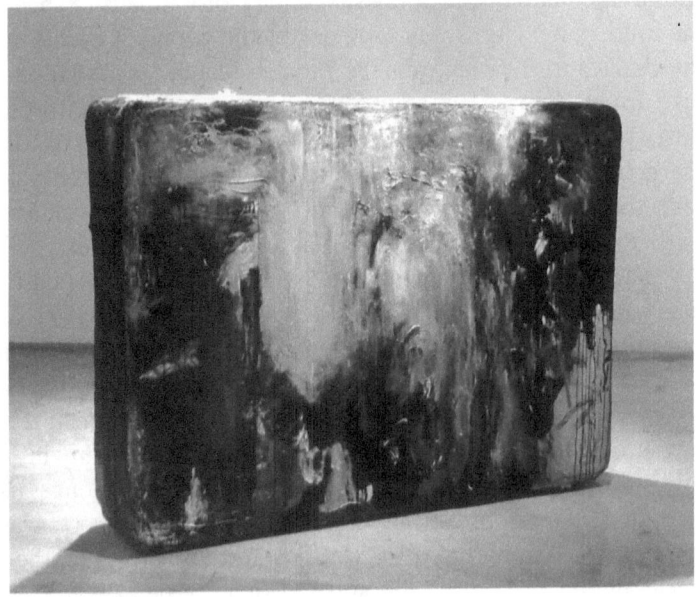

Slip Push Pull

The Ranch

Reaching overhead for the doorknob late at night from my mother's kitchen to follow a wooden path that led me to the two-seater outhouse was a regular nocturnal habit. I liked going down the steep staircase, through the living room, past the woodstove into the kitchen while the ranch house slept. At dawn, my big sister would come get me from my lower bunk bed in the little kids' room, whispering, "Come on, Barbie." I'd reach for my elastic-waist blue jeans and pull them on and whatever shirt mom had out for me.

My big sister and I would go down to the creek, under Three Billy Goat's Gruff Bridge (where we put on plays) and we'd turn our heads down and look for the little creatures that moved in the morning light through the shallow waters. Buttercups, wild ginger, and clovers, along with many wonderful plants and herbs flanked the microcosmic world. As the house stirred I could hear my dad whistling as he'd start his chores. I liked going up with him to the pump house on the hill. There were giant toads that lived in there, and the smell was dank from the old wood and dirt floor. Dad would pour water into the hand-cranked pump until it would flow through the pipes to a gravity feed into mom's kitchen. Mom would have the wood stove stoked and breakfast ready at a big dining table where our family of 7 ate all of our meals. Some days I'd go with dad to the barn, but it was a place we were not to play. The milk cows were in there and the feisty bull he named "Ike". The Clydesdales were in their stalls over night and needing to go to pasture. Some days, dad would take me in Dynamite, his WWII jeep with a red painted grill, out into the forest, where there was a ravine he'd dump the garbage. Many days, he'd drive me to an opening in the forest, where he'd chop a tree down, and split the other dried tree into firewood. I was like his puppy. When he'd tell me to stay, I did. I'd watch him from the jeep. Taking in the beauty of this place I'd watch him chop the wood, bring it to the jeep and unload it back at the ranch house outside mom's kitchen.

Some days, we'd have baths. This was a major undertaking. Mom had to boil pots of water on her big cook stove to fill our tin tub. On warm days, we bathed outside but the winters came early on the Olympic Peninsula, so it was often in her kitchen.

I'd sneak from my bunk bed at naptime to watch the magnificent rainstorm that often rolled down the mountain then. Old timers call these "freshits". Our ranch was situated in the midst of giant mountains; with thick forests all around the open pasture lands. As the rain moved down the mountain, it darkened the view, but light before it remained. It was quite the show! I was little, so I had to nap, but the older girls were out playing somewhere. I got up from my sleep and went to find them. Mom was making butter from the milk cow's supply. She was churning a cranked bucket. She asked me to get some cream from her cooler, a cupboard door that closed to the kitchen but was screened to the out doors, covered walk way.

I wanted to go find my sisters. On this day, I saw the Milk House door was a little open. I knew this clean room to be off limits. But I wandered in, anyway. Big stainless steel vats with valves and tubes were there. The room was incredibly tidy. There was a ladder. I climbed up into the attic. It was a tiny space, suitable for a playhouse. An old doll was in there. A strong feeling of remorse came over me. I wasn't supposed to be there and I grew intensely lonely for a sister. I left the Milk House. I found them playing down by the Canning Shed. Dad had tools outside the room where shelves of glass jars resided. All of these out buildings had their instructions to not disturb. We were never allowed inside the Smoke House, where the pigs and cows were slaughtered and hung to cure. I saw it once while dad and Uncle Fred were at work during the season. The garage floor had a trap door we liked to go into, that was where the root cellar was and potatoes and other vegetables were kept over the winter. My eldest sister led the way, when she wasn't in school. Whatever they did, exploring the woods with a little map and following the blazes in the trees, it was always an adventure.

When dad pulled in from the end of the long driveway after work, he'd honk his horn and we'd all run screaming his name. He'd give us a big hug and let us ride on the runner boards back up to the ranch house, across the bridge. He liked to listen to football games on a big grey battery operated radio. He'd prop his boots up on the edge of the little wood stove in the living room. It roared hot. I'd lay my face on the cool linoleum and listen, too. Dad worked on the Strait of Juan de Fuca during the day as an engineer. He drove up the mountain in time for dinner and sometimes catch the sunset on the front porch and watch deer grazing close to the house. Night times came early before we wanted to sleep. To lullaby us, they would serenade from the top of the stairs, mom playing the guitar and dad's beautiful tenor voice unwinding the storied songs.

http://www.barbarakerwin.com

Melissa Ann Lambert

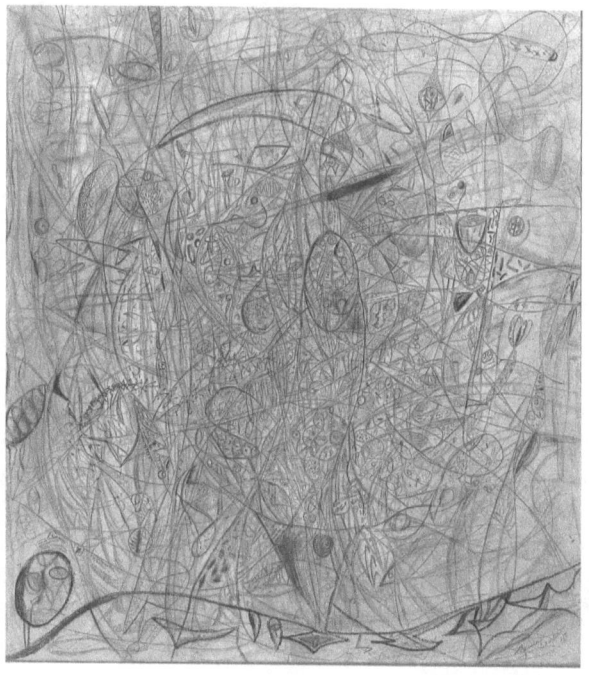

ASTRO PODS

My parental units did not know what synesthesia was; of course I didn't either. Everybody has hallucinations and sees auras and flashing light shows and hears, smells and feels textures; right? My synesthesia is a lot more involved than that, impossible to describe. When I do art, I go into another dimension. REPLACE Sometimes I go into another dimension. At times it can be extremely annoying. And when I'm tired, I cannot "turn it off". When I was younger, I could not see into a room because the auras were so strong. I've learned how to control it, but when experiencing extreme fatigue it's impossible to control. As surely as it is annoying I'm sure it has directly contributes to my artistic process.

THE DEVIL FACE

There was a very intense red light that reminds me of a laser point device. It was extremely tiny and seemed light-years away. Very slowly, it began to grow larger and larger. The next thing I knew, it was hovering right above my head, about 3 inches away. It was a scowling, horrendous devil face. It rotated 180° rapidly, and it was the most terrifying thing that had ever happened to me. I felt insane, it was so powerful. I did my best to muster up a feeling of control, which was incredibly difficult. Gripping the bed with my hands, I told myself "I'm JUST a little girl, I've done nothing wrong." It worked, but I was shaken and really upset. I never told my parents or brothers about it, I was ashamed. Only later, when I came across Jung's collective unconscious theory, did I add up that from "saints and sinners" both I descend from time immemorial.

The very first dream I remember as a child of six or seven: my parents had introduced me to the concept of God and the devil. I was flying with God Superman style and he gave me a choice of which time period to live in. I looked at the past, and being my logical self even as a child in my dreams; I realized people had too many teeth problems in the past so I didn't want to live there. I then looked into the future and knew there were too many problems with nuclear weapons and overpopulation. So even though I realized that nuclear weapons and overpopulation were a problem in the present day; I still decided to live in the present time.

In another dream it was Halloween all over the world. Rather than children going door-to-door however, it was the adult that got go from door to door. And these adults got to show off their best skill sets. Children under the age of 13 or not allowed to participate so my younger brother and I could not go, however my older brother and my parents left to "do their thing". About 10 min. after they had left, my brother and I saw a man come to the open door who was wearing a suit and a hat. He was carrying a stool and a briefcase, and he proceeded to set it down on our hearth. He glanced up at this, and asked "are you ready?" We nodded with anticipation. He then opened his briefcase slowly taking out large metal pins about 7 inches long apiece. Proceeded to put a pin to the left and to the right at either side of the ankles, the knees, the hips, shoulders, and the front and back of the neck. "Are you ready for the show?" he intoned. "Yes we are ready, we both said yes simultaneously." He then proceeded to tear his skin off starting with his calves then moving to his thighs, his torso, his neck. Then he turned to us and said "are you ready for the grand finale?" We were very eager to see the grand finale. He then tore the skin of his face off revealing his brain thinking. It looked like a lightning storm. I woke up feeling very excited. I remembered afterward that you could see the blood coursing through his veins, and it was absolutely fascinating. Was one of the most exciting things or rather dreams that I have ever had. I keep a dream journal now, I'm having a lean period the last few years but I still remember my dreams good enough to keep a dream journal. My shrink loves my dreams. I love them too.

I would lay on my bed every morning and stare at my hand and see auras around my hands. I saw auras on immaterial objects as well. For instance, an orange bottle always have a blue aura. It took until high school to realize that this was not "normal." Many of my teachers would speak in front of a white film screens. My favorite was my psychology teacher; here the wildest aura of anyone I've ever seen. A profile of his face would often jump out into space and travel to various students blending in with their auras. I've never seen anything like this before or since. Pretty amazing. I could never tell if it was really happening or if my eyes somehow invented this. I was careful who I told this information to us I thought people would think I was crazy. I did tell my father, because he knows that I am a very logical person who is good at math, and I figured he would not think that I was insane. I also told him how I fuck computers up, and I also stop watches. He said I should report this to some electromagnetic foundation, I assured him that they would think that I was a nutter and a loonbin. I like to joke I don't need LSD, I'm already on it. The only difference between my brain on acid and my brain off acid are trails.

http://www.MelissaAnnLambert.com

Peggy Sivert Zask

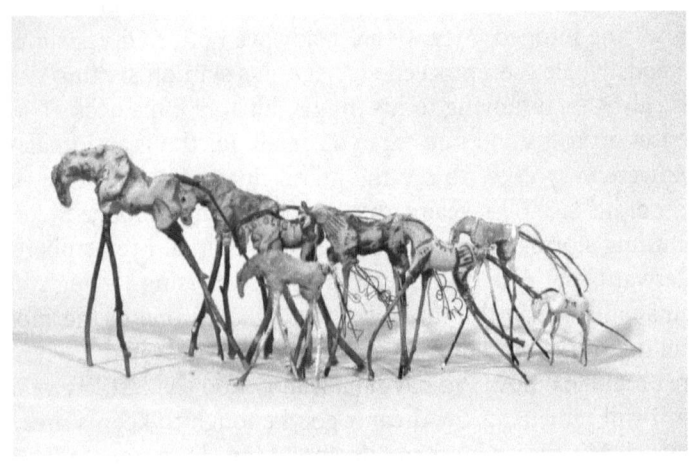

Herd

Horse Girl

A sloping curved cement stage carried the big red tricycle, adapted to fit my 4-year-old legs. A developing sense of importance began while adjusting roller skates with my skate key and playing the father in our games, rolling down the sidewalk into the driveway, home from an imaginary job.

That tricycle faded out of its role as my vehicle when we moved into the rural suburbs. The horses stepped in, the white fences surrounded them and my world started. It was a slow building of trust and balance with the horse, learning without lessons or rules, it was an introduction to nature.

Grooming was the entry point in the relationship with this big animal. A black rubber curry comb with red cotton strap that looped over my hand would circle over the horses entire body, bringing up the loose hair and dirt from its coat and finishing with brushes for the shine. Grooming tools were collected like new toys and hours would pass in front of the barn, the horse loosely tied to a post, patiently standing at rest.

The smell of hay and horse combined in a pleasant horse

home where the horses grew to expect me each afternoon. The musty barn was dark and enclosed, horses stomping, munching hay, breathing, and snorting. Dark eyes, curving muscles, a huge power on four heavy iron clad hooves would stand in greeting every day.

Walking into the California sunshine corral with a big water bucket, space to roll in warm dust and see the world, I hold a rope halter up for the horse, both walking forward we enter into this relationship of equine and humankind.

flies, dust, mud, mold, manure, pee, dog hair
birds, trees, Sun, hills, wind, clouds

Balance came over time, a few falls in the beginning and eventually I became part of the horse. Learning to ride bareback with no saddle, on a horse back of perfect symmetry, my tailbone meeting horse spine, curving up into powerful neck and head with ears reacting to every sound or shadow. As my fingers pulled through the course groomed mane I would talk softly, stroking the neck. The spine curved under me into a huge muscle mass, the rear end like the power source topped with a flowing tail.

Horse training became part of my practice in place of sports after school. Time in the arena gave me time to develop a precise communication with the horse, a vocabulary of body language. Navigating the neighborhood streets, maneuvering the horse around cars and obstacles, the communication with the horse was important to keep us safe. A prey animal, the horse is always looking, listening and expecting. On its back, never sure what move the horse may make suddenly, a constant awareness of horse senses was part of the balance.

The build up of surging energy could be felt in anticipation of the run in the unfolding open space. Legs wrapped around belly, hands holding leather reins and the rest was up to trust and fate in balance upon the strong backbone.

Year in and year out, horse and rider became a unity of transformative energy.

In the heat of summer, the horse lowered its neck,
Sharing sweat
Soft dust on trails creating clouds behind our path.

Moving shadow Patterns on the tan ground
Created by great sinewy eucalyptus trees.
In winter bundled in jackets the horse is eager to run.
Windy days even more, head high, nostrils flair,
Bit in mouth, reins in hands.
The spooky unknown, tense and alert.

A daily meditative practice has replaced horse care. My time is spent working creatively with the anticipation of something transformative — the memories of seeking freedom and peace on the horse are ever present.My lifetime has been a developing relationship with nature in anticipation of meeting the greater energy on the path into the unknown.

http://www.Zaskgallery.con

Keariene Muizz

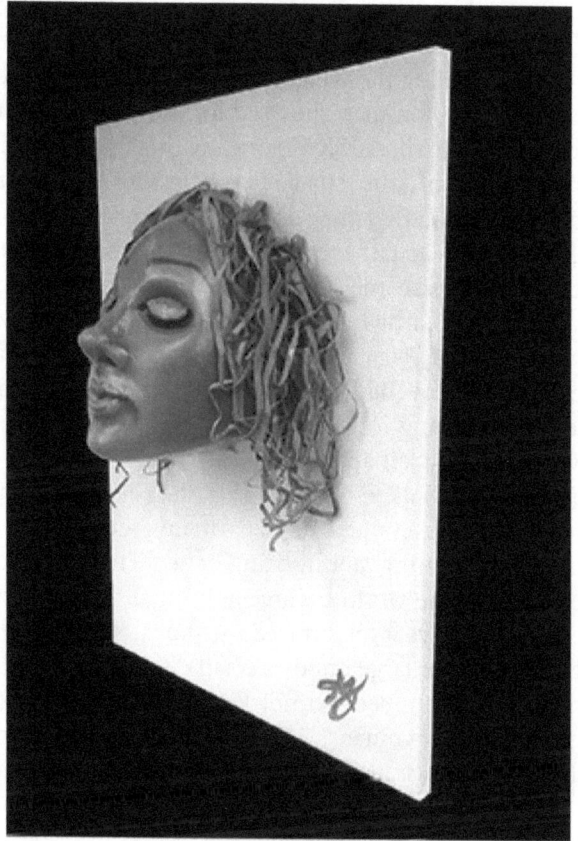

Days In The Dark

Good Girls

"The world may not like you some day," my mother said unexpectedly, erupting from the corner of the mattress after a long defeated silence. She did not look at me. But my presence in the doorway of the bedroom abbreviated the sobs I heard from the kitchen. The air in that room felt heavier than the sunlight as her golden brown arm glided in my direction, palm open and upturned, as though she was in search of rescue, like someone underwater who no longer felt the safety of the swimming pool's cement floor and suddenly became afraid of drowning. With one quick glance I examined her hand, followed the dark creases of her lifeline, heart line and fate line with my gaze, feeling the weight of her burden unfold so similarly to the accordion map she used for the five of us to flee to Los Angeles –us, in those days, being my three siblings and her. Uncharacteristic of our small two-bedroom apartment off Florence Avenue, earlier that day I found myself alone. I was washing dishes when the front door shut abruptly and my mother rushed past me without a word in her charcoal pantsuit. My mother had always been the best-dressed woman I had ever known. I gave her space to ignore me because I understood her day had begun by taking one RTD bus to another, interviewing to get a job as a nurse. That must have been when her day fell apart.

Undivided, I walked to the edge of the bed and put my left hand in hers. She cupped all ten of my miniature fingers. Because she was sitting, and I, being of elementary school age, was standing — the world became abnormally even, and for a moment we were eye level. I traced the moisture on her cheeks, stared deep into her large impoverished eyes. They were brown like mine. She continued, "If not because you are Black then because you are a woman." The corners of her magenta lips curled into a weak smile, adding reassurance to her warning, "But I want you to know that these are good things."

It was the first time I saw my tears gather in the corner of someone else's eyes.

What my impotent heart wanted more than anything in that moment was to confiscate her pain and overthrow the chaotic thoughts storming the recesses of my mind. I stood bravely before her for what felt like an eternity, unaware that I would be forever insulated from within by our intercourse. It was a growth spurt of a different kind for the skin of my ten year old body to stretch into. My pupils enlarged, illuminated by the lightening of awareness that I might be penalized by the society surrounding me for things that I could not amend but that I must be anchored to my own sense of self and be self-determining –hop scotch, if you will, through the barriers before me as best I could. Then I gave my mother a nod of reassurance conveying to her that I would never forget that I was made good.

http://www.muizzgallery.com

Barbara Nathanson

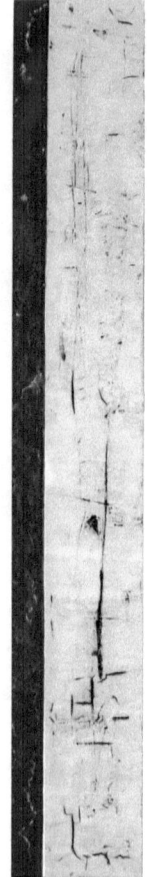

A Narative of a Moth

A couple of favorite early memories from my life.
A Bitter-Sweet Nap.

 Time frame: 1940's Sometime during WWII.

 Setting: Mid-summer on a farm outside Dayton, Ohio

 I was about 4 years old, living at the time, with my mater-
nal grandmother, grandfather, and 2 uncles about 8years and
10 years older than me respectively. My grandfather was out in

the fields working, my grandmother was attending a myriad of tasks, my uncles were off doing something fun together ...without me... "not wanted, little miss too young and a pain besides". I was bored and lonely. My grandmother shooed me out from under her feet..."go outside and find something to do" she said. I missed my momma, who was working somewhere in the city, wherever that was and my daddy was on a navy ship on the ocean, wherever that was. "What's a ship and an ocean?" I asked. "A big boat and a big water." "Like the pond?" I asked. "Way bigger than the pond, stupid" replied my uncle. Everybody was someplace else, doing something except me and I felt that "stupid" comment burn.

Feeling sorry for myself I ran out to a field behind the outhouse and threw myself on the ground and had a good cry. Lying on my stomach I finally stopped crying and started noticing a line of ants marching past my head. Each tiny ant was carrying a tiny object, following in a single line the same distance from the ant in front, keeping a consistent cadence. Curious. Fascinating. Actually mesmerizing me for a long time. After awhile I flipped over onto my back to watch the sky. Clouds were stretched and thin, it was very hot and humid. The sky was a hazy blue...blue was my favorite color. The grasses around me were tall and browning and very itchy. The sounds of the insects at this time of the summer were a constant, loud, buzz-hum. I liked the sounds. They took me away from my misery and put me to sleep.

A Bit of Mischief.

One year later...

It was now my paternal grandparents' turn to take care of me.

They lived in Elizabethtown, Kentucky, where I was born and partially raised.

Elizabethtown was small, consisting of a courthouse with a circle of stores around it...that was town then even though it first began as a town in the late 1700's.

I was happy to be living with Granny and Grampa since 3 of my younger cousins were living there too, for the same reason. Their daddies were also in the navy, on a big boat on the ocean and their mommies were also working to earn money.

Since I was the "oldest" and, I thought, the wisest now I was the decider of things to do to stay out of Granny's hair.

My Grampa was a carpenter and Granny, a homemaker, now had 3 grandchildren plus one teenaged daughter to care for. There were no modern conveniences to help with keeping a household humming, no washing machine, dishwasher, vacuum cleaner, television (whatever that was....at least I had never heard of such a thing yet) and a wood stove to cook on, so, like my other Grandmother, she was a very busy lady and we kids were told to go out and play and to not come inside until we were called for dinner.

Now my Grampa drank moonshine, made up in the hills somewhere (all of Kentucky is hilly). However, Granny, a staunch, teetotalling Presbyterian, did not approve of such bad habits. So Grampa kept his hooch hidden and took a swig now and then in secret. One day, my next oldest cousin and I happened to catch Grampa out in the shed taking a big, long drink then hiding the bottle back into its' dark corner. But Betty and I saw where he stashed it. After Grampa went back to work, we stole inside the shed, poured out the "whyte lightnen'" as it was called, and replaced it with the equally clear, but less satisfying water. Then we waited and watched for him to steal back in for a swig. It was our great delight to see him take a big drink, make a dreadful expression then spray-spit it out. We could tell he was MAD!! Knowing what our comeuppance would be if he caught us alone... we decided it would be a good idea to stay close to Granny for a good long while. The memory of our successful mischief was well worth the many days of sweepin' and dish dryin' we had to do if we were going to insist upon being underfoot.

(Please do an internet search for more info on the artist)

Wendy Smith

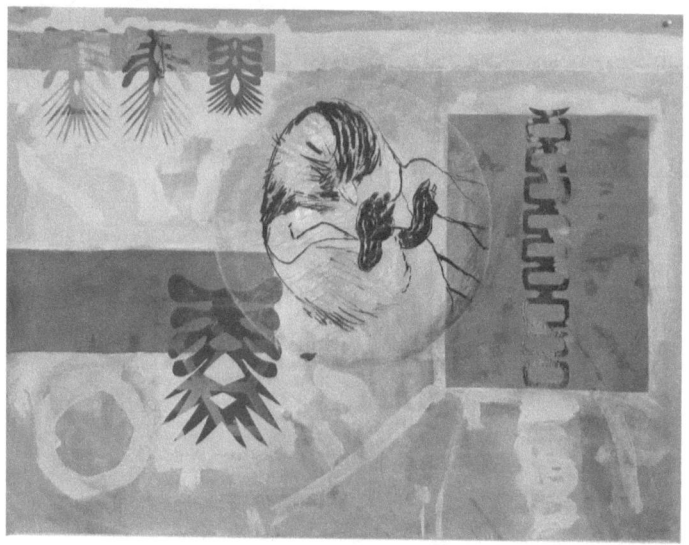

My son was home for Spring Break, a busy time as we were celebrating his 21st Birthday, a week early. He is now a physics major and has tried to explain some of what he is learning to me. He was talking about atoms and all the minute pieces of the universe that exist, so that if I touch a wall I am not actually touching anything. The wall seems solid to my touch because the forces of electrical energy keep all the atoms and electrons in place. In fact the forces between my hand and the wall push back, giving this illusion of solidity. We know that the reality of the atom is a vast space between the nucleus and the electrons. We experience the effects of these forces.

This made me think of an example of experiencing the effect of forces beyond our control. My Mum at 82 was thought to be a relative by a woman who saw her walking along the street. Apparently my mother looks very Danish, so she conferred among her sisters and discovered that her father's, father, my Great great Grandpa was in fact Danish.

One of the dishes I loved that my Mum made was, cod in parsley sauce served with mashed potatoes and peas, the fish is cooked in milk, I know this is a very Nordic way to cook fish and wondered if this family dish came originally from Denmark. So even though consciously no one realized we had Danish genes, we experienced eating a meal directly related to that heritage

http://wendysmithartist.com

Ann Mitchell

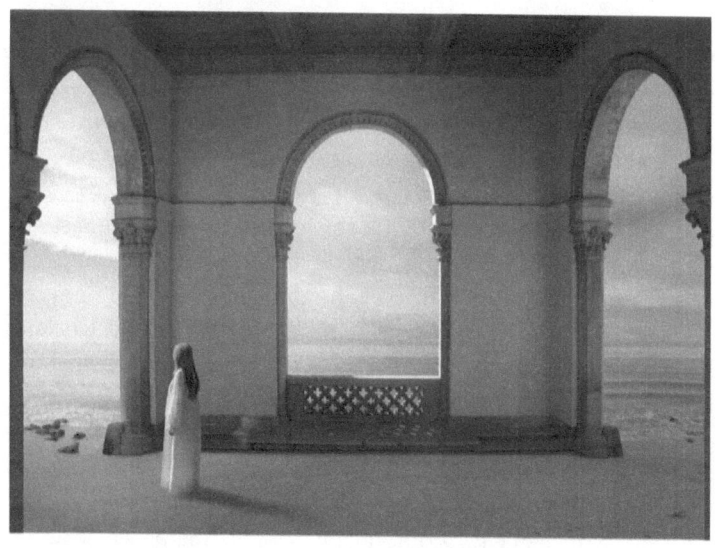

This past Christmas I spent a lot of time visiting my hometown and it has enveloped my bruised grown-up self with a warm mix of community and nostalgia. It's a small rural town in northern California, the kind where ex-cheerleaders slowly go to seed over the decades and your friends think you're more brilliant than you really are. Where the slow lazy days of summer get you out of your car and onto a bike. Where strangers say hello as they pass by on the street and everyone gives up the right of way at an intersection...except for young guys in pickup trucks...but they're that way everywhere. Most days are highlighted with the pleasant surprise of running into friends or relatives and you often find a jar of home-made jam on your doorstep from a neighbor. Hard to believe? I totally agree...but it does exist and I'm being wooed by it.

When I was growing up I couldn't wait to leave and get on with my life. Now I return two to three times a year on holidays, or when needed. As a kid I was oblivious to the incredible beauty of the surroundings. An agricultural center (rice and almonds), the fields put on a rhythmic and constant series of changing views. Over time, each visit home was also punctuated by pilgrimages to remembered sites: high school keggers, my first dance, first kiss...first everything. As the years went by the sites evolved and noticing those changes added a ghost-like layer to the experience.

Through several twists of fate, I now live in SoCal and what feeds me here is the constant banquet of variety it has. On one street I can go through Japan, Korea, Mexico, El Salvador, India...it's a movable feast. I like being able to find the last letterpress printer, driving through the last great rows of eucalyptus trees or eating lunch up in Panorama City – sitting between cops and the old women who remind me of my Aunt Connie. It's big, at times massively ugly, but it's been my home for a long time and I love its stories.

On the other hand, small towns have indie bookstores, accessible music scenes, real bike paths and a sense of connection to the people around you that I find soothing to the soul. It's said "you can't go home again" but in many ways home itself moves forward to meet you as you continue on your own path. New faces inhabit most of my old haunts...but the former imprint does remain and so the experience becomes this interesting blend of the new and old — connecting to my younger, wilder self without the intensity of the actual experience.

I fully understand that a big part of my gratitude at this homecoming comes from being somewhere other than the stage of my troubles...but what I've truly gotten from this experience is the reminder that there are many ways to live our lives...with many paths to finding home.

http://www.ann-mitchell.com

Pat Gainor

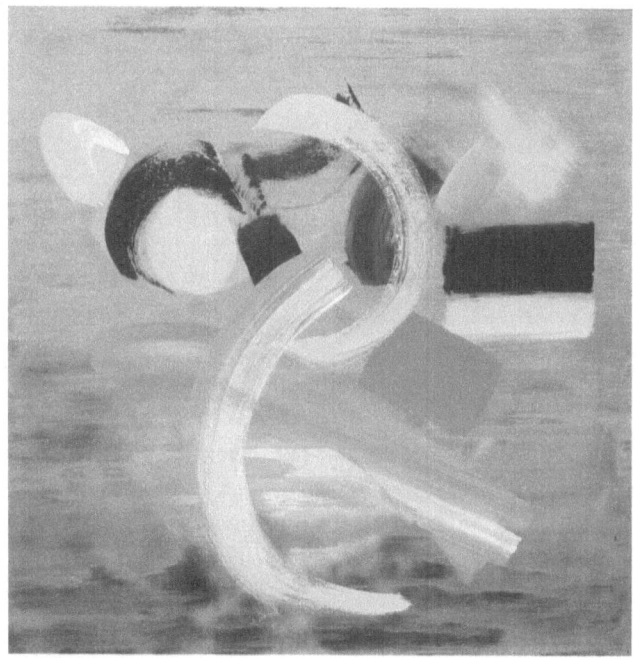

Interchange

ACT 1

On my first day after moving to New York I spotted a famous singer, waiting to cross 6th Ave. and proceeded to tell him how wonderful he was. Never missing a beat as we crossed the street he said, "You have a lot of chutzpah for a shiksa." Those words set the tone for my amazing adventures in NYC.

I was lucky enough to be accepted in the famous Rehearsal Club where aspiring actresses lived. Located on 53rd Street between 5th and 6th Avenues, it was a perfect location. The jack hammers would wake me up every morning and continue all day. My shared room was a four flight walk up. Nothing bothered me. I was in heaven.

I finally found a place that moved as fast as my brain was working. I embraced the city with the energy of a 20 year old ready to take on whatever it had to offer. Amazed and delighted I would order a burger at a café and it was in front of me before I could get out the money to pay for it. The whole town worked like that and I had found my "home".

I left my parent's house in Michigan with $225.00. I was on my own and it felt great!

Each day I 'pounded the pavement' looking for agents, going on auditions and "go sees" and scouring the show biz rags for opportunities. As I left the Rehearsal Club there was always a chorus of construction workers yelling down from the beams of the building they were putting up next door. "You're looking beautiful!" "Can you give us a smile?" "Come on gorgeous, just one little smile." "Make my day!" As a slight smile crossed my lips and they would break into applause. Those guys made my day! Who needs Dale Carnegie! They got my confidence up as I had to compete against the 'cream of the crop' of talented, beautiful women from around the world.

My friends at the Rehearsal Club were great. My new roommate and I would go out to the deli at night and our big treat was a cup of yogurt. She warned me how fattening that was. She had just made the cover of Mademoiselle. The girl across the hall was a Rockette and was always dieting. Every pound I lost brought me more work. My Mom said I looked like a skeleton but in NY I was just right.

We all tried to help each other. One of the girls recently reminded me how I recommended her for a modeling job and then lent her the clothes to wear. She went on to star in films and was bridesmaid at my wedding along with the stunning Liz Daly who I met on the steps of St. Patrick's Cathedral. She became a top run-way model at the time. We are best friends to this day along with her brother, Neil, who worked at NY's Carlyle Hotel.

NY is so concentrated you are always seeing people you recognize. One day, I was thrilled to run into the author of "Death of a Salesman", going into the Russian Tea Room. He was a big influence on my life as I had vowed after reading his play that I would never be like Willie Lohman. I was well on my way.

Five of my modeling friends from Michigan came to NY for a visit. I was able to finagle our way into being on the The Tonight Show! While talking to the host on camera I told him that we were big fans of his and would love to take him out to dinner. He did some wonderful double takes and got everyone laughing. After the show, his sidekick approached me to say the host would like to see us. We went up to his dressing room where one whole wall was television monitors and he could watch 20 programs at once. He was great and asked to take us to dinner. We all piled into his limo and were whisked off to Danny's Hideaway where we were treated royally. The entire evening was surreal.

During dinner I wanted to get some advice from the most successful man in TV as I aspired to hosting a TV show. I asked, "What was the most important ingredient to your success?" He said, "Talent." That was the extent of his advice.

I was learning you have to be on your toes if you want to keep up in NY. I briefly dated the partner of the most famous producer on Broadway and we would often all go out to dinner for where famous stars would float up and kiss all the men at the table. The producer once asked me what it is I want? I told him to host a TV show. Too bad Broadway wasn't my dream.

That year, I appeared in the advertising for a famous car company and posed on the car with a full grown, live jaguar next to my head. It made all the papers and TV nationwide. My poor parents!

This was just my first few months in the city. I have to save my "Bond Girl" stories and what happened when I moved to L.A. for ACT 2.

Suffice to say that I did go on to host my own TV show (with my name in the title) plus having successful careers in modeling and acting. I never became like Willie Lohman and am still that shiksa with a lot of chutspa. .

http://www.patgainor.com

Virginia Viera

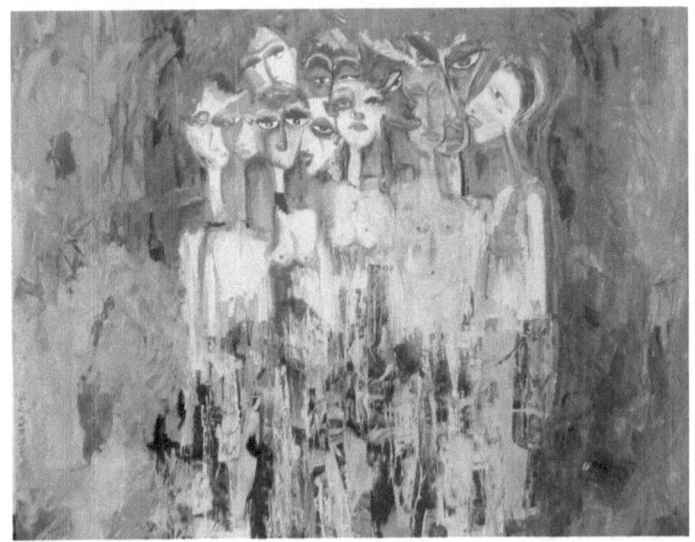

Family

When I was a little girl in Buenos Aires, every year, every summer we would take a boat to my Grandparent's house (Now this was not any boat but a fabulous creature the steamed and huffed and puffed its way up the river to the Island, the long wood floors with windows and decks overlooking the forests. Every once in a while some odd animal would raise its head, behind the hydrangeas and ferns)

Nothing seems to be better than this... I'm sitting here, on the grass, amazed by this beautiful view. This lake is bringing me memories from my childhood and everything came back to my mind so clear, so real... Suddenly I am looking at the little girl I used to be holding my father's hand and walking down the pier where a boat was waiting for us to be taken to my grandpa's house in the island. At that time, nothing would have been more boring than that! Don't get me wrong... I loved being with my grandpa while he spent long hours telling me stories of battles in the middle of the sea between the most violent pirates you could imagine! But besides those incredible tales, there was nothing to do there. I was only 7 years old and I spent my afternoons playing with my brother. After an hour of being together, the games turned into fights and fights turned into tears so every time this happened we walked away from each other promising not to play together anymore! Later I used to walk along the woods, trying to follow a running chipmunk or catching slippery butterflies. Every day the same walks, the same people, the same scene. Nothing was excited to me, I felt tired of the forest, the colors, the smells...

As time went by, something started changing... I was waiting for the summer, for my father's hand holding mine, for the boat. My grandpa was no longer with us which made me so sad and although my visits to his place were painful, I started feeling the need to go to that forest, to see those colors, to smell the wood. After a while that place turned to be "my place". The trees knew about my happiness and my sorrow, my ups and downs, my life. I enjoyed my afternoons there, laying on the grass, thinking of everything, solving this huge puzzle called world, living my youth as much as I could.

I'd wish nothing would have changed but it did. I miss the hand that hold me, the fights with my brother, the scary pirates. I would never have imagined my future missing those things but it's true. Not only I miss them but I need them because they are an important chapter of my life. There are who I am and sometimes I have the feeling that I lost them. Then I realize that the truth is I will never lose those memories. They will be with me forever as long as I have that forest in my mind, those colors in my eyes, the smell of wood in my nose.

To me, nothing seems to be better than that.

http://www.virginiaviera.com

Roland Reiss

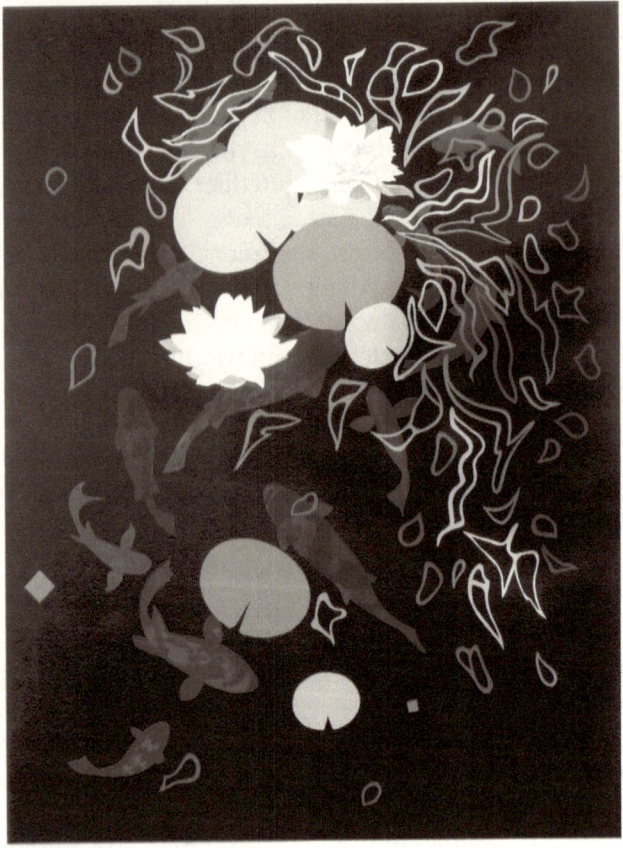

Flow, 2014; oil and acrylic on panel; 52 in. x 40 in.

I remember, as a little boy in Chicago, the radio broadcasts saying unidentified planes had bombed Pearl Harbor. It wasn't until the next day however that the president identified them and declared war on Japan. My mother, a housewife, became a machinegun inspector in a factory for a while before we left for California.

Early in the war we moved into an empty home in Pomona and the neighbors showed us where, in the linen cupboard below the bay window, the Japanese family had kept the wireless radio to communicate with Japan, because they were spies. We were told this was the reason they were taken to an internment camp. Japanese submarines had shelled the coast and we were all afraid of a Japanese invasion.

In those days, Pomona was also home to a lot of Pachucos, whose wild outfits and mysterious ways played into a conflict with U.S. sailors and service people. We thought they were draft dodgers and dangerous people threatening to our personal safety.

Later in the 1940s, as a high school boy, I worked during the summers at the L.A. County Fairgrounds when it was a prisoner of war camp.

Italian prisoners were given considerable freedom; deporting themselves like visiting opera stars and lovers. The day that the Italian prisoners were sent to San Luis Obispo, in preparation to being sent home, almost one hundred women catalogers employed at the fairgrounds quit their jobs.

The prisoners were mostly German, caught early in the war and sent to the U.S. We were not allowed to talk to them, but of course we did. They were treated harshly and with considerable discipline. S.S. types were highly restricted and limited to a fenced area guarded by high towers, barbed wire, and machine guns. Regular German prisoners were used to pick oranges in the groves and to process war materials for reuse. I saw American soldiers punish and abuse these prisoners in extreme ways.

One of the prisoners I knew, escaped and lived under a house in Ganesha Hills, which looked down on the fairgrounds. He became involved with the lady living in the house and this situation was later made into a movie.

My job was to provide acetylene torches and equipment used for cutting apart "ducks," those large amphibious landing vehicles used in the South Pacific, in order to salvage the metal in them. My other job was to administer first aid to the prisoners because a torch would occasionally hit a live round or grenade, imbedded in the "ducks," resulting in injury. Forcing prisoners to work on such projects was against the Geneva Convention.

During that time, the death camps were discovered in Germany, and large billboards were put up all around the fairground for the prisoners' viewing, showing those horrific images we all know. They claimed to know nothing about the camps, but did admit they were aware of mistreatment of the Jews. Since then, I have thought a lot about complicity in recent years, about how we know something is wrong in our own country but do not speak out about it.

(Please do a search for more information on this artist)

https://www.youtube.com/watch?v=AUdWOv25csc

Davie Lovejoy

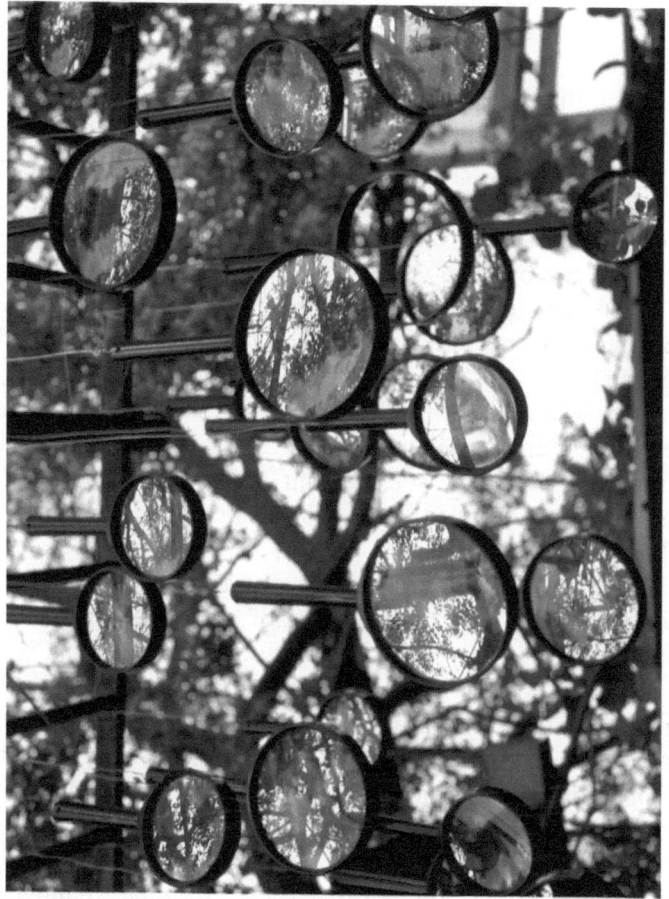

Oops, My Rad.

When we were young and light of income, in the days before cellphones, my wife and I were adjusting to married life. She stayed at home with our son six days a week – one day a week she had our old car to run errands. I worked at the nearby financial planning firm where we'd met. I ran the print shop, across the parking lot from the main building.

One day, I got a call from the Human Resources Director. "Dave, I have the police here with a warrant for your arrest." I quickly went across to her office to find two policemen who informed me I'd let an unpaid traffic ticket go to warrant. To make it go away, all I needed to do was pay the fine. But Vera had the checkbook. And the car.

At this same time, my wife had loaded up the car to go grocery shopping. She and our son wheeled their cart up and down every aisle, gathering ingredients for a week's planned meals. When she arrived at the checkout stand, she placed her items on the belt and got out her checkbook — only to find it empty. She noticed the carbon of the last check written was signed by me. I had used the last check and put it back in her purse.

My wife asked the checker to hold the groceries for her. We lived nearby, and she would get a fresh checkbook and return. She loaded our son back into the car, strapped him into his car seat, and pulled out of the parking lot to head home – when she ran out of gas.

The car had a broken gas gauge and stopped tracking the gas level below a quarter of a tank. To compensate, our deal was to always keep at least a quarter of a tank in the car.

I had used the car the day before, probably to pick up the thing I bought with her last check, and left it for her with only fumes in the gas tank. Now livid, and dangerously nearby, she grabbed our son and marched to the office where we used to work together.

She went straight to the print shop and demanded "WHERE'S DAVE?" My assistant leaned to look around her. Vera turned to see what he was looking at and saw me crossing the parking lot with two policemen flanking me.

I had told the policemen that if I could just go back to my office and call my wife, I'm sure we could pay the fine. As we crossed the parking lot, I saw Vera coming from the print shop and felt pure relief. "Oh, thank God", said I. "Do you have any checks?"

Vera smiled like the Grinch.

"No," she said. "You used the last one. I found out in the checkout line at the grocery store. I was on my way home to get more when the car ran out of gas."

Everyone was silent for a moment.

The officers looked at each other, then took me away. They drove me to my bank and waited in the car while I went in. Then they took me to the police station. I waited in the lobby while the officers went behind the counter, paid my ticket for me, brought me the receipt and drove me back to work. They knew they could trust my wife to impose my sentence.

Protect and serve.

And yes, we're still married 34 years later.

David Lovejoy, Thingmaker

http://www.lovejoyart.com

Debbi Swanson Patrick

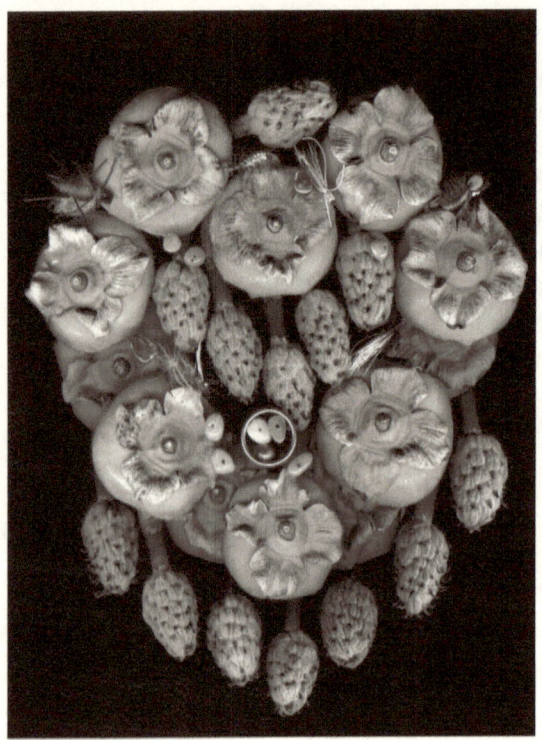

A Day at the Beach

Steve emerged from the rough bay, white with astonishment.

"You won't believe it, " he said. "I can't believe it."

I was sitting on the rocky beach of Two Step on the island of Hawaii near Captain Cook, the location where lies a monument to the famed explorer who was slain by the natives on what is now Valentine's Day, 1779.

My husband and I had been told the story of the dolphins there, but it didn't seem possible, even as smart as they are.

Turns out, it was.

***

We'd gone to Hawaii in 2008 for Steve to tour and study the cabling system of the Keck Observatory telescopes on Mauna Kea. Once an Imagineer at Disney, his childhood dream job, he'd moved on to run his own business designing major rides for Universal including Earthquake and Back to the Future. A highly sensitive guy, he was thoroughly depressed when the King Kong ride burned in early 2008. By then he had moved on to JPL/NASA where he helped design rock crushers and the landing balloons for the Mars landers.

Bored with the politics and pace of that, he moved to a unique engineering company in Vancouver, BC, led by a Scotsman who had been knighted by Queen Elizabeth. Steve was a kid in a candy store, working on both the highest-end amusement rides, and on the massive Thirty Meter Telescope being planned for Chile.

"You gotta push back the darkness," he'd say, believing in both science discoveries and having fun.

Though we grew up near each other, we were five years apart and didn't meet until I was nearly 50 and he was going through a hellish divorce. We met on Match.com and we connected in nanoseconds. His bio was open, honest, disarming even in his sensitivity. We met for a glass of wine and stayed for dinner. Eighteen months later we were married—privately. Then we married again on April Fool's Day for family and friends. What a hoot. Steve was a magnificent force to behold and I'd never been so happy.

The 2008 trip to Hawaii was a total vacation for me. We stayed in Kona and picked up the book "Spirit Walker," by Hank Wesselman, recommended by our yogi chiropractor. It's the story of Wesselman's first shaman experiences while living on the island in Captain Cook. So while Steve was working at the Keck, I started reading the book, got a massage, roamed, and at one point was on the top of Kilauea while he was atop Mauna Kea. Once done with work, we were free to roam together. We visited my old boss near Hilo and walked to the edge of the volcano's lava as it steamed into the ocean.

But like Wesselman's magical story of his Captain Cook experiences, we were to have one there ourselves, with Steve's old family friends who had retired there. Maria, a former lawyer, and her beachy, unlikely husband Craig, a casual pot dealer and artist, lived in a gorgeous tropical home, complete with a meditation cottage, drumming circle pit, and pet geckos that I fell in love with. Craig's cousin Doug and his wife were also visiting while we were there. While we drank cocktails by the pool, Maria told us how she snorkels nearly every day, and most days she encounters the dolphins.

"You wanna go?" asked Maria. "I have rash guards and all the other gear." Of course we did. "There's no guarantee you'll see them, but if you do you have to play the leaf game. Doug blew it the other day so the dolphins deserted him."

Steve was puzzled. "What do you mean, the leaf game?"

"Here's the thing...a single dolphin will single you out. Then it will retrieve a leaf from somewhere, bring it to you, but first it will swim around you, moving the leaf from its mouth, to its fin, to its tail. When it drops the leaf in front of you, you have to pick it up and throw it, just like you were playing with a dog."

"I didn't throw it," said Doug, redfaced. "I hadn't heard the rules yet!"

"You're kidding!" yelled Steve. Clearly, we were going. The next morning we got on our gear and headed down. For me the water looked too rough, so I bowed out, opting to sit on the rocks and read.

I kept an eye on Steve and Maria as best I could with the choppy waves. I finally spied them swimming back into shore just as I saw the dolphins breach about 200 feet behind them. I stood up and screamed, "Dolphins! Dolphins!" They caught what I said and headed back out. I tried to see if there was any interaction, but I was too far away.

About a half hour later they swam in. Steve, in amazement as he shedded snorkeling gear, said he got to play the leaf game. "I saw a school of dolphins appear from the deep blue, spiraling up toward the surface, then one split off," he spurted out. "It came right at me, with a shredded wreck of a leaf. It swam around me, moved the leaf from his nose to his fin to his tail, then dropped it for me, about six inches away. I picked it up and threw it like Maria said. The dolphin retrieved it and we did it all again, and again. Finally it looked at me like it was saying thank you and swam off. Oh my God, what an experience. Never, ever, anything like it in my life!"

Maria was glowing and I wished I'd gone with them. Steve couldn't stop talking about it and Doug was kicking himself. We went out the next day but no luck. It was a once in a lifetime moment, and meant for Steve. And at that time we didn't know that he didn't have much time left. A few months later he was diagnosed with kidney cancer, and he passed away a year later at age 59. He forged a relationship with the author Hank Wesselman during his illness, and because of his spiritual curiosity, we both had soul retrievals with his wife, Jill. That helped Steve accept his life was ending and heal his childhood wounds. I then had my retrieval shortly after Steve passed, so it helped me reconnect with his beautiful soul and remember that I still had a rich path to follow while I'm here. And so I go on.

http://www.tellingimages.com

Ben Zask

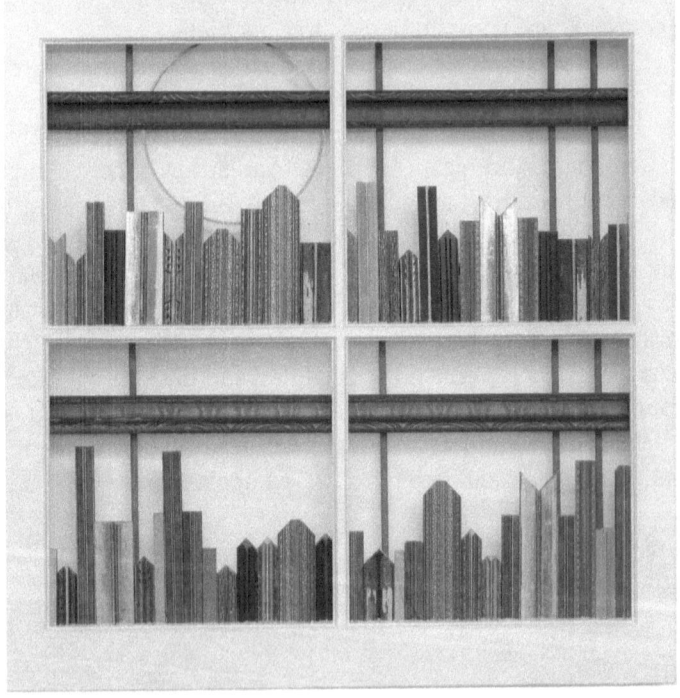

City Window; 2015; 36x36x4; wood, paint, antique frames

Cab Story

In the early 1970's I was driving a cab in NYC. One winter night a gentleman hailed me down on the Upper East Side and then he escorted a lady into my cab. She was an elegant and beautiful lady in her 50's and I was wondering why she was alone.

I was heading towards 5th avenue but a big black car in front of me was crawling along on the narrow street so I began honking my horn to let him know that he should pull over and let me pass. He stopped his car.

I sat there for a couple of minutes it felt like hours, but nothing happened. I started honking again, still no movement.

I reached my boiling point, I opened my door with the intention of going to the side of his car and kicking the shiny black paint with my boot. I was half way out of the cab when my passenger, the elegant and sophisticated lady started freaking out. It was a crying scream telling me to change my course of action and to stay inside the cab.

I got back in, closed the door and observed my passenger in the rearview mirror. She was extremely upset and gradually composing herself. When she calmed down she told me a story:

She was in a car with her husband a few years back when he got into an altercation with another driver. Her husband was a big man and he got out of to confront the other driver. Her husband got punched in the jaw, fell backwards and hit his head on the curb killing him.

I didn't think of my mortality when I was in my early 20's but sitting there looking at the black car in front of me I started to. Who drives that kind of car late at night? Mafia? Secret Service? As the car started moving I realized that my beautiful passenger might have saved my life or at least great bodily harm. I encountered many more altercations after that night but I never left the cab. I used my steering wheel as an offensive and defensive weapon.

http://www.Zaskgallery.con

Yoshie Sakai

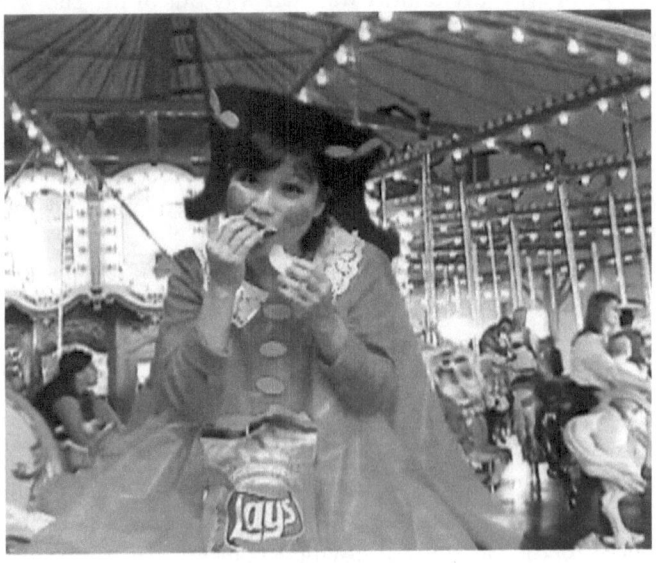

My mama thinks my body type takes after my papa's side.
I don't think so.

My mama, Kasumi, an Issei, a first-generation Japanese woman from Wakayama-ken, Japan, tells me all of the time in Japanese: "You better be careful because you're prone to get fat." Thanks a lot, (Asian) mama.

Though there may be dispute in terms of physical similarities, I believe that I took after my papa in temperament and personality. When my papa, Hiroshi, a Nisei, a second-generation Japanese-American man, born and raised on Terminal Island, California was still living at home and talking, he would always say to me "Don't take after me, Yoshie. I hope you take after your mama."

Well, sorry papa, but I think I take after you. Mood disorders like recurrent depression, I think, went undetected quite a bit for Nisei like my dad who passed away at 89 years-old last year. But for Sansei or Nisei-han, third-generation Japanese-American or 2.5-generation, like me, there seemed to be less shame in admitting or declaring that I was depressed, at least to my peers, but I remember being fearful of telling my parents that I was severely depressed and that I was about to drop out from the graduate program in Classics at Berkeley. It wasn't that I was getting bad grades, as I had "A's" and "A-'s" in my classes, but I clearly wasn't happy. I had a hard time getting out of bed in the morning, but still being the good student that I was, would manage to get to class somehow. This was in the spring of 1995. I really was like the Zoloft anti-depressant commercial not too long ago that had a cartoon head (a circle with some dots as eyes) walking around with a dark cloud over it, and when it rained, it rained only on that head. That was me.

I would always wonder…. How did I become this way? Was it my upbringing? Was it that I lacked self-confidence and self-esteem? Why weren't I loving life like everyone else?

This is where I feel like the apple doesn't fall too far from the tree. My papa, although he was the eldest son, lived in the shadow of my uncle, his younger brother, Isao. Isao did well in school and eventually became a dentist, and my papa was a good son but did not have the same academic opportunities like Isao. Even if he would complain and mutter to himself things he would like to say, they would never be said out loud or in conversation with my aunties and uncles. My mama thinks his siblings had taken him to be the fool and always ran right over him in terms of important family decision-making and therefore leading to low self-esteem. I feel that I grew up feeling the same way. I was the only child, and I don't think my mama ever thought she was putting me down in front of her friends by telling them, why I couldn't be like THEIR children ("Oh, your daughter is so good and so helpful around house, unlike MY daughter…. She doesn't do anything!" etc.), but it always made me feel badly even though I think for her it was a form of humility and agreeable behavior.

So, I went on with life, rarely being told I was good or good enough, which perhaps contributed to my success in school because I always had to work harder than everyone else to keep up, but if something good did happen like being Valedictorian of my high school or getting into one of the best graduate schools for my field of study in Classics, I never believed I was smart enough, and it would eventually lead me to self-defeating behavior by way of depression. I felt I didn't belong. I was miserable, and I finally told my mama that I was dropping out, and surprisingly for me, she didn't give me a hard time. All the while in my head, I was thinking I had an obligation to my parents and all the teachers that wrote all those praiseworthy things about me in the recommendation letters so that I can go to a good school and that I was being most ungrateful by leaving Berkeley, when I had a fellowship with a stipend. I felt so badly about dropping out when I was given those things and felt crazy and thought people around me would think the same of me. I finally told my mama all of these things that were going through my head and she understood. She told me the most important thing was for me to be happy and that I should take care of myself and come home. She even started reading up on depression from Japanese books she borrowed from the library.

Years later and with the help of anti-depressants and therapy and after having moved to Hawaii for five years, I was feeling better. But I can't help but wonder if my dad suffered from depression after he retired, as he slept A LOT, but everyone would just say it's because he has worked so hard all his life that he is resting now, but my papa and I have a tendency to focus single-mindedly on one thing, for him it was working and providing for the family and saving money, and for me it was academics. But when that one thing you focused so hard on all your life is gone in one way or another, what is left?

http://www.yoshiesakai.com

Kerry Kugelman

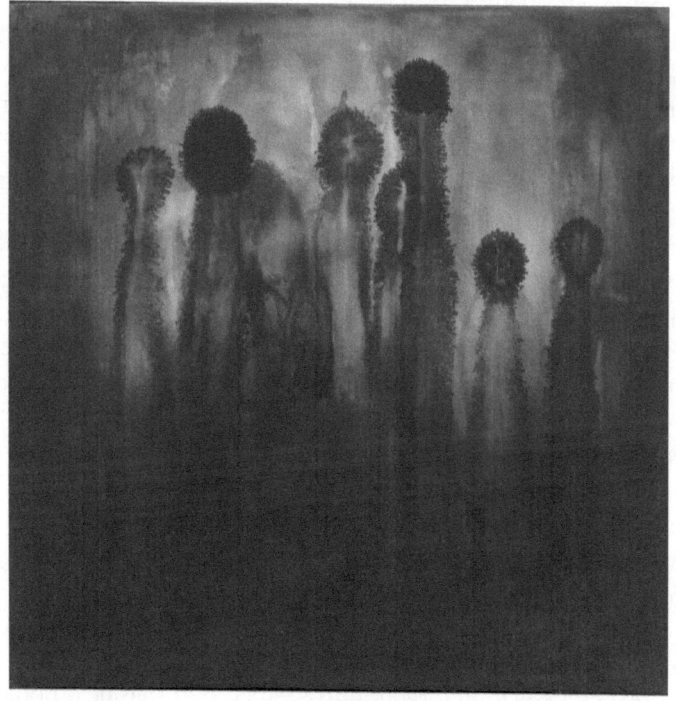

Ohn Titel (sentinels II

I had a transformative experience in 1989 while attending a Tibetan Buddhist retreat, a moment that resonates to this day. Accompanied by my yoga teacher at the time, we went to Ridzin Ling, a teaching center nestled in the Trinity Alps, near Redding, California. The area was formerly a placer gold mining site, hosing away whole hillsides and extract small bits of gold ore. I couldn't help but see a parallel in those of us coming to find some flakes (if not nuggets) of golden wisdom in the dirt of our material selves. Certainly, my expectations were high for some kind of breakthrough moment, though having such expectations gets in the way of having such moments!

First, a bit of context: some Eastern spiritual traditions hold that there are energetic areas of the body along the spine (sometimes called chakras) that play a part in spiritual growth and evolution. Generally speaking, the lower centers of desire, appetite, and power (in the pelvis and solar plexus) are where many people focus their energy; reorienting awareness to the higher spiritual centers (the throat, "third eye," and crown of the head) is the work of the spiritual path. Hold on to this general idea, as it is key to understanding the impact of the event I witnessed.

Staying in a large yurt on the grounds, we went to empowerment teachings, and also performed duties of various kinds around the center — washing dishes, helping craftsmen, even digging trenches — to pay our keep and practice karma yoga, non-attachment through selfless work. At first I found myself frustrated, almost angry, by having to do such mundane work — Washing dishes? Really? — when I had built up shiny expectations of moving toward enlightenment by just sitting and listening to a Tibetan guy. I'm being flip — I didn't really think it would be all incense and saffron robes — but it was a humbling experience. After a day or so I felt myself warming to the tasks.

There was a guy at the retreat from Portland, Oregon, a dour, "glass-half-empty" type. For now I'll call him Don, but his real name is long forgotten. It seemed odd that he'd bother to attend a workshop that offered the possibility of greater self-awareness, and no small degree of effort, as well. Surrounded by beautiful scenery and supportive people, and in the presence of a Tibetan lama, Don consistently remarked on everything in a negative way. Nevertheless, here he was, so at some level he seemed to be seeking some kind of growth.

On one of the last days of the workshop, Don and I were assigned to a trench-digging crew for some electrical cables. The day was bright and hot; working continuously in the full sun soon had us sweating profusely and blinking off the perspiration from our eyes. We took off our shirts to catch the breeze. Don talked while he worked, and wasn't particularly negative about anything. I mused to myself that perhaps his time at the center had effected some small change in him for the better. I paused for a moment, leaning on my shovel and looked around at the ocean of nature surrounding us, under the bowl of a cloudless blue sky.

I heard a shout from Don that yanked me out of my reverie, and I turned to see him gyrating wildly, and holding his shovel blade even with his hips, jabbing at something. "Lookit the size of that thing!" he exclaimed, "It's huge!" I followed his gaze and saw that, improbably, his fly was unzipped, and a large green caterpillar was hanging out of his zipper. It was a fantastic scene. For one thing, I was trying to confirm that it was a caterpillar and not something else (it was a very large caterpillar, it must be said). As Don continued to thrust his shovel in the direction of the caterpillar, I wondered if he'd neuter himself in his efforts to kill it.

Then I looked up and the moment shimmered, not from heat but with a vision. On Don's shoulder there was a large butterfly, hanging on despite Don's tarantella of caterpillar fear. Its pale wings were highlighted by the early afternoon sun, and moved only slightly.

The moment crystallized for me as a living tableau of awareness, suspended out of time: Don, relentlessly negative, was figuratively and literally looking at his lower center, and at a caterpillar — a creature that symbolizes potential transformation — with fear and alarm, seemingly ready to risk striking himself with the shovel in an effort to kill it. He was oblivious to the lightness and beauty of the butterfly on his shoulder (level with his throat chakra), a symbol of transformation and new life. Even Don's posture placed the caterpillar in shadow, and the butterfly in full sunlight.

I was transfixed, taking all of this in without any internal dialogue. At some level this rare and ephemeral vision seemed a harbinger of the choice always presented to us, to live from a place of fear, darkness, and violence, or to seek light and transformation. In that moment, I felt transformed in some luminous, ineffable way.

Our other co-workers by now were coming closer to assist Don, and the spell was broken. I don't remember now if the caterpillar was allowed to escape, or when the butterfly flew away. What I do remember is that no one else had seen what

I saw, or remarked on it — they had only been aware of Don's flailing and shouting.

It was really just another moment in the day, but for me it held great portent. I was primed for it (those shiny expectations? Or maybe from washing all those dishes?) and it was in a special, spiritually charged location. It was, ultimately, a lesson in transformation and awareness, that by really trying to see and understand, there can be many such moments in our lives.

https://kerry.kugelman.com

Dawn Arrowsmith

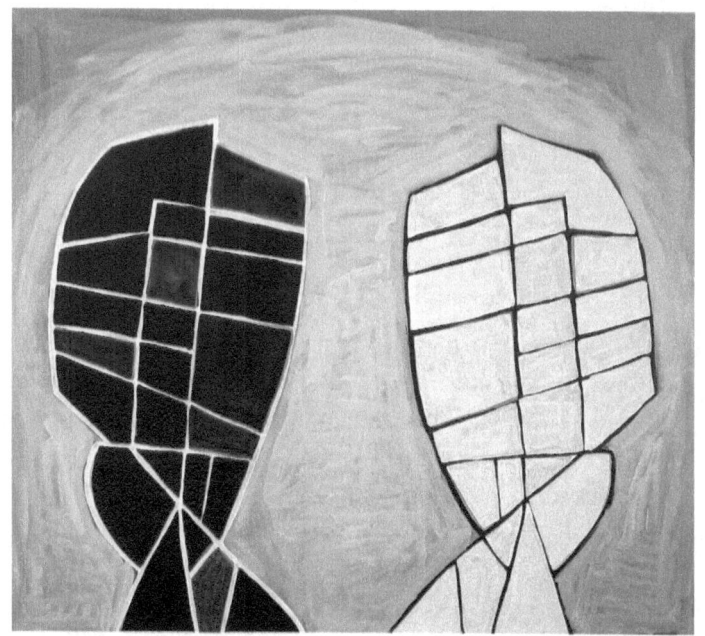

A Place to Talk

It's early morning, a bit chilly at 30 degrees below freezing and I'm bundled up in thick layers of wool and down standing outside my tent on the Khumbu Glacier Base Camp, an elevation of 17,600 feet. I'm looking up at the icefall where climbers begin their summit to the mountain the Nepalese call the Goddess of the Sky or Sagarmatha and we westerners know as Mt. Everest. Taking in the huge frozen chunks on the steep icefall path that leads upward to the top of the world's highest mountain at 29,025 feet, I say to myself, "I do not need to climb that." Happily, I turn around to join my trekking companions, Sandy and John and climb to the rocky, snowless summit of Kala Patther at 18,200 feet. We are light headed and thrilled to sit on rocks surrounded by our planet's tallest mountains. Several avalanches erupt and tumble down in the distance as we absorb the view of Everest with perpetual clouds of snow billowing off her top-of-the-world peak.

After building small, stacked-rock temples in honor of the mountains we pack up and rush back to meet one of our Sherpa guides who has stayed with our fourth companion, Mike, who is seriously ill with cerebral edema, an altitude sickness. The day before, Mike refused to descend to a lower elevation but now we must get him down to a doctor in the village of Dingboche as fast as possible. The Sherpas will carry Mike down on a shorter but riskier trail. We three, exhilarated from reaching our trekking goal, feeling in the best physical shape we've ever been, will follow. We lean back, literally dig our heels in and run down the steep dirt trail that is right next to cliffs that drop 2000 feet below. We are fearless, but I shudder now when I think back about that incredibly dangerous trail.

Mike survives and is flown out to Katmandu. We three continue our rapid descent that has become easier and faster in the lower altitude. I'm moving quickly on a wide downhill path when suddenly I trip, do a complete forward flip and land on my feet. I stand there astonished at what just happened, feeling like there must be some kind of weird magic in this amazing place. We pass colorful prayer flags fluttering in the breeze and thick dusty green moss hanging from the trees. We reach the village of Namche Bazaar and celebrate with a dinner of delicious yak steaks and for the first time in the two-week trek, sleep in real beds.

The next morning we wait for the famous Captain Wick who pilots a Swiss Pilotus Porter, the six-seat airplane known for terrifying short take offs and landings. In that quiet village you can hear the sound of a plane approaching. Everyone stops and listens, then recognizing the sound of his flying style, they shout, "It's Captain Wick!" and rush outside to watch this crazy pilot zoom in with his loud, low flybys and dramatic swoops before landing. Sandy, John and I nervously hop in and the good-humored Captain Wick takes off reaching about 20,000 feet where he announces, "Let's take one more look at Everest!"

and proceeds to bank and circle around for another spectacular, heart-stopping, over-the-top view of the Goddess in the Sky.

Back in Katmandu, I'm now on my own as I cycle around this ancient city, down wide tree-lined streets with hundreds of bats hanging in the trees and flying over my head in the night sky. I meet a couple who have been traveling for a year through India and they convince me it is safe for a woman to travel there alone. It is December 1976 and I want to see the Taj Mahal.

On the plane to Varanasi, I meet Julia, a friendly American traveler who shares hotel info. After checking in she invites me to walk to the ghats, the stairs leading down to the Ganges River where we sit watching a golden sunset while we eat homemade chocolate chip cookies her mother has sent from Iowa.

A couple of days later in Agra I arrive at the Taj Mahal for sunrise. The sky is clear and the light is perfect. I spend the entire day exploring the Taj as it glows in the sunshine. That night it is bathed in the light of the full moon. It is Christmas Day and this is the gift I have desired: to experience the difference of cultures on the other side of our world.

http://www.dawnarrowsmith.com

Vicki Barkley

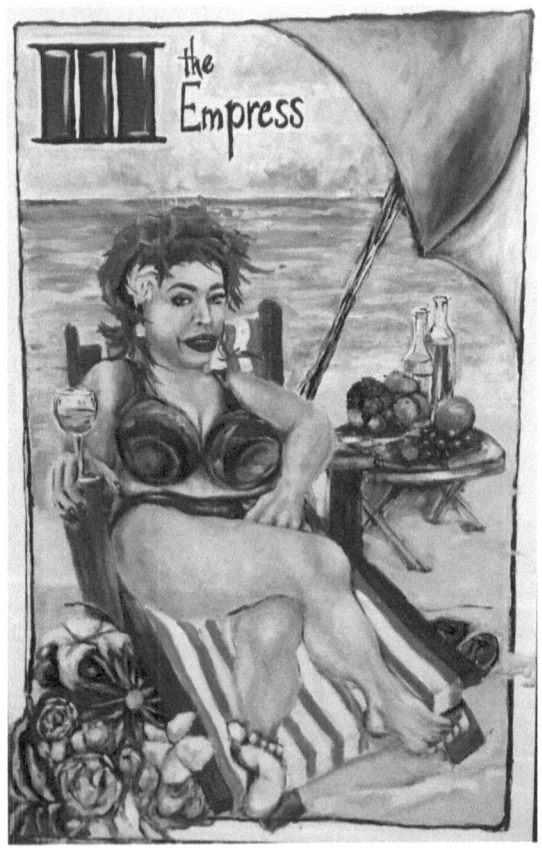

I moved to Southern California soon after graduating from college, in 1986. For the first two years I lived here, I eked out a living at various small print shops in South L.A. After the print shops, I thought teaching might be a good option. I learned that a substitute teacher needed a bachelor's degree and a passing score on the, CBEST, California's literacy test for teachers. So, armed with my test score, and my updated resume, I got an interview with the Long Beach Unified School District, and became a substitute teacher.

My first gig was at the high school four blocks from our house. I drove twenty minutes to get Jackson to daycare, back home, parked my car, and walked to school. I remember moving with the sea of teenagers down the street, to the entrance of the building. I was 27 — about ten years older than the kids I would be working with. It felt familiar, and jolting, and foreign, and exciting.

The Home Ec room was in the school's oldest building, from the 1920's. The linoleum floors and cabinetry of the kitchen area looked newer, maybe a 1950's remodel. The stoves, refrigerators, and washer/dryers looked like they were from the 1970's. At lunch, the other teachers said when this lady retired, the course would no longer be offered. The conversation turned to high school Home Ec experiences, and they welcomed me to their school, on my first day ever teaching.

The kids all spoke either Cambodian or Spanish, and each group had a bilingual aide, another student, who translated for me constantly. The teacher left a lesson plan, which indicated that she would to be out for over a week, and she'd left instructions, tools, ingredients, schedules, and data charts for me to use. I had no idea that most substitutes wouldn't follow such a plan, instead supervising the students while they sat and did written work. The other teachers told me this during lunch, also. Their guidance and encouragement that first day, and the absence of a disapproving boss looking over my shoulder were revelations. I had been working blind, just figuring everything out, in every job I'd had since landing in California. Those jobs never had instructions! The lesson plan I followed that day was clearer than a sketch on the back of an envelope, explained by a harried boss, that's for sure!

The student aides were both helpful, one cheerfully bossy and extroverted, the other shy, but very helpful in translating measurements, and talking to the students about metric and American/English systems. The kids worked in groups of four to six, each with its own personality, I discovered. They operated like noisy families. Some had more conflict, some less. Some were better at cleaning, and some made great cookies. Since I had no idea how to give grades, the aides took care of it.

I remember standing at the demonstration table, the mirror angled above so they could see what my hands were doing – the point of view of a cooking show. I followed a standard chocolate chip cookie recipe, making sure to enunciate, working slowly, while the aides translated. The kids seemed thrilled. Everyone had those glowy faces, like in a commercial. I told them, "Go cook!" or something equally inane. Somehow, the day worked. I talked on the phone at length with the Home Economics teacher that afternoon. She hadn't found anyone who would cover these classes, and do the cooking labs, and I was happy to finish the time she was out. This teaching gig paid twice the money per day, than the print shops. I liked the students. It was a respectful workplace, and except for a few individuals, people were friendly.

I did this for about a year and a half. In 1991, I needed a summer job, so I jumped at the opportunity to cover a maternity leave for someone in the Nordstrom Display and Design Shop. Nordstrom was my fanciest job, ever. The benefits also, were the best I've ever had. The pay wasn't as good as substitute teaching, but unlike sub pay, there was growth potential. After six months, as Nordstrom's Holiday 1991 campaign wound down, my supervisor asked me what I wanted to do next. I wanted my work to mean more than my paycheck. Nordstrom treated its employees well, but it wasn't the direction I wanted to take. Teaching, on the other hand, might allow me to contribute to something global and permanent. I thanked her, and in January 1992, I went back to being a substitute. At the beginning of April, I took over an empty position teaching 7th grade English. I finished the year with those kids, and the school offered me a regular position the next year. I stayed at that school for two years, then moved over to the Los Angeles Unified School District, where I've been working since July, 1994.

(please do a internet search for more information on this artist)

Roxene Rockwell

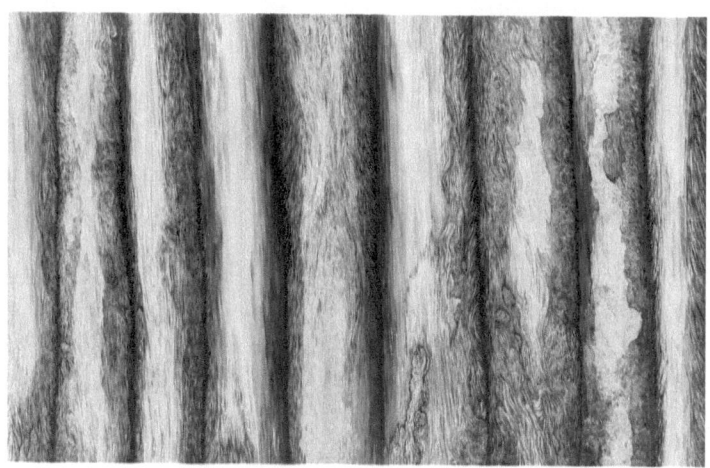

At two and half I moved with my parents into a house on the end of an idyllic cul-de-sac on the side of a hill in the Santa Monica Mountains. There weren't any sidewalks just cobblestones trimming the quiet street.

Our house was a "Hawaiian Modern" with a driveway that wound up around the hill at the very end of the street. The front of the house was actually in the back with a wall of windows facing a canyon. This was a wonderful location with a magical view. However, the house and our lives there were far from magical and idyllic.

The house had a damaged past, like we did. My father got the house as part of a real estate trade; the owner had built it for his parents. His parents moved out after a boulder came through the living room ceiling, barely missing one of their grandchildren.

My very first memory at 3 years old was in this house. For years when I remember it I became so chilled to the bone, and fearful that I had to learn to step away from the memory. Most of my childhood memories are of being scared. Many of them are full of what most people would say were irrational for a child growing up in an affluent neighborhood. I was a small quiet child. I had problems talking because I heard the world differently than most people. And instinctively knew I that I was not to be seen or heard.

I fear the dark and the wind whistling through the trees. I remembered trying to decide whether or not it was better to sleep with my back or front side facing the large window in my bedroom, in case I was shot thru the window during the night. In the end I decided that sleeping on my stomach was the best position to survive a gunshot.

I felt that I had to stay awake until everyone was home and asleep, no mater how late my father's car came up the driveway or how late my mother stayed up. I would pretend to be asleep, but in reality I laid awake listening to the blood curling fights between my parents.

The public areas of the house were decorated with hand painted doors, hand painted furniture, custom wallpaper, antique light fixtures, custom white carpets, and custom white furniture. This was important because my parents gave large parties. If any guest had gone beyond the powder room down the hall they would have seen that none of the bedrooms were decorated. This was not due to lack of funds, but because no one would ever see the bedrooms, they were not important.

My parents large bedroom had a fireplace and his and hers dressing rooms. Their furnishings consisted of two twin beds on frames about four feet apart from each other, and sitting on the floor there was a phone and an alarm clock. No nightstands, no headboards, no lamps, and nothing to sit on but the beds.

The outside world never knew about what was happening in this house; after all, nothing ever happens in affluent neighborhoods. One day, without even a goodbye, my father disappeared and the yearlong odyssey of hiding in the dark from process servers began.

When my mother, my younger sibling, and I left this house the view remained full of beauty and mystery. The house, however, was a reflection of our lives there as a family, it was damaged and neglected. The lot was sinking badly in the front towards the street below and on another side; the house was pulling itself apart.

http://www.roxenerockwell.com

Steven Fujimoto

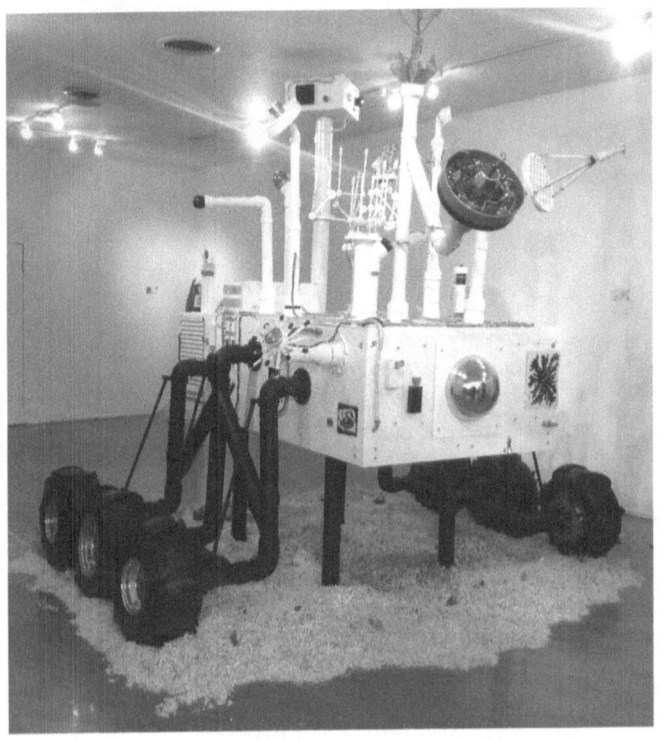

Although my Grandfather passed away long before I came of age, he was a wonderful teacher nonetheless. He showed by example the importance of perseverance, steadfastness, and forgiveness at a time when life's challenges and hardships seemed insurmountable. My Mother and her siblings drew on the strength and guidance of Grandpa as he navigated his family through difficult times; of war, internment, prejudice, relocation, and personal tragedy. In doing so, he passed along life-lessons to my Mother, which she in turn shared with her children.

Grandpa came to America to study medicine at the University of Southern California. He loved the challenges that higher education afforded him—yet he also yearned for a simpler lifestyle. In his senior year and much to the dismay of his parents, Grandpa left USC to pursue his true passion: Cooperative farming. Located in Venice just west of the 405 freeway along Jefferson Boulevard and extending to Lincoln, their label was "Cream of the Crop." This modest plot of land is where Grandpa grew celery, string bean, spinach, and other vegetables; it is also where my Mom and her siblings were born and raised, and where life's lesson on the meaning of temporal was learned first-hand.

1939 was a year of uncertainty for many. War or rumors of war were raging overseas and here in the States. It was in this year that lawyers for Howard Hughes visited my Grandpa. Backed by the might of Eminent Domain but seemingly humbled by the frugal but sincere lifestyle of his family and other farmers, the lawyers for Mr. Hughes spent considerable time explaining the strategic importance of strengthening this country's defense—and how my Grandpa might play a vital role by relinquishing his farm for the love of country and greater good. The following year, Mr. Hughes broke ground on his R&D facility and airport on the land that once yielded a sea of leafy greens. And it was short time later that my Grandpa and his family were sent to a relocation facility in Manzanar, California.

The winter of 1942 in the foothills of the Eastern Sierras was exceptionally cold. Filtered views through icy air of a distant Mt. Whitney amplified the sense of vastness of the region. In spite of the harsh conditions, my Grandparents created a warm and safe haven for their four children to grow and flourish amid difficult circumstances. Animosity gave way to acceptance and hope, and the bitter winters and scorching summers became more bearable as snow fights, communal gardens, softball games, and art classes arose from the dust of the desert floor.

Years later and by way of Seabrook, New York, and Chicago, my mother returned to Southern California. Sporting a husband and newly-minted twin infants, we settled into a modest home in Culver City—a mile east of where the farm once stood. I remember hearing the periodic roar of jet engines as testing continued at Hughes airport. And long after the airport was shuttered, a tractor-pulled tiller remained on the edge of the property, visible from Jefferson and a remnant of my Grandpa's farm. My Mom and Dad still live in the house in Culver City where I was raised.

http://www.greeniearts.com

Marla Fields

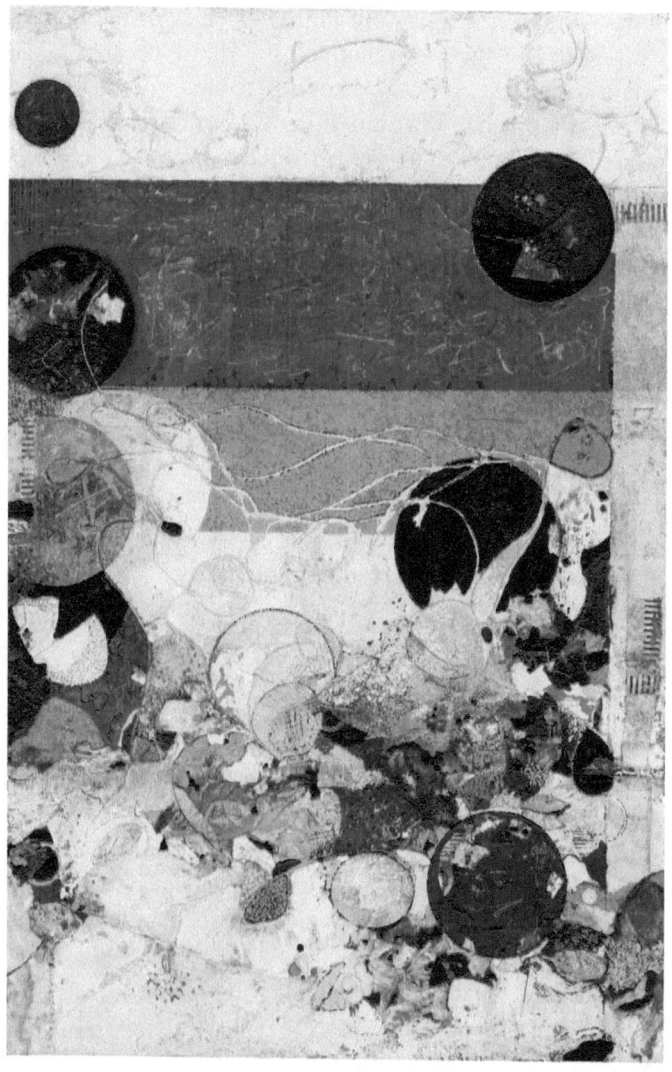

Shattered, sharp fragments of glass blasting out a few inches from my head; cabinets open with all the contents scattered everywhere, broken and destroyed. The never-ending hallway to reach my children, only eight and three years old. Could I even get to them? So scared...

These are memories, but still remain in my psyche, that one morning a little after four am when the earth shook hard in Northridge. This event changed my mindset forever. As I climbed over stuff to get to my kids rooms, moving in slow motion, afraid what I would find. Gathering them into my arms, feeling like I was a kid also, what now do I do?

Somehow my double bolted front doors exploded with the tremors and my neighbor came screaming into my house and said to get out. The entire block of neighbors stood outside, wondering with all the transformers exploding, was this the end? I remember an hour or so later going to my freezer and taking out my newly baked chocolate chip cookies. I recall a person I didn't recognize, numb with shock, come up to me, blood on his forehead and arm, but regardless he definitely wanted that cookie. I wanted to help, and I suppose this was my way, passing out sugar treats to all.

I learned a lot about life and people that day and the weeks that followed. I stayed with my kids in this war zone without electricity or gas. We flushed the toilets by gathering water from the pool. It was crazy. All around us there was mass destruction, people that perished just a few blocks from my house. All our fortresses were not safe.

But my block came together. One man had a generator and we gathered there and ate and watched TV. Our very own haven in the San Fernando Valley, a place to raise young families was not the bargain we signed up for. This experience was not only felt with my immediate block, it was with everyone and everywhere around me. We each had our own story. It was a time of listening and reaching out and sharing our community grief of what we went through.

Because the aftershocks seemed as powerful as the main quake, the family always slept in the same room for at least six months. I learned much about myself then. I didn't realize how strong I was. In some ways, I viewed it as a great adventure, first the quake, then the cleanup, the insurance issues, and dealing with contractors and unfortunately at times their greed. In many ways, as the rebuilding of the area began, I too was also being put back together and made whole. Having Kids, at times you get so caught up in their needs, that you lose sight of your own.

Going through this experience made me evaluate my life choices and most definitely woke me up! As the people came into my home to repair, I too was working on my creative process.

(Please do an internet search for more info on this artist)

Jane Cantillon

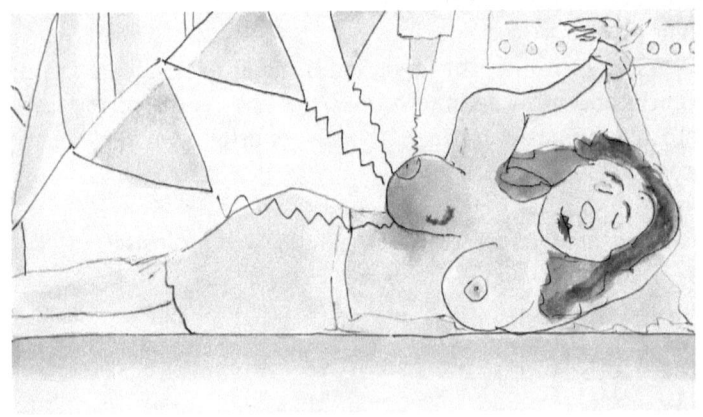

Jane of Arc

Like going into a sunny Embassy Suites, I slip into the Disney Cancer Center and smile at the receptionist, a perky Doris Day look-alike with her earnest "How are you?" Probably, I'm thinking, another survivor. My right breast is tender now, after five weeks here; second degree burns spread in the shadow of the pendulous one in question. I mechanically move toward the locker room, down a nondescript hallway marked with a beige painting of a California mission, I push open the door and peel off my shirt and virgin white hospital bra I was given after surgery, and under the fluorescent lights I gaze at the angry sneer of a scar on my breast, pulling the camisole around my waist and quietly chanting "hey sweetie you alright? All quiet in there?" I begin to gently massage my right breast. I read a recent report that said breasts that get more loving and massaging are more likely to be cancer free. I am curiously feeling myself up, just like when I first found the tiny bump, when a crooked woman comes through the door just out of treatment – a scarf wrapped neatly around her head, a slender and obedient patient marching out of the breast cancer factory. I know this woman. She always did what she was told, cautious and thoughtful in her life, a good student, then fine wife and mother, and now a perfect cancer patient.

"Hello" she murmurs a daily nod and she seems to be growing weaker everyday. I am one of the lucky ones who don't need chemo. Lucky, I shrug. I then climb into my fresh laundered hospital robe and push the door open to the inner sanctum waiting room. A Big 3D screen with scenes from a beautiful and fictitious white sand beach — pixelated seagulls appear to greet me there like a Disney ride gone terribly astray. Next to it is a small kitchen with burned coffee and traces of Coffeemate from the anxious early morning customers. I now have a secret ritual of placing my left hand over my breast and whisper "Oh now now girl, promise not to let those nasty little cells run wild again." Like clockwork, a large bearded Russian man comes out, "Miss Jane, we are ready for you." Down a long hallway I walk to the other familiar technician that knows every cell of my right breast, he looks at my chart while mumbling hello. I then remove my gown waist up, lie down on the electric gurney and place my arms above my head.

I'm locked in—shackled like a 17th-century prisoner in the belly of a steely ship as they spout out numbers and measures. "Do not move," they say as they position my body as if to prep a large holiday turkey. The remotes are pushed, machines like cannons move to each of my blue mapping tattoos, the three positions of my right breast begin to throb. They are now ready to fire the radiation into my body, then the nurse routinely says, "Your name and birth date please." "Jane of Arc, 21st Century." I laugh as the technicians scatter behind the thick barrier walls. "What was that?" the nurse says, safely hidden away.

The beams seem to float in the air as I try to stay still in the twisted position. The sound screeches from the cannons. I glance up at the other screen on the ceiling, another calming pixilated scene of birds and mountains over a cool lake. Was that supposed to be heaven, I think?

https://www.facebook.com/jane.cantillon.5

Stevie Love

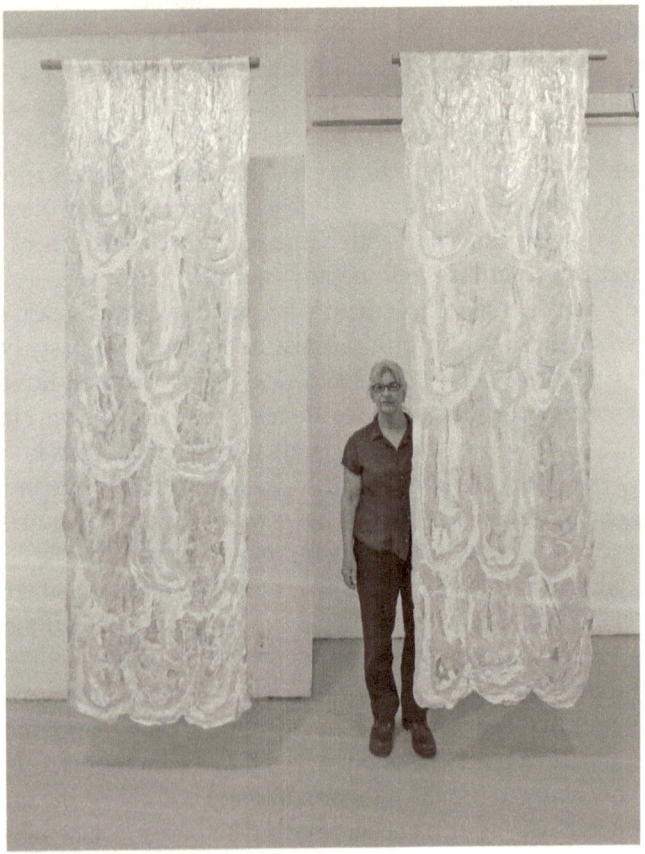

Doppelgangers

Bruce and I built an adobe house by hand making all the adobe bricks ourselves with a little help from family and friends and four guys we hired from the corner who came every weekend to our ten-acre plot in Juniper Hills, located on the north slope of the San Gabriel Mountains, overlooking the Mojave Desert. One summer of weekends driving up from Riverside and camping at the house site resulted in 14,500 adobe blocks.

After the blocks were done we built our adobe garage, sold our house in Riverside, put all our stuff in storage, sold the business, and lived in the garage for two years while we built the house. The whole process took about seven years. We experienced many surprises along the way, and here is one of them.

The house pad was cut into the hillside, and a little to the north, down slope, Bruce dug a deep rectangular hole with vertical sides with his Bobcat where we planned to put the septic tank. The concrete septic tank which was about 8 x 8 x 10 and weighted a ton was delivered and placed snugly in the hole with about 18" clearance on all sides.

It was around Christmas, and we left for a week to spend the holiday with family in northern California. After we got home late one night we went to bed and got up in the morning and were looking around the site when we were shocked to find the septic tank on its side in the hole, and the two concrete lids that had been on top of the tank were lying in the hole next to the tank. How could a huge concrete tank, with only 18" clearance on each side, turn over on its side in the hole? There were tracks in the dirt around the hole and we thought perhaps someone had tried to steal the tank while we were gone, maybe they were lifting it with some kind of hoist and had dropped it, but that seemed a little ridiculous. Who would do such a thing?

Bruce went to work with the Bobcat digging a long ramp down into one side of the hole so he could roll the tank upright, which he did using multiple logs and various invented uses of levers and pulleys. In the meantime we were talking to neighbors about this strange mystery, and one of our neighbors whose family had been dairy farmers in El Monte figured it out. There had been torrential downpours while we were gone, the hole filled with water and floated that big heavy tank up high enough to where it turned over on its side, the lids came off, it filled with water, then sank back to the bottom. When the rain quit, the water in the hole drained down through the earth, leaving the tank on its side in the hole, a surprise indeed!

http://www.stevielove.com

Mike Street

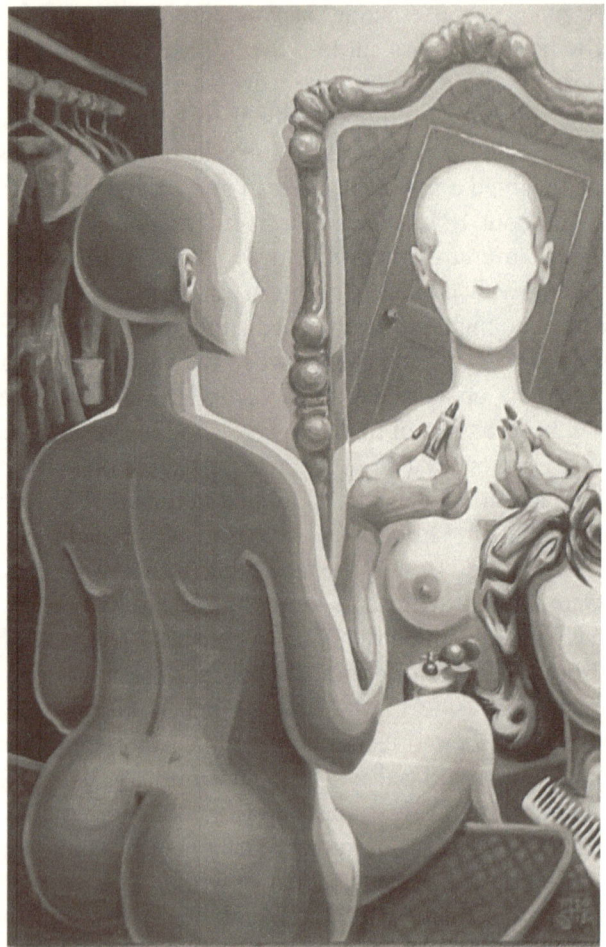

Lipstick; oil; 36x24

(Phone rings.)
MIKE: Hello?
PAUL: Hey Mike!
MIKE: He-e-ey Paul! How's it going?
PAUL: Aah, you know. It's going.
After 48 years, phone calls to my friend Paul Stiver were down

to a few per year. But they were always warm and friendly. Having shared so much continuous past together, there was no need for pretense or starting over. Communications could be quick or long depending on anything newsy about a mutual favorite subject, film. In Paul's case, I'd certainly call it "cinema." His academic and historic approach coupled with his enthusiasm and knack for words made his scholarly analysis accessible to anyone. A brilliant man cloaked in eccentricity, humor, kindness and generosity.

We met as freshmen in a San Fernando Valley Catholic high school by way of alphabetical seating, "Stiver" then "Street." He was already a supreme movie geek, and my own creative interests were firmly in place. Fate was simple, and this passionate "outsider" common ground of imagery was good enough to begin and maintain a long close friendship. I saw the back of his slightly squarish, light brown head for 4-years until we went to college, the same college. We became roommates on campus, then off in our own apartment. We lived together beyond graduation as well, about 10 years in all. Throughout those years, movies remained our major pastime. Part of our Sunday ritual together was grabbing the TV Guide and circling the broadcast movies we planned to view during the upcoming week. Meanwhile, we imperfectly scrambled monthly to pay the rent — and for our next Silver Screen fix.

In hindsight, our zany movie adventures could rival the madcap antics of Lucy Ricardo and Ethel Mertz. Our ongoing quest was not just attending new releases but special screenings and panel discussions, revival theaters, marathons, and even conducting our own interviews for modest publications. Somehow we managed to meet some of our "auteur" heroes like Alfred Hitchcock, John Ford, Sam Fuller, etc. Paul also developed a relationship with an aging Groucho Marx, film critic Robin Wood, a young Susan Sarandon, etc.

In the early 1980's, I finally moved out. As Paul and I carved our own separate paths over the last few decades, we stayed in touch by phone and met for occasional cultural events and waning movie-going. (He hadn't liked the overall direction modern Hollywood went.)

Paul Stiver died of a massive heart attack early last year. He was 61 years old. He was my friend and probably as close to a brother as I will ever have. His body was found in the apartment we shared for many good years. I was told the television was still on. I wondered what film he was watching.

I wept, and I mean wept, for about a month after Paul passed.

Even though the telephone calls and Xmas cards have abruptly ended, Paul still speaks to me as one of the respected little voices in my head. His influence and standards were that important. And there isn't a motion picture I view, old or new, without thinking about him.

http://www.mikestreet.com

Alex Schaefer

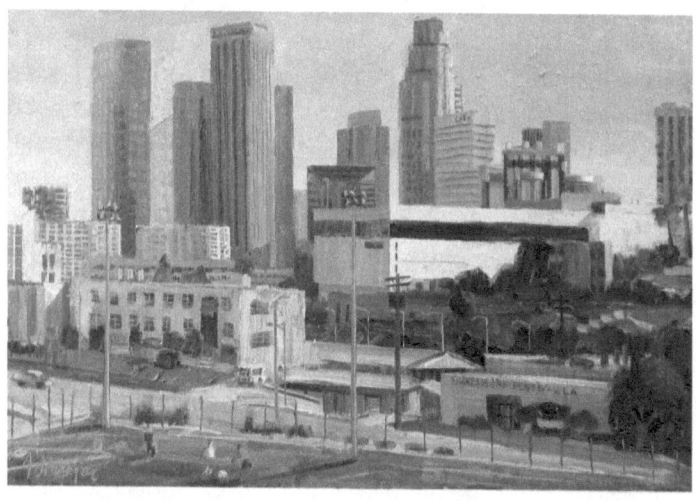

I was in a place in my life where I was tired with where I was living and what I was doing and who I was with so I decided to leave. I wasn't leaving any attachments like a wife or children, I wasn't running from any crime. I just wanted out. of everything. I lived a month to month life, it was the early 90's and I was in my early 20's. I was working for Disney with a great group of people, really enjoying a new phase in life. I was self-sustaining, and then some, for the first time in my life and the full understanding of all that entails was dawning on me. I was slow to realize that past a certain point, the life you're living is entirely up to you. And mine ended up an accumulation of accidents. Clothes, car, apartment, girlfriend. I had a 'this is only temporary' mindset for so long as my overarching aesthetic and direction. I was the type of person who got in line for 'life'. but for the first time I looked around and asked myself why? I wanted out. None of this had to be my life. I was young. I was immature. I still thought Bukowski was cool. So I packed up what was most important to me into my car, a two door honda prelude so it wasn't much, and moved into a motel near my job in Burbank. The Providencia. it was fantastic! like pressing restart on life. I lived there for nine months. It was a crummy motel and I enjoyed it very much. For $460 a month I got a bed, a shower, two chairs, a desk, a dresser and TV. All I needed. plus time to be alone and think and make some reasoned decisions in life. I learned a lot in that motel room. The funniest thing I always like to share that I learned about motel rooms was people go there to make a lot of noise at all hours of the day or night for two reasons: to fuck or to fight. The first one is obvious. We even have the expression "Why don't you two get a room?". The second was a surprise, frankly. for every two times I'd hear people in flagrante delicto, I would hear a couple arguing about this or that: kids, infidelity, money. It's all part of life but they didn't want the neighbors to hear or the kids to find out so they rent a shitty room and have at it. The sounds of Sex behind one wall and ranting anger behind another. Love and hate. It was the perfect storm. And then there was me calm and happy, between a rock and a hard place. In love with the light in the room.

http://www.instagram.com/paintwithalex

Terry Arena

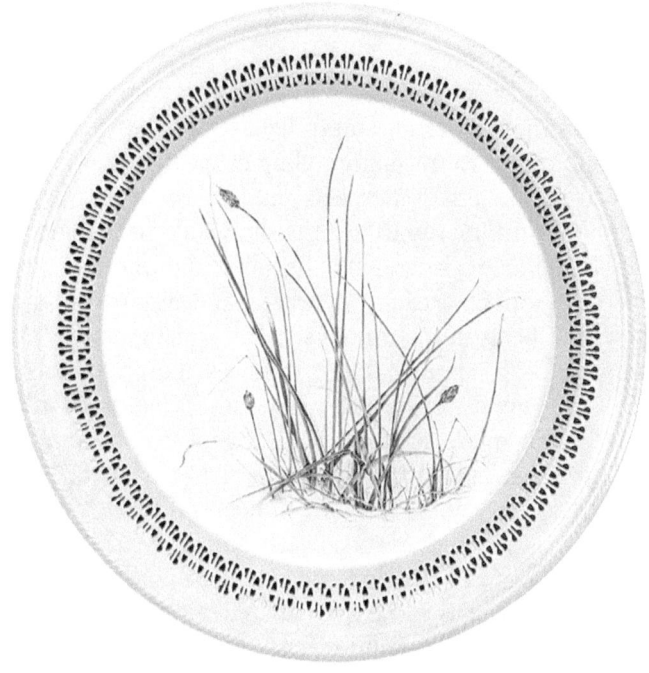

Chives

I did most of my growing up out in the sticks in a little town named Bonsall. When we moved to town, there was one stop sign, a post office, and a Mexican restaurant, El Establo. There were plants and animals and lots of land to go for all day rides on my horse, King. He was a misshapen old dude with a thick neck and slight hindquarters. I thought he was the most handsome horse and we were partners in crime. We would leave the house with the family dog trailing, and ride for miles poaching fruit from the local orchards, galloping, and exploring most of the land in that little town. The whole experience was all pretty dreamy for me.

You couldn't see a direct line to your neighbor, if you had any. It was the kind of place where dogs ran loose and would dart up at their property lines, posturing frenetically if you got too close to their claim. A more brazen Siberian husky bit the head off one or two of my "pet" chickens. And cats, they either learned to be in before dark or would eventually succumb to the coyote population.

On a typical weekend, I had bathed my horse and took him across the way to an empty field to dry him in the sun. He was notorious for instantly rolling in the dirt after a bath to return to his preferred state as a mud caked mess. When he was dry I jumped on top to ride the short walk back to his paddock. No saddle, no bridle, just the halter and lead rope. It was a lazy day. Sudden rushing of weeds and a surge of energy passed from beneath me. And a sense of some guttural animal sound. Standing. Spitting things from my mouth: rocks, dirt, weeds, and fragments of teeth. My father's voice called my name through muddled dark. To the garage floor and more voices over me. Laying in the back seat of the Toyota Celica with my head in my sister's lap I think. And a week of interrupted sleep. Later, there was talk amongst the neighbors regarding the fate of the dog and the horse and what would become of the girl down the street. In a week I was back on the horse with a jostled head and stitches. I was twelve.

http:// www.terryarena.me

Craig Sibley

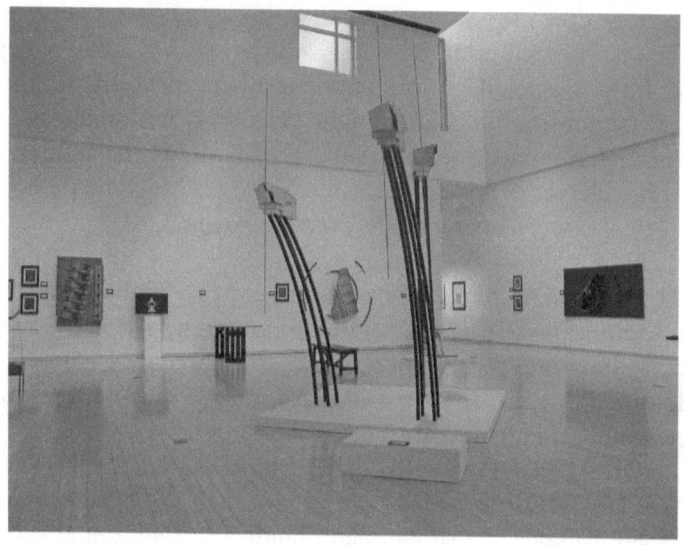

The Advance of Architecture

Being born a native "Hollywoodian" there are a few stylistic fashion nuances I had during the '80s that some might say were a tad different from the rest of the country. I arrived in Atlanta (my first ever visit to the South) arrayed in my vintage Teddy Boy tiger-striped loafers. This was probably a good indication I wasn't exactly a local (my '80s "Flock of Seagulls" pomp might have been another). The music store I'd entered was quite infamous. "Rhythm City" was owned by local legend (nut-job?) George Luther, a man famous for taking on a bet that he couldn't drive his brand new Corvette through the front entrance of the store. Interestingly enough, it turned out he won the bet. Although his brief sortie through the store's façade resulted in a slight modification of the Corvette, now minus two doors.

I navigated my way through a sea of guitars, keyboards, amplifiers and drums and finally found George. Apparently his favorite morning pastime was downing copious amounts of Courvoisier Cognac, mixed with diet Pepsi in a Solo Cup (the

little conical cups which required a plastic handled holder...
his of which was missing, making it impossible to set the
beverage down for even a second).

I politely introduced myself; "Hi George, I'm Craig Sibley.
I'm from the Roland Corporation, and here to do the synthe-
sizer demonstration clinic tonight." His reply was so classy. In
a perfect Hanna-Barbera "Deputy Dawg" drawl, he muttered
"Ahh yeah, yer that f*cking California Yankee faggit pussy boy"
(albeit, Deputy Dawg would never say "faggit").

Nice.

From there things just got more surreal. Without batting
an eyelash (or setting his Solo Cup down), he reached under
the counter and pulled out a sawed off "riot control" shotgun.
He says to me in a Cognac and Pepsi-fueled ramble... "Les jus
see whut kinda man you is!!!

OH MY GOD...WHAT THE FREAK HAVE I GOTTEN
MYSELF INTO?!?!?!

So, he takes the shotgun and holds it straight out at arm's
length and says... "I bet ya'll cain't hold dis here gun out your
side longer then I cans!"

By this time, a group of his "boys" had gathered around
the counter and were hootin' and hollerin' almost incoherent-
ly... "You show 'em George! Yeeeeah boy!" My only thought
was that somehow, inexplicably, I had been transported into a
scene of the film "Deliverance", and that the next thing I'd be
hearing is "Squeal like a pig!"

So, what do I do? Instead of doing the rational thing and
walking immediately out of the store, I say, "Uh, okay." Oh
God, what a freaking moron I am.

So, he holds the gun out, and the "boys" start their count-
down. "Wun, tooo, threee, foh, five..." until – his face beet red
and grunting – George finally drops his arm at the count of
"twunty-aight!!"

Well, due to some idiotic misplaced agenda, I was determined I was going to regain my manhood by holding that gun
out at my side for longer than he did. I'd been a pole-vaulter in
college, so I was quite strong. As I lifted the extremely heavy
WMD. at my side, the count began anew. "Wun, tooo, threee,

foh, five..." until they reached an agonizing "THURTY," upon which I dropped my aching arm.

So, had I redeemed my manhood? Hell no. Now George was totally ticked off! He rapidly made a beeline over to his security guard and said "Leon, give me your Colt!" Dang, I thought to myself, is he going to shoot me?!?!

Leon un-holstered and pulled out his sidearm, handing it to Luther, who snapped back the catch with a resounding CLICK. Now locked and loaded he turned to me and said... "See that big ol' gong over yonder in da corner of da store?" Uh, yeah, sure enough... there was a gigantic gong hanging in the upper corner of the store near the roof. George continued... "I'll bet ya twunty bucks ya'll cain't hit that sucker!"

I'm thinking to myself... There's NO FREAKING WAY he's going to fire off a gun in downtown Atlanta, at ten in the morning with employees and customers in the store! In retrospect, it was a feebly inaccurate and inane thought. And even more ridiculously... I retorted, "FINE... make it fifty bucks and YOU'RE ON!"

To my horror, the venerable yet acutely inebriated Mr. Luther turned and took a shaky, wide, wandering aim (looking a bit like a warthog in the middle of a Tourette's Syndrome-induced spasm) while still clutching the Solo Cup in his other hand. He pulled the trigger and...

BLAM!!!!

Sure enough... he hit it. In the far bottom left of the gong's rim there was now a perfect, fresh bullet hole. DANG not only was the blast impressive, but the sound of a room full of musical instruments RINGING after the explosion was downright otherworldly!!

Immediately, customers were dashing out the front door in panic and employees were diving behind amplifiers or plunging to the ground while covering their heads! It was total, cacophonous, uncorked mayhem.

Every guitar and drum (not to mention the store's windows and my tinnitus) were sizzling with a tone that was utterly stupendous!

To my dismay, he turned, gave me a cocky look and handed me the gun saying... "Yur turn pussy boy."

Crap. I'd done it now. My heart was racing with an adrenaline rush so hard I thought it might explode. Thankfully, my dad had taught me how to shoot as a kid and I'm a bit of a crack shot... but I'd never had the anticipation of potential felonious incarceration while practicing at the range.

So, I took a deep breath, assumed the "Highway Patrol" position of kneeling on one knee, held both arms out gripping and steadying the weapon (and probably looking like a total ass in my '80s New-Wave garb while doing so), took careful aim, and gently pulled the trigger, resulting in another deafening...

BANG!!!!

... followed by more spectacular sizzling and ringing tones of every cymbal, drum and guitar in the place! And when I say I nailed it, I mean I hit that gong dead center!!

Now standing completely alone with George (because everyone else had run for cover), he looked at me for the first time with admiration in his eyes. "Yur not so bad for a West coast pussy boy" is all he had to say. After which he poured me a Solo Cup full of Courvoisier and Pepsi (holder missing of course).

From that point on, I couldn't do any wrong in Mr. Luther's book. That night at the scheduled public product demonstration, he introduced me with redneck splendor. "This here's Craig Sibley. He's from California, but don let that bother ya none... he's a dyed in da wool, good ol' boy... I tell ya whut!!"

I was honored... and thankfully didn't even have to spend a night in jail as a result of the accolades!

P.S. - I've told this story hundreds of times, but one night while recounting it at a business dinner with about a dozen Pro-Audio professionals I couldn't help notice a guy named Bill who was acting quite differently than others I'd told the story to. He sat there with a stunned, peculiar look on his face (a combination of disbelief, yet knowing). After I finished the story, I later asked Bill, "Hey Bill... I've told that story hundreds of times and couldn't help notice that you didn't react like others. What's on your mind?"

Bill asked me, "What year was that?" I answered, "Around "'87."

He replied, "HELL, that explains it! During that time I worked for Aphex (a pro-audio equipment manufacturer), and we had a product returned from Rhythm City for warranty work because it was inoperative (DOA). When the tech opened up the unit, there was a BULLET LODGED IN THE CIRCUIT BOARD!!!!" BWAHAHAHAHA!!!"

Turns out that directly behind that big 'ol gong was Rhythm City's warehouse, where new products were stored!

I love it. Years later... Bill placed a very nice cherry right on top of my story!

http://www.craigsibley.com

Abby Schachner

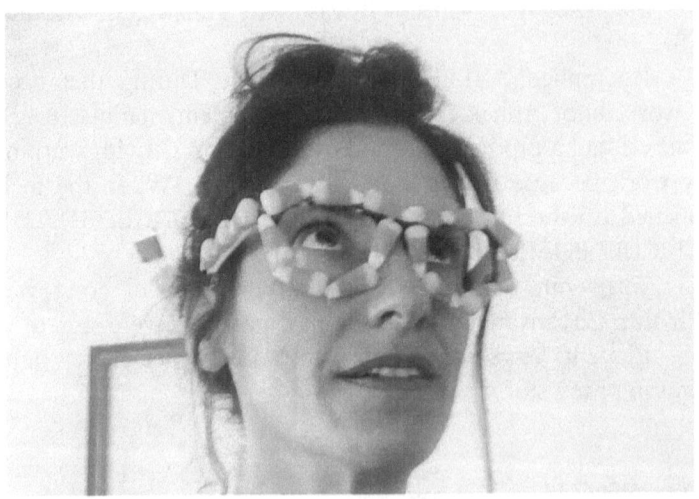

When I was a kid, one of my favorite things to do on Sundays, was go to the hospital with my father. Visiting patients, sneaking into surgeries... the hospital was like an amusement park to me.

Being that my dad was an otolaryngologist (an ear, nose, and throat and facial plastic surgeon), his most common surgery was a tonsillectomy, which included lopping off the adenoids. So I'd see my dad take out a lot of packs. Basically, a pack is the gauze that keeps the blood from oozing out, packed up inside the nose.

When he wasn't working, sometimes he shared about various cases. On one of our Wednesday visits, my dad shared the news that changed me.

"So... there was this guy today..." he said, pulling the turkey legs out of the oven, "who's head was run over by a truck." I had to ask my series of questions. "Is he living... How'd it happen?" My dad nodded. "It was a big truck, too. A semi."

I was mesmerized and asked if I could see him. Days passed, and I asked him again. When we got to the hospital my dad joked with the nurses and then asked them about the man. I followed my dad down the hall and snuck quick peeks into the other hospital rooms... seeing families... or people staring off into their TV sets, but my focus was mostly on the room at the end of the hall.

And there... he was. I could see him through the glass. The man whose head was run over by a truck. Except, as I followed my dad into his room, I noticed he wasn't really a man. He was a clump, laying in the fetal position with stitches all over his head.

"See the wax?" My dad said, gesturing to his face. "They had to wax his eyes in, because his eyes were bulging out... He's a vegetable... but he's living."

I scanned his room looking at the Get Well cards on the walls, the partially deflated balloons, the machines... and I realized, in this instance, maybe living isn't all that it's cracked up to be.

I didn't ask about the mangled, motorcycle man much after that, but months later, when my dad told me that he died, I felt better.

"Sometimes, dying... is living," I thought.

But most of all, I knew he was free.

http://www.yourfriendabby.com

Hung Viet Nguyen

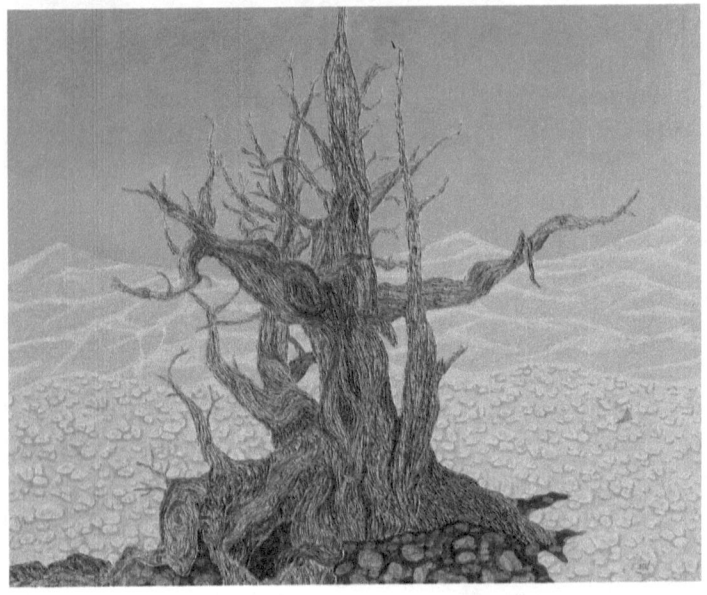

Ancient Pine # 13, oil on wood panel, 48" x 60", 2016

DOWN TO THE RIVER

"Warning: Do not attempt to hike from the rim to the Colorado River and back in one day. Many people who have attempted this have suffered serious illness or death."

I showed the note on Grand Canyon visitor guide to a ranger lady and asked:

"Does that mean people can't do this hike in one day?"

"People do it anyway. But don't do it unless you're marathon runner".

I paused for few second and thought "I'm not really a runner, but I did run some marathons, so it will be okay for me to do it in one day, I guess-I wish". She also told me the best way to hike down the river was by South Kaibab trail and hike up on Bright Angel trail, and take along plenty of water plus electrolyte replacement.

Next day, I woke up at 3:30 am, walked out of campsite at 4, through the darkness of early morning on South Rim. The sky was full of stars, half moon hanging over above the pine trees and shone upon the road, no one was around, the only thing I could hear were my footsteps and steady breathing. I took the earliest bus to the South Kaibab trailhead.

At trailhead, I rechecked everything and started to hike down at 5 am. I was walking smoothly at a good pace, enjoying the sunrise, fresh air and quietness of the Grand Canyon early morning. Sunrays were touching rocks, soil, plants and myself, I would feel I became one of these elements, I would hope to get closer and be accepted into the environment.

The trail was steep, plenty marks of mule-hoof, their fresh dung drop here and there. It was beautiful along South Kaibab trail, especially when sunrise. But there were no shade and water supply, one needed to carry own water. After the cedar ridges, then several switchback down to Tonto platform, the trail got level. There was an emergency telephone located at Tip-off. In case, a rescue needed: back up to the rim by helicopter, one had to pay around $2,000 *so don't leave camp without a credit card.*

During the time descended to the river, I caught two rows of mules going up. Mules always had a right of way, I found a safe place to stand still and let them passed by. It took 3 hours to reach the river, I crossed the 1st suspension bridge, The tight floor of the bridge was installed to prevent the mule from frighten by looking down to the running water and the height of the bridge. After walking through the bridge, I took a break, dip my feet under the cold river at same time the sun was so intent hot above. I walked another half mile to Phantom Ranch logging, passed Bright Angel campground for backpacking hikers. I visited ranger station, met a lean-rough looking lady, collected some information about the Bright Angel trail which I would hike back to the South Rim. She suggested to soak-wet head, hat, and back of shirt to start going up. I walked back to the river, crossed the 2nd suspension bridge to a cabin, I filled up tap water and re-soaked myself. First part of the trail was not much steep, I had good time strolling along the ridge, later parts of it were very steep and much expose to open sun around Devils Corkscrew. The the trail went side by side with Garden creek, water from the creek provided vegetation with shades. I had lunch under a shade of a big tree, took off my hiking boot, I could feel sign of black toes on two little toes, caused by downhill walking.

After lunch, I walked a short distance and reached Indian Garden, a flat area with plenty of trees. There were mule barn and campground for overnight hikers. I was lucky on that day, temperature was cooler then normal, it was around 90F instead of 110-125F. From here to the next water stop: Three-Mile Resthouse was less than 2 miles, I only needed to refill just 2 litters. The trail got steeper and had no shade, it started getting hotter, the landscape was pretty much plain of dried bushes and cactus. I hiked slowly; left-right, left-right, one foot in front the other, and it was it, simply motion, no special skills, thinking nothing. When legs and feet were tired and sore, every small barrier like rock on the trail became a high hurdle. If I could not raise my feet high enough to land on top of these rocks, the shoes would bang at the rocks and toes were hurt. I refilled water at Three-Miles Resthouse. It was very hot and dry, trail went through lots of steep switchbacks. I walked slowly, water bottle on hand, sipped water constantly, prayed my mantra *"om mani padme hum"*, listened to every part of my body. I reached 1.5 Miles Resthouse, it was a little tower with water faucet under a shading tree. After refiled my last water enough for the last 1.5 miles, again going up hill. The last part of the trail was tough, I could see more people, more tourists, who would like to get some Grand Canyon dirt on their feet or even dress shoes. It became like a park, it had to be safe for me, but I lost the charm of being alone, as mountaineer Reinhold Messner said: *"… loneliness that was no longer a handicap but the strength"*, if I could not feel it at that moment, perhaps later I would.

Finally, I got up to the last steep of the trail at 2:30pm. Standing on the trailhead at South rim, looking down the several switchbacks, I talked to myself *"That's it"*. And of course there was no medal, no certificate, no internets' result, no one cared about, only the wonderful memories of today would be on my mind for long, long time.

Writing from the note in June 1998.
March 2016

http://www.hung4art.com

Joy J. Rotblatt

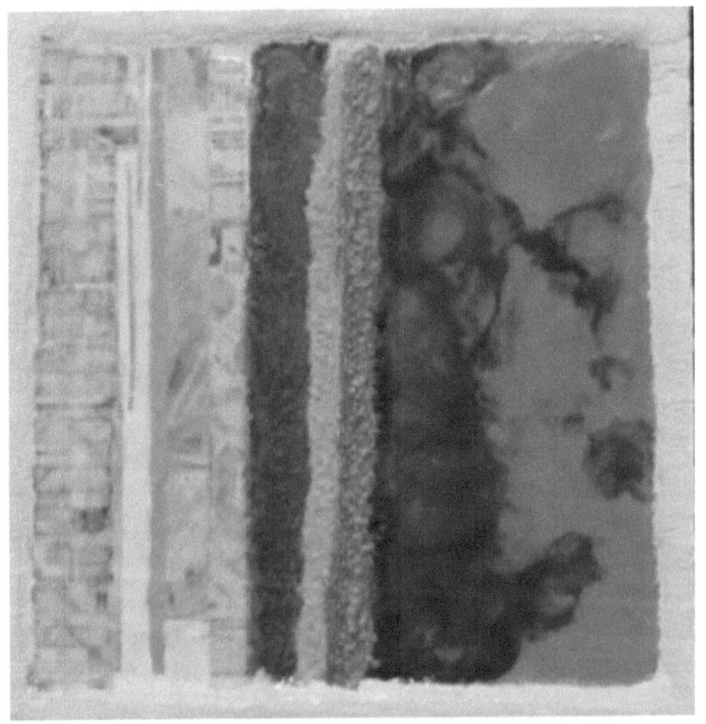

Cusco

It was magic! My grandfather gave me a birthday gift of Richard Halliburton's book, "New Worlds to Conquer" when I was a young girl. The adventures described in this book, especially the time he spent in Peru at Machu Pichhu, sparked my imagination. I read the book many, many times and the desire to one day be able to visit those fabulous ruins was born. As an adult I was fortunate to have traveled to wondrous places all around the globe, but Machu Pichu remained an elusive goal. The altitude, I was told, could be a problem and the trip was not an easy one. It remained the ultimate challenge for me.

I was on my way to recovering from breast cancer in 2009, but had not reached my full strength yet when a friend of mine, a travel agent, presented me with the opportunity to join her tour to Peru, specifically Machu Pichu. I wanted to jump right in with a yes, yes, yes, but even though it had been my life's dream, I spent a long time considering if I could actually undertake the trip at this particular time in my life.

After much deliberation and assurances from my friend that there would be assistance should I require it, I booked my trip. When I arrived, it was everything I had ever imagined, and so much more. There were sights I had never even heard of. One of the most memorable evenings was spent with a shaman, watching him go through his ritual to give a blessing to "Pacha Mama" (Mother Earth). The salt flats and terraces we saw were visually stunning. I managed to climb all over the ruins quite well, most likely on adrenalin, without as much as a walking stick. I learned that the Peruvian civilization was very advanced when Machu Pichu was built. There are viaducts running alongside the ruins to carry water to the valley below. All of the structures are aligned with elements of the cosmos, and the dressing on this particular cake is that the Peruvian people were wonderfully friendly and helpful, and were ready to communicate with me knowing only a bit of Spanish. The food was so remarkable that I have sought out and found several restaurants in the Los Angeles area where I can, for a brief time, relive the wonders of Peru. The sights, the market places, everything about the trip fulfilled all of my expectations. I feel I was so fortunate to be able to actually make the magic happen that I had dreamed of for so long.

http://www.joyartist.com

Lillian Abel

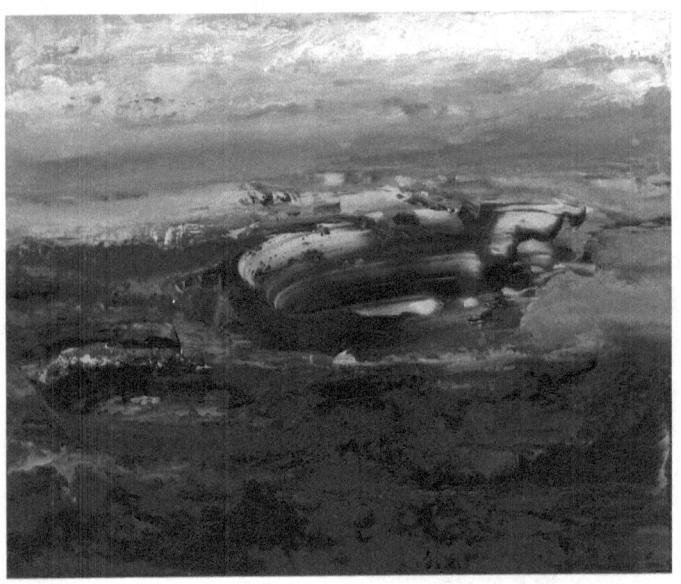

The Attack

It was a warm summer evening in Chicago. My best friend, Simone and I were at one of our favorite beer garden hangouts for dinner. It was a festive and lively ambiance as usual. We laughed, talked and shared secrets for an hour, having our usual great time together. After we ate and paid the check I went to the restroom, which was down a long flight of stairs in a lighted, deserted area.

When coming out of the stall, I saw a tall, thin man standing in the middle of the bathroom. The lights were strong, however, his eyes were shadowed in the brim of the hat he wore. I smiled at him and said, "You are in the wrong bathroom." To my naïve surprise he walked toward me, without saying a word, and put his hands around my neck. I felt panic at that moment, yet kept in control. There was no escape as he was in the middle of the room and therefore blocking my exit to the door as he continued to tighten his grip on my neck. I looked into his piercing, dark eyes, placed my hand at arms length on his chest and repeated quietly, "No" firmly over and over as I slowly moved sideways in a circle toward the door, fearing I wouldn't make it that far. I could see in his demeanor that he was confused. At last, somehow, my hand was on the door and I flung it open as a horrible, ripping scream came out of me, so loud and distant, it sounded as if someone else was screaming. He immediately released his grip from my neck and ran up the long flight of stairs.

I could hear shouting and banging coming from the floor above as I ran up the stairs after him. I could see in the dim light of the restaurant at the top of the stairs there were many men waiting for him. As I came to the top of the stairs, they were punching him and throwing him against the wall and across the bar. Chaos ensued as beer mugs and chairs were flying everywhere. Immediately I felt a wave of guilt come over me as if I'd done something wrong! Now I know, this is the way women sometimes feel when they are attacked. One of the men asked me if I was all right and I immediately started telling him what happened, now breathless and in a panic as I allowed the pent up emotion to rise up. In the meantime, the other men are throwing my attacker on the floor and holding him down. They called the Police after he was punished to their satisfaction and under control.

Women have not been treated fairly in these kinds of situations, even in rape cases. The owner, who was a gentle, caring fair-haired man, brought me a beer, giving me comforting words. He then asked me if I would press charges when the police came, and he explained that prosecution by the courts would be a difficult journey. By this time the ordeal I had just experienced was sinking in and anger was replacing panic. I told him "Yes, of course, I will press charges!" The police came quickly and put the man in handcuffs. They inquired if I was all right and then interviewed me and asked if I wanted to press charges. Yes, again!

http://www.lillianabel.com

Beanie Kaman

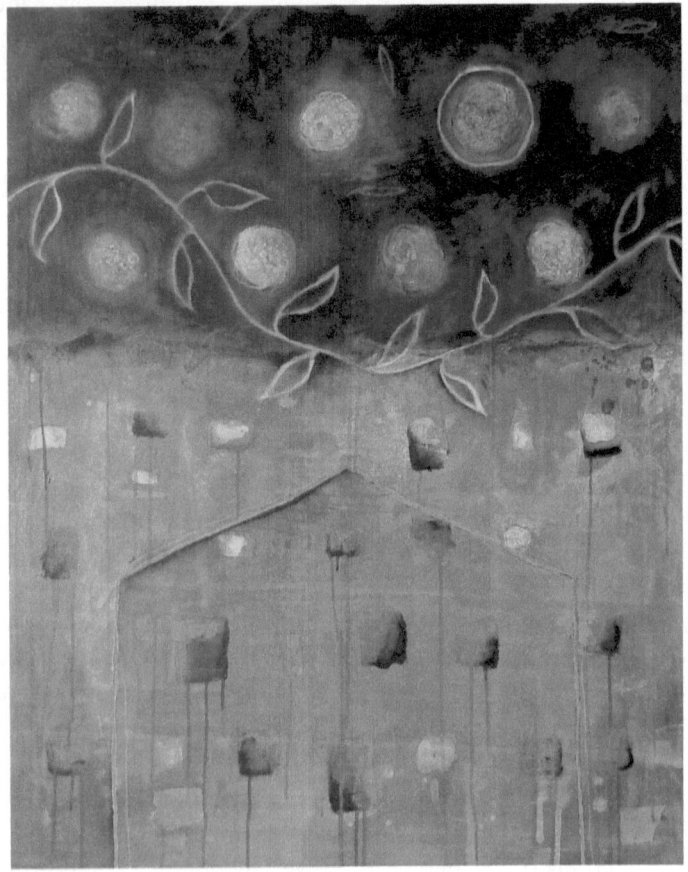

Walking the Stone Wall

New England is full of stone walls. They came about as a natural process between man and nature. The ground is so rocky that as the farmers cleared their land for pastures or building, the rocks were piled into low walls as property line markers. I'm sure there is truth to that, but the walls might also have been a convenient way to simply pile the stones. As the walls age, gravity pulls and moss grows, and they become an integral and beautiful part of the landscape. Some have been there more than 300 years.

Where I grew up, we had 4 long stone walls dividing our property. They were great places to play on, to hide things in – all sorts of games could be played with imagination. They delineated the four pastures for the cows and sheep.

Behind the barn was a long low wall that ran the length of the pasture. That wall was particularly old, and the forest beyond it held a certain charm that kept us coming back. We would climb over the stones in different spots, venturing into the trees with a sense of adventure. Wandering, we discovered a rusted old Model A Ford. It was only the chassis; the tires were gone, the doors were left ajar, and it had turned the golden rust color that let it become part of the forest. Who abandoned it like that? We climbed in and out of the windowless doors; dead leaves were now the floor. We discovered old cans equally rusted, and thought maybe it was an old campsite, where some poor soul lived in the car. Or maybe someone was hiding out in it, keeping a low profile for some shady reason. Each time my brothers and I went there, we would make up different stories and the joy was knowing we would never have an answer.

Once we had exhausted our curiosity at the old car for the time being, we would keep walking along the wall to our next discovery of a long heavy rope with a loop at the bottom. It was tied to the branch of a huge pine tree about 16' above us. There was a small clearing, from the edge of the wall into the trees, just enough to give you room to swing around. The thrill of putting your foot in that loop, holding onto the rope, jumping back up on the wall and pushing off with the other foot was unending. The rush of the wind would pass through your hair and for a few seconds it felt like flying. If you had enough of a push, you could bend and sway, go round in circles or any which way. Because you were standing, not sitting, the experience included your whole body, completely visceral in every way.

It became a constant place to go. Friends would come, and we would all take turns, seeing who could go out the farthest, or who could go the highest. We were young and agile; no one ever fell off. Your weight kept your foot safely in the loop. Sometimes the cows or sheep were in the pasture, and they might follow us over, but they would never cross the wall. They would simply watch, and wait for us to be done to give them hay from the barn.

Now I live in Los Angeles. My memories from such an innocent time seem like a dream, but yet they live on to remind me of who I am and where I came from. Walks up in Topanga Canyon or the Santa Monica Mountains bring shaded recollections of how it felt to be free with nature, to know no fear and be one with the earth, trees and sky. If I am up high enough in the mountains to find the big trees, I can imagine where the best spot might be to swing up to heaven and remember that glorious feeling of flying for an instant.

http://www.beaniekaman.com

David Glynn

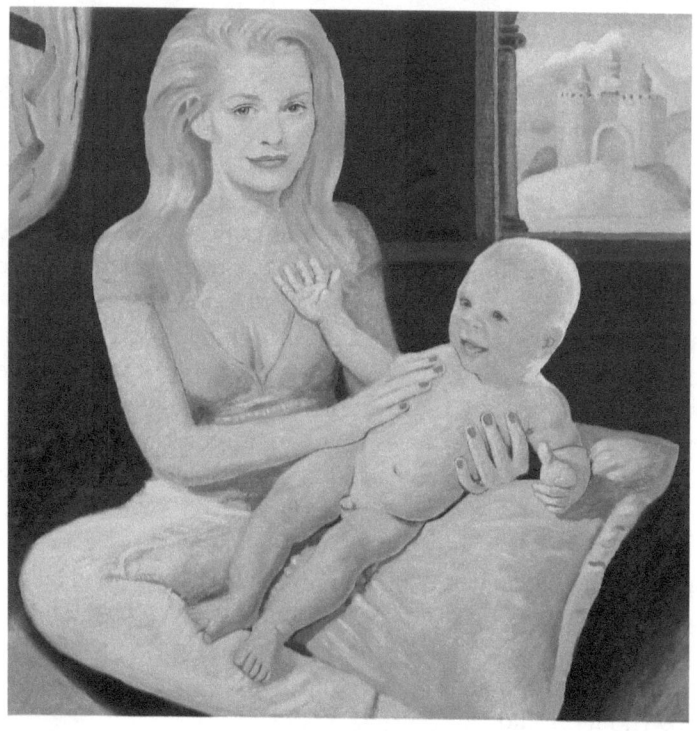

Basketball was a big thing. I had spent a lot of time again in the summer playing ball almost everyday at the Rec. center. Every season we would take a bus to Exeter and the sport shoe store near Phillips Exeter Academy. The team was supplied with matching sneakers and we got Adidas low cuts for everyone. Coach Baron had had injuries to both knees and had lot's of opinions (about everything) and thought high tops were worth less as they added no additional support. He said you would need a shoe that had laced braces that went half way up your leg to make any difference. I had had a few sprained ankles in my career and could see his point. The season started with a multiple game Christmas tournament in neighboring rival Portsmouth. In spite of doing well in practice, I didn't get in much game time and as we lost the last game with Gary Jewell missing shots badly, I just stormed off after the game and coach Baron came following after me with the team behind him. We got into the locker room and he started going off on Gary about blowing plays and then turned to me and said "glynn, you are starting next game."

This was good for me. We were about to start a nearly 10 game home stretch. I played serviceably well, didn't excel but didn't mess up. So this was how things went for most of the stretch. The starting line-up was Ned at point guard, Jay, the nephew of the coach (and the other guy who played both JV and Varsity sophomore year in the "77 champion season with me) as wing man/ guard. Me as wing man/ forward. Ed the big man and Scotty the sophomore with a good shot and height. After a few game of this I got a little grumbling from Gary and also Kevin, who had started some games over me last year when we were juniors. Gary would go on to be voted "most athletic" as in addition to being a natural shooter, he was also good at baseball and football. Even coach Baron had talked to me about needing to get more points out of my position and how would I feel about letting someone else start. I just said honestly that I wanted to play and he didn't change the line-up. Though it did change.

Coach Baron's back started bothering him and he had to stay home for some games and have the assistant coach Fran McNally fill in. McNally didn't change the line-up either. We were playing the last game of our home game stretch. I was doing well, In the first quarter I had 8 points in as many minutes. As the second quarter started it happened, I was running down court and some guy kneed me in the back of the calf. I was in pain but mostly I was limping badly. I was out of the game. I went home and wasn't sure what to do. I put some ice on it and by the next day I was using crutches. Apparently I had torn a muscle. Later coach Baron would say he would have been able to tell me what to do and I should have made the 10 cent call. Anyway we hit the road and I went along for the ride but I didn't suit up for about 8 games. I had a good game against Pinkerton Academy against a former junior high team mate, scoring 10 points coming off the bench. My long shots were improving and in another game I hit a 20 footer which would have been a 3 pointer if they had that rule at the time. In the mid seventies only Dr. J and the ABA had that rule, though he still managed to make some impressive dunks while finally playing in the NBA for the Philadelphia Sixers. We had a winning season overall but not championship level. When the State playoffs came around at UNH coach Baron's back was again acting up. In one game McNally put in a junior big man he was grooming over me at a key point in the end and we lost the game.

Later, coach Baron would tell me that he had been listening on the radio and would have put me in if he had a phone to the bench. That was basketball season. Because of my convalescence with my regular routine of dipping my leg in the whirlpool for therapy back in the locker room I had started to distance myself a little early from high school and began the transition into another phase of my life.

My aunt Queenie had given me some real contemporary fiction including Tom Robbins Another Roadside Attraction which I enjoyed and would go on to get into reading in general and him as one of the particulars.

http://www.DavidGlynn.com

Anna Marini-Genzon

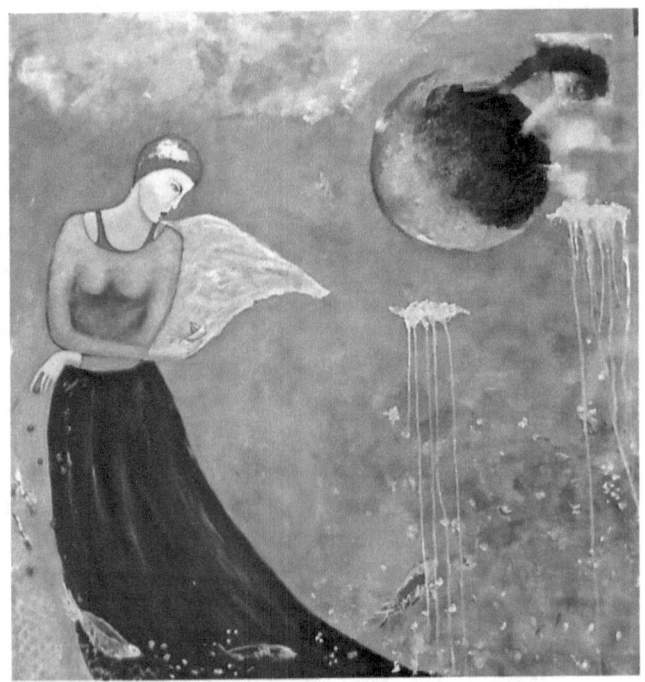

TheFisherman Story; Oil, Acrylic; Canvas; 48"x48"

The Story

As my Italian grandfather use say Mangia, Mangia!
Which means Eat!!

My grandfather like most Italian families had lots of siblings they were nine in total.

All together with their own children and grandchildren, they were a lot of people.

We had a big house; I guess our house was the one that could accommodate a multitude like this.

That is why the holidays were celebrated in our place most of the times!

Around the holidays my grandparents would get the plans for the meals early enough so when the time came around we had plenty of pasta to satisfy a large crowd.

My grandpa had a chicken coup and a nice orchard.

The ceremony would start by getting several chickens ready to be transformed in ravioli filling!!

He would go to the chicken coup select two or three young chicken, and then he would grab them by the neck, twisted them and finally cut the heads off.

I remember looking with horror how the chicken would continue waking headless for a few minutes!!

Next, was the feathers; my grandma had a large pot with boiling water ready for the poor animals to take a steamy bath. After that, the feathers would come off easily.

The next day my grand father would start making the dough for the ravioli and the spaghetti.

Once the pasta dough was ready they would cover every single table in the house with flower and then stretch the dough like thin soft sheets.

At the time of mixing the ingredients my grandfather would get lots of garlicky cloves. My sister, my cousins and I would play around looking with curious eyes. My grandpa would grab a piece of bread, he would cover it with olive oil and put inside a whole clove of garlicky. He will tell us Mangia, Mangia, this is good for you!

You will grow nice and healthy!!

I grew up loving garlic; I use in most of my meals. Every time I cook I remember the sweet memories from childhood playing around and my grandfather gfeeding us garlic.

http://www.amgart.com

Amy Kaps

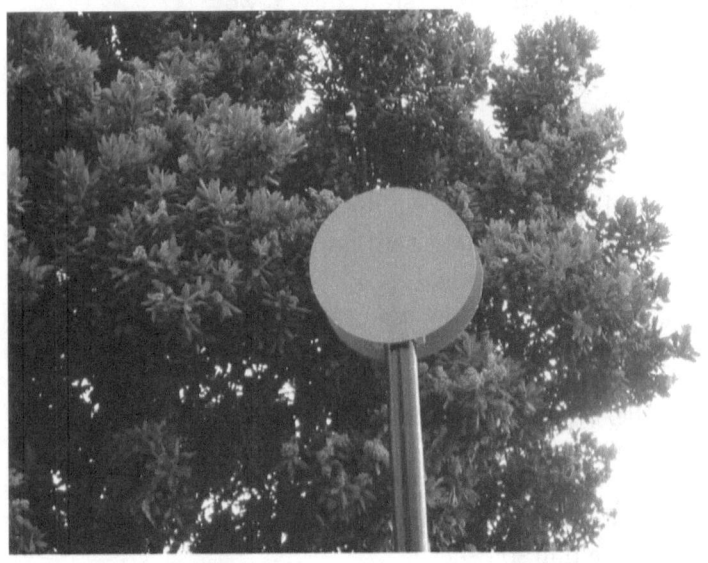

A New Zealand Sign, 2006

An Emotional Exorcism

Several years ago, one of my best friends and collaborator on planet Earth, died.

Soon after that, a few friends and I embarked on a trip to Joshua Tree; and a trip on magic mushrooms. Sitting in the back seat of the car, driving through downtown LA, I contemplated slipping out and taking a bus back to Venice. I felt as if a dark cloud was hanging over me, and as good friends as they were, I didn't want to subject them to my morose mood. It was not fair to infect them with my powerful gloom that might ruin their experience.

Upon our arrival at the Inn at 29 Palms, I found myself alone in a room with one of my dear friends, someone who is like a sister to me. I told her my worries, especially about taking hallucinogens when I was already in such a wretched emotional state. She gently advised me to sleep on it and maybe take just a little bit. We all wanted to share the magic of the desert and each other.

If you have ever been to the California desert, you know of its deceptive beauty. Gentle and jagged rocks nestled with sagebrush and fossilizing bones. Violent acts of nature suspended in time and space. At first glance, everything is just Beige. But as you acclimate to the vastness, and your eyes get used to the light, you begin to see the nuances in the shades of brown and white and green. At sunset it is most misleading as the rocks reflect the pinks and oranges. Distances become very difficult to judge. Disorientation is a real danger. Responsible drug users that we are, we had alerted a few friends staying at a near by campsite of our journey, so someone came looking for us to lead us back to camp around the magic hour. Of course we were only a few hundred yards away.

I went into the desert crying. And upon seeing a fresh green stalk shooting out of a seemingly dead and withered plant, I began to smile. Here it was. Absolute proof. Ashes to ashes. Here, in the middle of the desert, right before my eyes, was Life sprouting from Death. I was relieved. A certain calm came over me. I was able to laugh again. I was able to sing again. I was able to see beauty again.

My first psychedelic experience was in college. It was a warm and rainy day in Saratoga Springs. And ever since that day, I have an appreciation for grey days because the world seems so vibrant. I wasn't seeing anything that wasn't there. I was simply seeing.

I'm not advocating rampant drug use. But I do acknowledge that the ingestion of these organic substances, often used by indigenous people for transformative purposes, offer a key to a different level of consciousness. It was such a powerful experience. I refer to my last desert trip as an emotional exorcism. Nothing esoteric, just real.

http://amykaps.com

Milo Reice

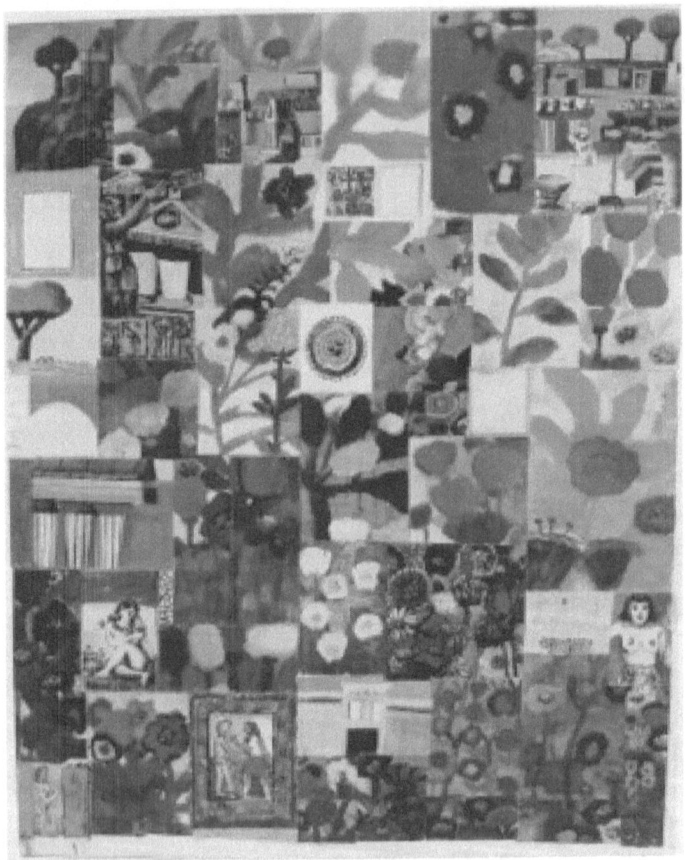

Free Verse, 1990; 84"x70"; Odyssey Revisited #9

Milo Reice /Troy and a bit of Baclava

The Directress of services at Istanbul's Hilton directed me to the local bus depot; it resembled an ancient bazar set within a peristyled court full of buses rather than hawkers and stalls. It was hot for May and dusty- the sun refracted by the dust making it more Constantinople than modern Istanbul lending verisimilitude to this, my trip to the site of Troy. This was

1987, I was the lone foreigner on the standing room trip unless you considered the chickens and goat that accompanied their masters, as aliens as well. I was a tourist — a stranger in a land I knew from book-learning only; so, "Rapt" I embraced this advance education. After a several hours drive half of which one side of the bus drove in dying sea waves the other on beach sands I disembarked with my baggage in the town of Canakkale several miles out from Troy. Weighed down I managed to leave my back pack, my 30 inch plus portfolio of paper and drawings and weighty suit-bag in the care of the local bus kiosk and taxied up to Ilium.

The taxi "would wait for me". The entrance was manned by only one man who went back to his sleeping after taking my money as I entered into the past. And it was a past disturbed only by my awe, my thoughts, and footfalls for unbelievably during my entire time there I was the only entrant. No guards were about, no other tourists, however ghosts were manifested in little sudden and short-lived siroccos whistling across my path or from within the beautiful ruinations. But I conjured up things that were no longer there: everything from pet dogs and cats, horses and oxen yanking wagon loads of goods, outdoor cafes and bars. I imagined the famous like Priam and Hecuba, Paris and Helen, but mostly I thought of the countless everyday people who'd lived there: loved, argued, played with their kids, the visceral's of real life.

Back in the modern town, a lovely dinner in it's central square having a few hours to kill I walked a bit and then went into a bakery and bought some Baclava not one slice but a whole Baker's tray for as a non Turkish speaker I'd pointed to the pastry and in his believing I wanted a tray's worth the proprictor beamed happily in his unusual fortune, and too the exchange was, well 1987 exchange making of me albeit for only mere moments King Croesus; I'd not the heart not to follow through with my purchase. Returning to the town square to await my next transportation I ate thrice a NY restaurant's serving until I could eat no more and yet I'd still essentially a full tray's worth of honeyed tastiness.

At mid-night I boarded the bus to see Pergamon the ancient spectacle of a city built on the side of a mountainous steep-slope, the home of parchment, the site of Galen's psychiatric hospital, the place where Scopas's Alter of Zeus and Athena resided, the site of the second greatest library after Alexandria's, et al.

About 4 A.M. the bus driver kindly woke me and directed me in the direction of Bergama, explaining that the bus only dropped people at this crossroads 7 or so miles from, town. Ok, not a local whereby my wife or a friend might be awaiting me with a car, and being the lone foreigner not wary of late night travel in the middle of no-where, I found myself suddenly all alone surrounded by dense darkness and silence on a lightless road no different than it would have been 2,000 years ago. So after a somewhat comical routine of juggling I managed the best way to carry my valise, my portfolio, my back-pack and my newly acquired boxed and stringed Baclava, I headed on listening to my walk-man and thinking perhaps a car might come by if not lions, tigers and bears (oh my). But really, I probably imagined all sorts of passersby of long ago: religious pilgrims, philosophers and writers, patients seeking Galen, even perhaps ancient world brigands but I largely marched on blanked rote silently counting my footfalls rather than imagining I might meet Eumenes II. So I trudged onwards, occasionally re-adjusting my load, somehow maintaining the box of pastry's level relationship to the ground, the box's string marking my alternating hands with the grooved canals of Mars.

Gradually the Sun began its rise and commercial traffic slowly materialized and eventually too a car of 4 men on their way to work picked me up. Via broken Italian and broken English we communicated and then I'd my Eureka! I opened the box of Baclava and passed it around: "Here Take some." "Enjoy! it's all yours, Thank-you Guys!"

They drove me around Bergama un-rushingly showing me the town's sites till they managed to find me a Hotel with a vacancy, checked in and comfortable.

In all these years since I 've not eaten Baclava again- I simply overdosed-having eaten too much at that sitting years ago, but those 4 men intertwined with Troy will forever cause me to smile, and forever serve as a postscript to Blind poet Homer's Iliad.

http://www.miloreice.com

Yvette Gellis

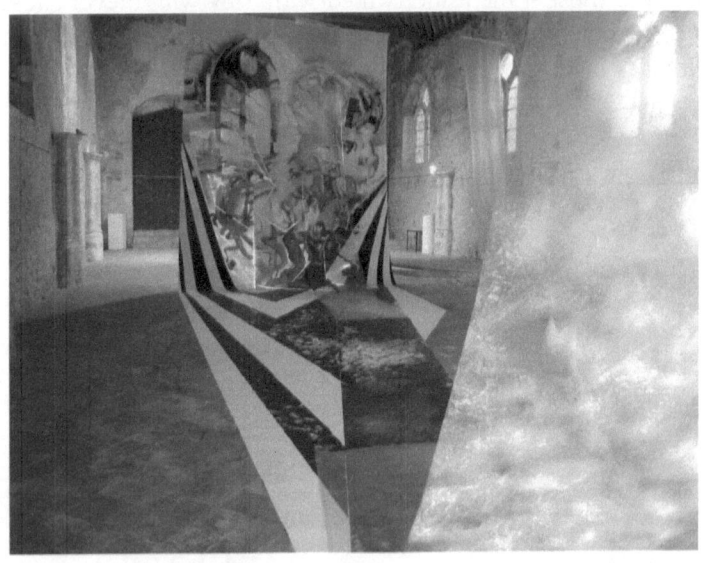

For our honeymoon we wanted something adventuresome and exotic, as well as romantic. So my newly minted husband and I spontaneously flew from Lisbon to Marrakesh, Morocco. After wandering through the Souk, being mesmerized by the cobra charmer, and navigating our rental car through the Atlas Mountains, we were ready for a more traditional honeymoon experience, so we asked the hotel concierge to recommend and an exceptional romantic restaurant. We set off that evening in a strange taxi that took us deep into the dark abyss of tiny abandoned alleys and miniature roads until he stopped at what looked like a vacant warehouse. We thought surely we were to be robbed and disposed of – our bodies never to be found. Courageously, we continued on our way. In the dark corridor of some strange place, we knocked on the grungy tin doors. To our delight the doors opened to a lush courtyard, where water fountains twinkling with candlelight and the sweet aroma of roses settled our fears. The transition was astonishing, as if a dark spell erupted into a magical dreamscape like OZ or the

Garden of Eden. As we entered paradise, a trail rose petals and candlelight led us to a table into the middle of a beautiful dining room dripping with gold fixtures, satin linens and soft music. The very air oozed romance.

Promptly came the champagne. It was poured. I smiled at my new husband and felt the rush and longing of a newlywed. We clinked glasses — I most slowly brought the glass to my parched lips. As my mouth barely touched the edge of the glass I saw it — a large, translucent scorpion perched on the opposite lip of the glass, inches from my face.

Ahhhh!!!! I screamed and hurled the glass across the room. I jumped up from the chair, knocking it over, feeling like creepy things were crawling up my legs. The Maitre'd rushed over. "Madame, are you okay." My husband gallantly pointed to the table where the scorpion sat wondering what all the fuss was about. It didn't survive long enough to find out as the Maitre'd nailed it with the menu and then, with apologies and new glasses of champagne, moved us to a new table.

That evening, Fate let me know that life would be a roller coaster full of extreme dualities, the promise of which has never wavered.

http:// www.yvettegellis.com

Sharon Suhovy

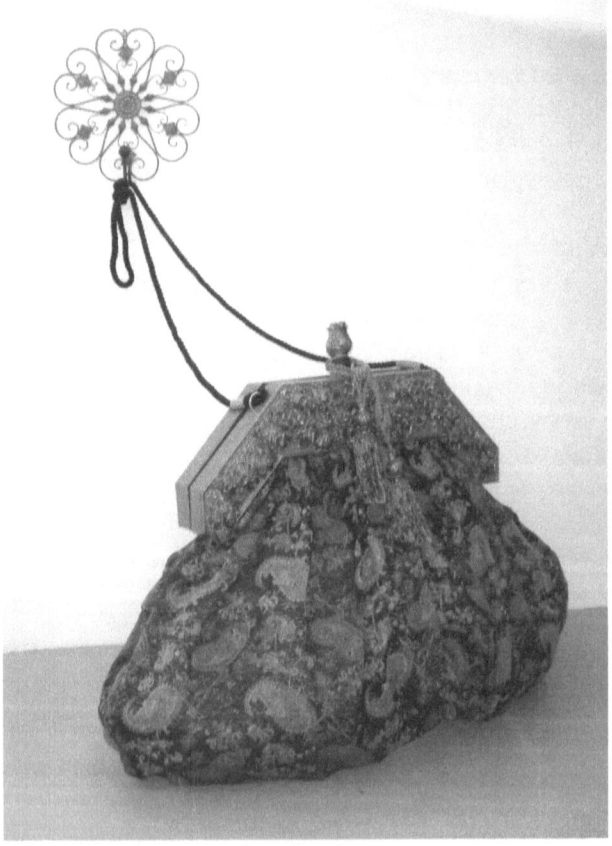

Chantelaine Purse

Being Foreign
Sharon Suhovy VanderMeiden

My grandfather, jedda, had just passed away and my husband and I were driving to the service in LA. I hadn't seen jedda since I was a child, just after my parents were divorced. The next time I would see him he would be laid in a casket in the Russian Molokan church.

Though it's customary to wear black at American funerals, that isn't the case for the Russian Molokan's that left Russia. Russian Molokan women had stopped wearing black dresses and shawls when they immigrated to America. There would be no black at this funeral. I needed to respect that. It was also sacred for women to have their heads covered. That morning, my sister and I decided to wear the peasant scarves that our grandmother had once worn. They were colorful, and bordered with hand-painted roses. I wore a colorful dress; no black.

When I was young my mom's parents lived across the street from the Russian Molokan church. My grandfather was once the minister of this church, and when we (my siblings and I) would come to stay with them, we practiced their faith and attended church with them. Since his passing I had never been in the doors.

It was tradition to wait at the church doors for someone of faith to escort you through. My husband and I were anxious as we waited with family members. My Dutch-born husband reluctantly supported me by going to the funeral with me. He would rather have waited outside for me, but I coaxed him into helping me get through this. He had never really been aware of my Russian culture. He spoke Dutch, but I didn't speak Russian. He never saw me as a foreigner, but that day, I would be.

Eventually, a woman came to the door and escorted the four of us women into the hall. The men also waited for a male usher who would lead them to be seated. We weren't late, but everyone was already seated. I guess the family comes in last. The women were escorted to a long row of wooden benches which faced another long row of wooden benches where the men were seated facing us. The casket was resting at the end of the benches, opened.

The Russian Molokan women were draped in colorful pastel chiffon dresses and scarves. I couldn't help thinking how beautiful they looked, and how foreign. I knew we were outsiders and I felt like that. I had been to the Russian Easter services as a child many times, when the women dressed in colorful hand-screened scarves, skirts and aprons. They looked like Russian matryoshka nesting dolls, but now they looked soft.

Being there opened up a flood of memories, and the tables of Russian food; hundreds of boiled eggs, the borsht soup, the egg bread and lamb. My parents had socialized me American with undertones of Russian heritage, but my cousins all spoke Russian. I remembered the endless prayers and chanting; stomping on the wooden floors, until someone was suddenly filled with the Holy Ghost. There was always a series of prayers where you were on your feet, than on your knees, and up again. Up and down for maybe an hour. This day would be one of those.

When the funeral ceremonies were almost over I seemed to relax a bit, taking in the room. The men's choir of Russian chants echoed in the room. The bare wooden walls were almost like a casket itself. The room felt small, claustrophobic. I was submerged in my own world of thoughts and memories. We were trying to fit in, but with our vanity of American fashion and mismatched head scarves, we looked almost comical. We had become the colorful nesting dolls.

Relieved that it was almost over, I searched to see where they had seated my husband (the Dutch man in a blue suit). He wasn't sitting with my dad or the men facing us. He was nowhere to be found, leaving me to believe that he had chosen to stay outside. We started whispering to each other of his whereabouts. The service was coming to an end; the chants were resuming, and almost all at one moment, the four of us turned around to the six men sitting behind us; the choir, and there he was. He stood when they stood. He sat when they sat; his lips moving with the sounds of the Russian men chanting. Of course we all wanted to know how he ended up in the choir. He said that a man walked through the door and said, "Follow me."

https://www.facebook.com/Sharon-Suhovy-157946574216476/

Stephen Rowe

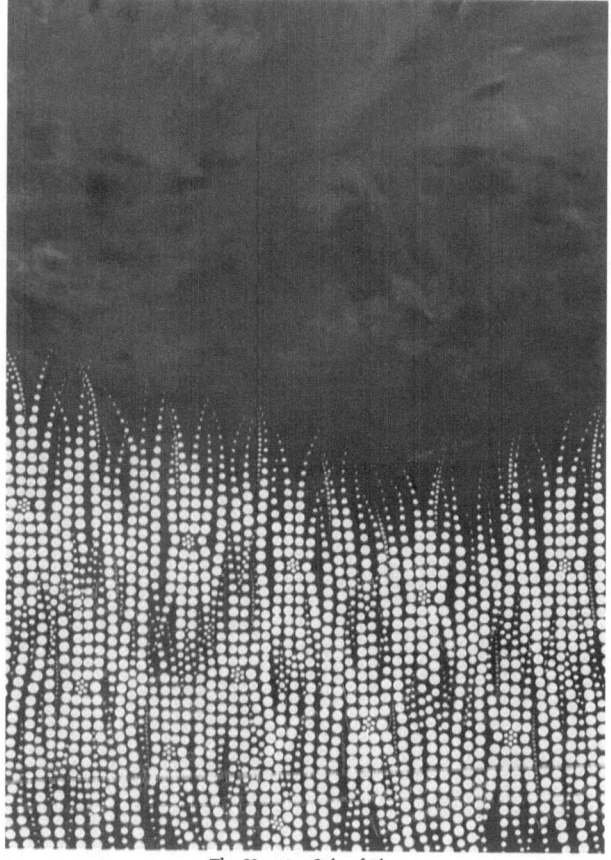

The Happier Side of Blue

I was born in a mining town in the outback of Australia, called Broken Hill. I left school at 14 and 9 months, became a carpenter, did boxing to be in shape for motocross, and was sponsored by a local Suzuki dealer. I started classical ballet at 16 and went onto a ballet career for 17 years as a professional.

This story starts with me following my fiancé (I got engaged at 18 years old) to Adelaide for a 2 week ballet camp. At the end of the 2 weeks, the director of the school called us boys into the office and said that he felt that we had potential to become ballet dancers. The course was two years. I told him that I couldn't afford the tuition and as we were leaving the office the director asked if I could stay behind for a chat. They offered me a scholarship for two years, so I said yes.

I drive back to Broken Hill and told my dad that I was going back to Adelaide and that I was going to be a ballet dancer, he didn't believe it. I packed my suitcase, put it in the car and drove off to Adelaide for my new adventure.

Wow, what change from carpentry! During this time I was doing really well as a motocross racer and Suzuki called me into there dealership and they offered me a racing deal to ride for Suzuki, haha! When I said that I couldn't take the deal, they asked why? And I told them why "I am going to ballet dancer", their jaws dropped, haha!

But I made the right decision, and I started my new life.

http://www.stephenroweart.com

Lena Moross

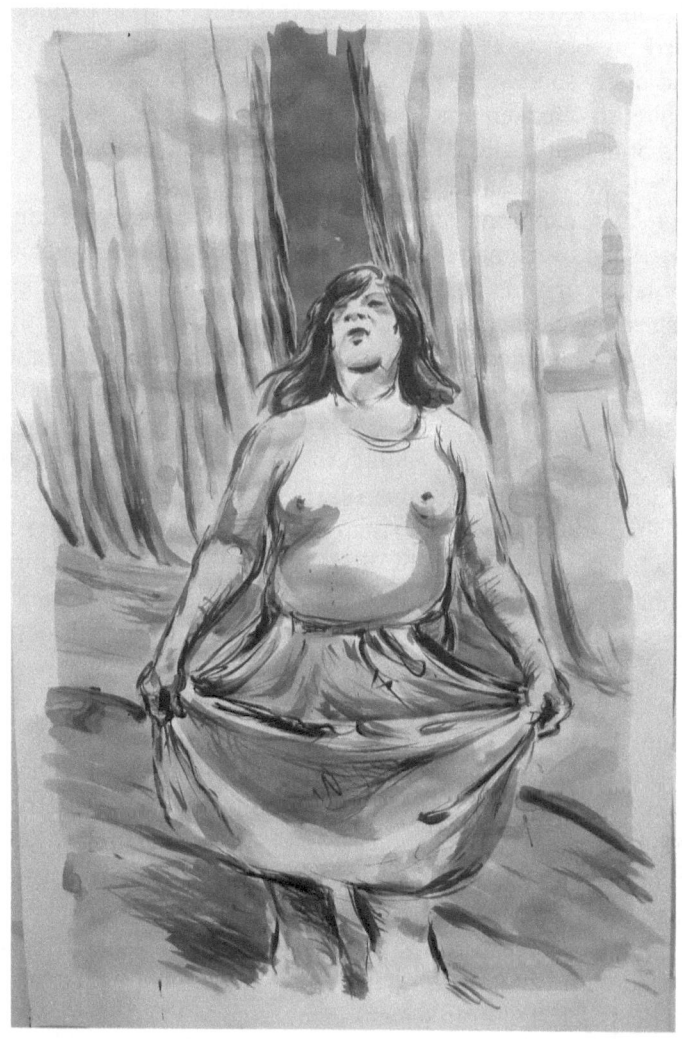

OK, I know exactly how it began — my cooking adventures.

I read a book by M.F.K. Fishers "The Art of Eating". The writing was so beautiful so elegant and reflective...

Her words made me taste the food, smell it, feel it, long for it. I understood that food is not necessarily only recipes, that it's connected to memories, places, and time — from then on I tried my best to re-create the smells of my mothers cooking and pretty soon my apron began to smell like hers — a mix of gefiltefish, chicken crackling, and caramelized onions ...with lots of dill, dill, dill ... mixed with boiled potatoes fume.

It was 25 years ago.

After exploring indulging, discovering, experimenting, obsessing, over my new found passion, I began to victimizing my family, friends, and strangers with creating/cooking ethnic dishes, my childhood comfort foods, and new technique discoveries — learned from random chefs...the diverse mom-and-pop hole-in-the-wall places in which Los Angeles so bursting with...

I became arrogant enough to hire myself out as a cook to someone I didn't know personally but befriended on face book. In France. A couple who happen to live in the middle of nowhere, surrounded by fields and in a 16th century monastery. I asked how much it cost to rent a room, he said it rents by the floor that has five bedrooms and three bathrooms — at an unimaginable, unaffordable price for me. But then I offered my cooking abilities to him and his wife for staying there. AND, they kindly accepted.

The journey begins with a 12 hour flight, to a five hour train ride, to a two hour bus ride, and a one hour car ride through the fields to the monastery. My first day started at 7AM on our way to the open market, shopping for food. "What was in season?" And my decision not to cook French food.

So I decided to cook Russian food. My first lunch meal started with frittata and beet soup! — and ended with peaches. Items selected from remembering from M.F.K. Fishers book about buying deformed ugly fruit and that they gave the best flavor.

My 10-day stay involved creating, exploring the country, food shopping, and without any friends — I kissed every old man and received free wine! And each evening I was in the kitchen, modern and mid-evil, cooking, sharing my "private food collection" with honesty, sincerity, and love.

Made evident to me each night when the couple were loudly fucking in their room on the ground floor while I was in my room on the third floor … knowing my food is being well used!

http://www.LenaMoross.com

Bradford J. Salamon

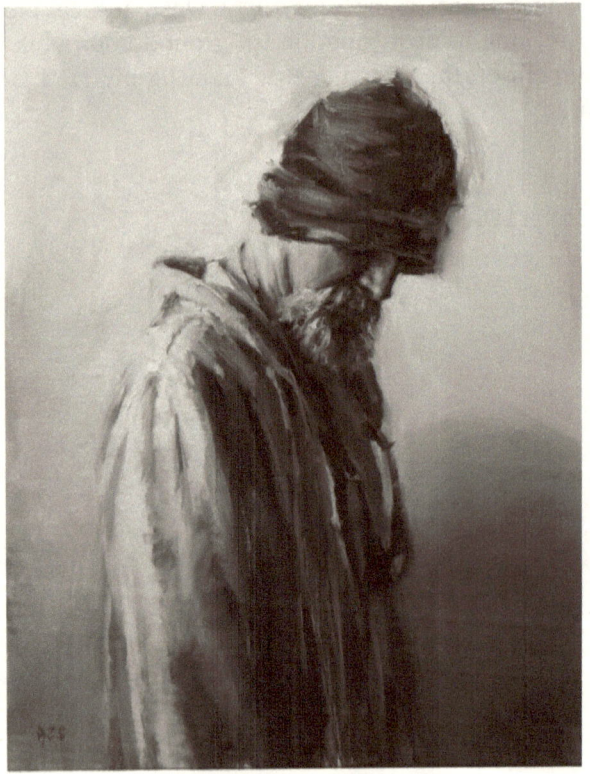

William Wray, 20x16

While the war in Vietnam was coming to a painful end in the Spring of 1975, I was living in Huntington Beach, California with my mother and 2 brothers. That summer the Russians and the Americans had worked together to join, in orbit, the Apollo/Soyuz spaceships. Gerald Ford was our president. Richard Nixon's resignation in August of 1974 and the Watergate scandal were still in the news.

Scott Richman was my best friend that year. I hung out at his house every day after school. We rode his minibikes, chased girls and watched his family's big color TV. Scott's mom was a tall blonde who just had the first boob job I had ever heard of. One day her breasts suddenly looked like two rockets about to take off. Scott's dad had dark hair, was handsome and quiet. During a dinner one night at Scott's house his mother suggested I might want to join them for the summer in Colorado. They decided to move and buy a small restaurant and run it themselves in the small town of Grand Lake, Colorado.

I wasn't sure my mom would let me go, but she gave in easily and didn't even talk to Scott's parents whom she had never met. So in early June of 1975, we headed for Colorado in a big banana-boat Lincoln Continental. Two twelve-year-old boys in the back seat, driving over the Rockies trying to out belch each other to pass the time.

Once there, I was introduced to the current restaurant staff and shown my living quarters in the back of the small restaurant. The next day I was trained for the work I was expected to do in exchange for my food and lodgings. I had the morning shift. I cleaned floors, scraped the grill, wiped down the booths, cleaned the bathroom and took out the trash.

Within a few short days I never saw my best friend again...or his mother. Scott's father stayed around to run the restaurant.

It's been forty years now and I still can't recall what happened between my best friend and I to end the friendship. Perhaps Scott's parents separated and Scott's mom didn't want him near his father? Who knows? However, it's inconceivable to me that Scott's mother never checked on the 12 year old boy she invited to stay with her family for the summer.

Before I left California, I had promised my brothers and a few friends, that I would not be coming back until the summer was over. My pride kept me there longer than was remotely sensible under the circumstances. A 16 year old kid named Greg lived behind the restaurant with me. Greg slept in a bed across a room we shared. He told me of his future plans to be a truck-driver and gave me advice on the finer details of how to seduce a girl. I smoked grass with him for the first time. We went a few places together. Mostly I was on my own; wandering down sidewalks and watching local characters run their errands...scurrying about, trying to avoid the hot, dry summer sun. I recall a candy shop next to the miniature golf course in town. It must have had air conditioning because I remember sitting in that shop, sometimes a couple hours a day, listening to the top 10 radio hits over and over. Countless times I heard "Philadelphia Freedom" by Elton John & Frankie Valli's "My Eyes Adore You" during that summer in the mountains.

One night Greg set me up on a date with a dark-brown-haired girl named Jessie who was also about twelve-years-old. The Exorcist was playing at a cheap bargain theater at the end of town. It was the only entertainment in Grand Lake so the movie was packed. We had smoked a joint in the car before we went in. I was so frightened by the film that I desperately wanted to leave but my pride kept me there to the end. It was a horrifying experience.

After the movie Greg and his date split. Jessie and I went to her house where we bypassed the front door and entered her room from a small door off the alley. I remember seeing her father through a crack in the door, sitting in a La-Z-Boy, watching what looked like re-runs of the Winter Olympics. The scary movie we just saw freaked her out too. We were both real hyped up. We had just survived something terrible together.

I put some moves on her right away and it didn't take long before we were really going for it. I suggested that she shut the door so her father couldn't see us, but she ignored me. She quickly got under me and pushed my pants down and pulled up her skirt. My previous experiences with girls never got past the shortstop. She was rounding third at full speed. I still remember how small she felt under me and how her thick dark hair was covering most of her face.

Once I was inside her, I had no idea what to do next. I didn't move. I just laid there on top of her thinking to myself, "well this sure is over-rated ".

Jessie was getting frustrated so she started guiding my hips up and down with her hands. Then as quick as you can say, "small town"...I was no longer a virgin. Years later, I figured that the man watching TV in the other room must have had way too much to do with Jessie's precociousness. After that night I never saw Jessie again.

Most mornings back at the restaurant a balding, sweaty man, around 50 would have breakfast and give me money after he ate. I didn't normally get tips. One day he asked me to sit down with him. I did. We talked for a while. He was jittery and a bit too nice. He suggested I come see his big house sometime. He offered to even have me come live with him. One day I decided to at least check it out. I was tired of the dark, hot, smelly room I lived in with Greg behind the restaurant.

Then came the moment that changed my life. I was walking between the booths for the front door to get in this man's car, that was running outside. Scott's father was walking the other way to the back of the restaurant. He stopped me and whispered in my ear, " did you know that guy is as queer as a three dollar bill? "

That was all he said. I paused...not really understanding this riddle. But it was just enough. I looked out at the man in the car who had a very worried look on his face. I didn't go with him.

That was the day I realized that no one was really looking after me. I never saw the world the same way again.

As the summer ended I called my mother to say I wanted to make plans to come home. She had not tried to contact me once while I was gone and had no idea that I was basically on my own. My father, who was divorced from my mother had no idea I had even left.

When I got home the door was locked. I had no key. My little brother answered the door with long blonde hair and a dark, end of summer tan. When my mom got home from work that night I remember her giving me a hug and saying she missed me while she made her first cocktail. She turned on the TV. No questions about anything. No one else home.

The next day I started 8th grade.

http://www.bradfordjsalamon.com/

Jill Sykes

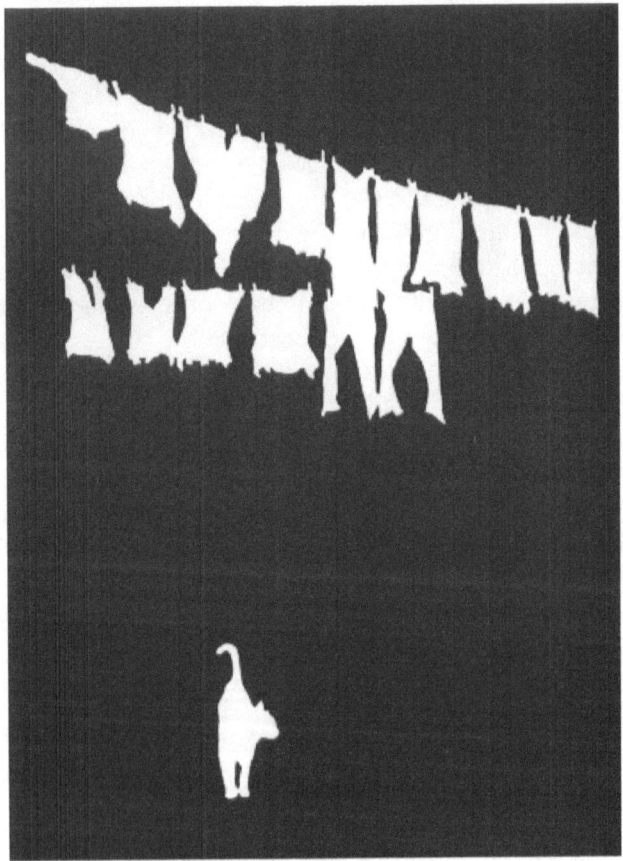

Heather's Cats II, acrylic paper, 18.5x14.5

How I learned to Change a Tire

I was 19 years old and found myself wintering at a "photography school" in Northern Denmark – an incredible 4 month long adventure I was able to pursue during a break from college, and yes, it was exceedingly cold. For a brief period I had access to a sweet little green panel truck. Hand-painted on each window-less side was a large, colorful tree and the word

EARTHGAARD. The owner was an Ecologist – first time I had ever heard the term. One day I ran down the outside stairs of the old farmhouse we were all living in to find the right rear tire of the EARTHGAARD truck completely flat. Damn. So I ran back up the stairs to ask the lads I was living with to come help me fix it. Four of them were just sitting around doing nothing, so they cheerfully hopped up, bundled themselves for the cold and we all ran back downstairs. They had me open the trunk, take out the tools and patiently instructed me how to hitch the car up with the jack and unscrew all the lug nuts, etc. etc. Slowly it dawned on me that none of them had moved anywhere near the car – they were all just standing there smoking and giving me directions. I was steamed...but I just got on with it because clearly they were no help! Ultimately the spare was in place and I drove off – furious! Eventually I realized that they had tacitly, as a team, taught me an incredibly valuable skill: how to change a tire. Even I had to laugh.

A few years later back in California I was driving my own little red VW Squareback and had a blow-out. There was no phone, no garage, no AAA – just me on the highway, hours north of San Francisco. I changed the tire, got back on the road and headed home to the city and college. Amazing.

Decades later I was picking my kids up from school one day and was once again faced with a flat tire. My eldest – maybe 11 at the time – and I got to work cranking off the lug nuts and swapping out the spare. Then we nabbed his little brother from the playground, went home and all was well. Years later he reported telling a friend – after tending to a flat of his own – that yes, his mother taught him how to change a tire. That felt pretty great.

Several years after that my younger son, in college at the time, called to tell me about a big fight he'd had with his girlfriend: her car had a flat. His first thought was not to change it for her but show her how to do it herself – she was about to go off to college for the first time and he wanted to know she could take care of things on her own. She complained bitterly, and since they were at her parent's house she eventually called her mother outside to talk some sense into my son. Mom was very angry at him and said to her daughter "Oh honey, you don't have to worry about that. You're so pretty – someone will always come along and help you." My poor son was so confused – in putting forth some good intentions he'd gotten into a big argument with both of these ladies and didn't understand what he'd done wrong.

"Nothing," I told him. "You are an excellent boyfriend."

I don't know any of those young men I wintered with in Denmark so many years ago, but in teaching me that grubby, rudimentary skill on that cold winter afternoon they did me a very great favor whether they meant to or not. I doubt I ever thanked them.

Independence is a wonderful thing.

http://www.jillsykes.com

Ada Pullini Brown

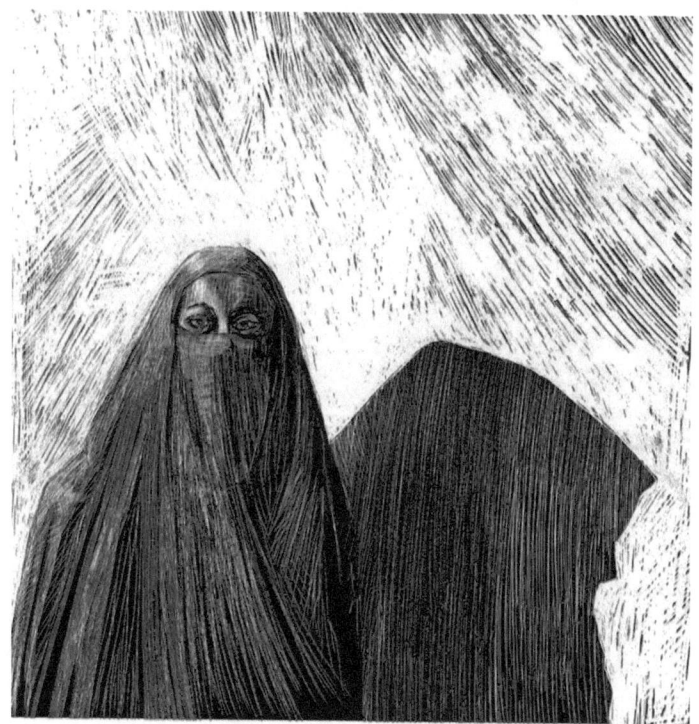

Veiled (stratch-board.) 10 x 10

No Mo' Hoes

Over the years our lofts in the garment district of Manhattan had seen it all. An elevator broken for years, two winters with no heat or hot water, and a leaking roof, but the current landlord was the worst of all.

The fifth floor of our small building was rented, renovated, and running to a busting business over the long Labor Day holiday weekend. I had my suspicions by the looks of the items being delivered, but no proof until I came home Tuesday evening to find Screw magazine on the elevator floor. The back page ad read "Junko Erotic Massage" with our buildings address.

Over the next few months the flow of clients took on a constant rhythm. Mornings brought the 30-60ish suit, tie, and attaché case carrying office workers. Afternoons brought in the blue-collar workers and the seemly unemployed. Early evenings, again the suits before catching the train at Penn Station home to suburbia. And then late nights and weekends brought the "bridge and tunnel" twenty-something's (always in groups of five or more) drunk, boisterous, and incapable of finding the right floor as they pounded on our doors in the middle of the night trying to gain entrance.

The only "tenant" we saw come out was an older woman. She swept the hallway, sometimes left for a few hours, but was usually stayed inside with the girls. You could hear their voices through the vents in our bathroom below. Sometimes there was giggling, sometimes crying, sometimes yelling, and what sounded like fights. Often there was one loud male voice shouting and scolding. The police were called and once again we were told it was not their jurisdiction. "Enforcement knows about it, they are working on it. Call the Enforcement Office in the morning." Repeatedly we were told it takes three to five years to close a whorehouse legally. This was not the answer we wanted to hear.

Then one afternoon the building next to ours collapsed. Another tragic NY story about corruption and illegal contractors. It was the media's interest in our street that changed the slow course of events. Our Press Release "Buildings are not the only things falling down on 31st Street," brought an article in a small community paper and then the TV reporter called. "What can I do for you?" he asked. "You can help me close a whorehouse," I responded. "Get the tenants together tomorrow evening and we'll interview you."

That next evening as I walked in the front door, signs were taped to the glass, "JUNKO: Closed By Order of the Court." During the day before our scheduled interviews the reporter and cameraman went to the Enforcement office and chased the politicos to the elevators as they tried to flee the cameras, asking, "why haven't you closed that business?" Within a few hours, and well before our scheduled interview, the police closed JUNKO down.

The interview went on as scheduled, but this time the reporter stood in front of the yellow taped fifth floor door taking full credit. It ran on the eleven o'clock news as the "Erotic Eviction."

It was early December and we could smell something was rotting inside and worried about rats. We weren't supposed to open the fifth floor until the court lifted the order, but we broke in anyway. It was all as they left it that day a few weeks earlier; small private rooms with beds, lots of towels and cases of beer. The beer offered an opportunity to celebrate the closing of the whorehouse. We decided to throw a party and everyone can take some real whorehouse memorabilia home.

We created a flyer and sent it to all our friends: "Ho Ho Ho — No Mo' Hoes "– come dressed for the role of pimps and hookers."

The place was emptied in one night with music, dance and lots of beer.

http://www.adapbrown.com

Mike Mollett

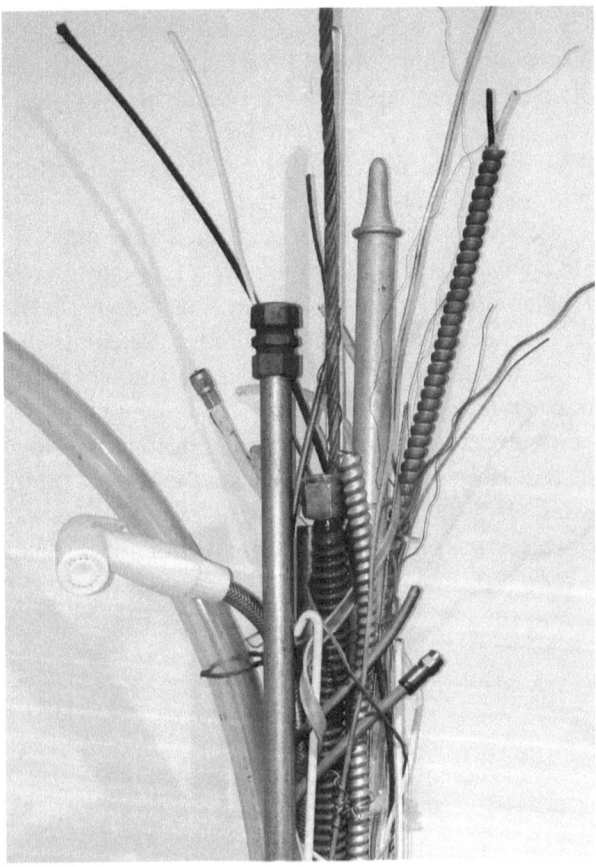

Life going on-line (Version 1a)

I was stupidly innocent. Without fear. I was 23 with long-hair & wire-frame glasses. Younger than I knew. Older than I realized. Time & experience was about to gallop. I was the rider & the creature under the saddle, wide-eyed new.

I will abbreviate...

I was writing poetry, a solitary relationship, probably since mid high school. (I'd publish my first book within a couple of years of this adventure.) I knew that bio sci, my thru-the-microscope major in college, wasn't what I was to follow & make a career out of. A TRUE SCIENTIST I WAS NOT. But what? & WHO IS THIS PERSON? I was asking...

I hit the road. Stepped onto a plane in Los Angeles, CA. Climbed out of another plane into another country. Luxembourg. Winter. A few days before Christmas. A world faceted into other worlds. This was to be my great odyssey of discovery.

I had: 3 or 4 hundred dollars in travelers checks (after selling the VDub) in a thigh pocket wallet next to my passport. More pockets in my leather pants. A down bag. Wool sister-embroidered coat. A down sleeping bag. Good boots (I thought). An oversized backpack with tube frame (a future hash stash). Rabelais's Gargantua & Pantaqruel. Black Spring by Henry Miller. A notebook for poetry, writing, & notes to remember. Wads of possibilities stuffed everywhere. More innocence. & the great unknown.

I'd turned in my senior project- a behavioral study with cactus-living wood rats... Good-bye university. Good-bye America. Good-bye Mom & Dad, friends & what seemed like security. I said adios as well to what I thought I knew about myself, who I was.

Deliriously crazy, in English, French, & Spanish I said hello to who I was to become. I just didn't know who that was yet...

What a wondrous adventure this would be without a plan. Ready. Set. Go. Go. Go... Into the snow blanketed European winter. I loved it.

Place spot/what not.

Foot-print discovery.

Hitch-hiking mostly. & walking to save money. The less I'd spend, the longer I could travel. Working was not an option.

At first, thru forest & field arriving at hostel after hostel, often in a castle... most hostels were closed. White cold & hollow. Not enough travelers foolish enough to venture in the snow & wind & uncertainity. Just me on my quest of self-dis-covery.

Sleeping along the road-sides, winter then spring into summer. Climbing over fences of construction sites, out of the way places, under bus-stop roofs protected for a few hours. I slept in parks. On top of city boulders. In garrets, one with drying leaves of tobacco. Flop-house cot halls, tin bowls for breakfast, lunch, & dinner. Beside fountains, moss, & stone. An army barracks too, to meet a friend (evading the MP's); finding "safety" there in a boarded-up mess hall in the dark; fuzzy frozen rats for a morning surprise.

Surprises into surprises, on top of in between; over 10 months. 10 countries. Vistas. Panoramas… Montage…

Wet/dry hopes never flagging for too long, along the way, along the roads taken & not taken. These lines inside & out of me. Me. I thought I was with everything. & everything was in me. But

I needed a mirror. I needed some friends. I needed to be grabbed & shaken-up. I needed to let go…

Yes, Dear Readers, there are people in this story… People, & people, the people I met & who met me. Pulled me in. In every country I was taken in at least once… warmed, fed, & housed along the way. Humbled with love by those who lived in each country, rode that donkey, drank in that tavern, walked that street. With that smile.

& the travelers, from all over the planet, not unlike me I came to realize, in spite of my solitary, shy nature like a hermit. I was button-holed again & again to hang out and listen, talk share communicate… relax…

Who are these people? People who wanted to be with me? Was it I who had become lost? Lost in another bag with stuff tied upon me inside? A heavy bag waiting to open into an air of opportunities?

I was a hard nut to crack. Not an easy learner even now… I needed a key. Not in a pocket, but on the table, with wine and wisdom.

As it was in this transforming nutshell, day by momentous day, the lines of connection grew nearer & nearer… some began to touch! The moments of understanding began to shine thru… Holy shit! The people I continued meeting, the travelers who pulled me in, the people I became friends with, the wanderers who were maybe searching too… We were comrades in community on the same roads this lifetime life line. I could see myself in the mirror now…with these people…

After nearly a year I realized…I was an explorer too.

http://www.mikemollett.com

Karrie Ross

The publisher and coordinator of this book series.

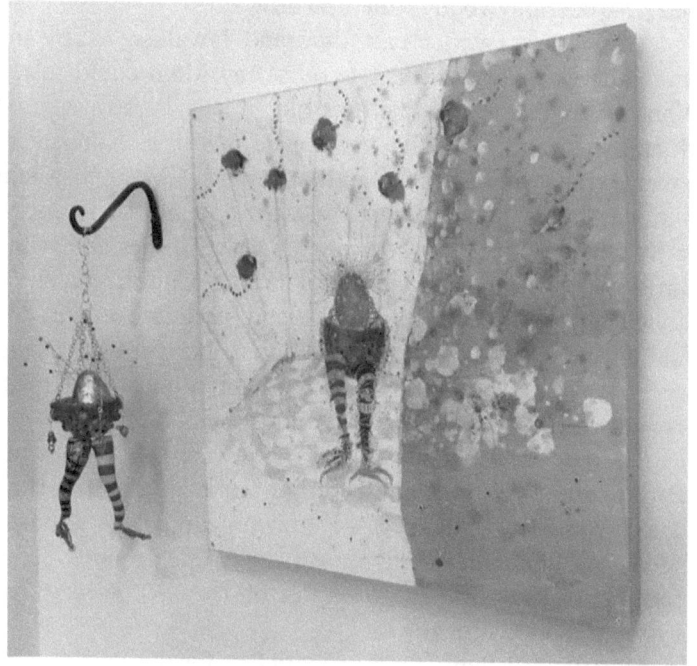

The Egg Walking; 2015; 24x24; mixed media. Sculpture: The Egg Walking; 2015.

Embarrasment Is Wasted On The Lost

I like Chinatown. I always have. When I was 16yrs old packing a newly acquired drivers license I would drive to downtown Los Angeles, and explore, Chinatown. Park my car where it was free and walk to the wishing well to throw my pennies in and make my wishes. I would then walk through all the shops, it seemed like there were lots more back in the mid 1960s. I loved to look at all the little gift items for tourists—fans, shoes, umbrellas and puzzle boxes, but I never bought anything, I didn't have the money. I would cross Hill St. to the courtyard, sit on the bench, and watch—watch all the people dressed in plaid shorts and Hawaiian shirts, hats, sunglasses, camera's — Tourists! The game I played to keep me busy was trying to guess where they were from and make up stories about where they were going next — was it Disneyland, Knott's Berry Farm, Hollywood ... the beach!

This was a favorite past time and I was so happy my parents let me use the car. Of course my Mom could relate. When I was just a kid, like 8yrs old (it was 1958s), we, my Mom, sister, and I, would hop on the bus from Norwalk to downtown to "have a day in the City!" my Mom in a suit (she was raised in a big city, Chicago) and my sister and I, native Californians, in our fancy little girl clothes and white gloves to go shopping and have lunch at Clifton's Cafeteria (grilled cheese, french fries, a Coke, and black forest cake). My mother underwent several opperations to her petuitary gland over the years and paseed in 1972 of a massive stroke. Downtown Los Angeles always reminds me of her.

Anyways, as the years passed there were fewer moments for this type of outings and more of work and family. Time passed into the 1990s, my son growing up, two marriages ended, my life changed, living on the Westside now. Some good friends moved to Pasadena just off the 110 freeway that runs right by downtown.

I would visit them on New Years Day for the Rose Parade and got into the habit on my way home, of being in the fast lane that automatically exits into Chinatown and my favorite Dim Sum place in a-kind-a-mall on Hill St.. And one day after eating...I ventured out into the stores like I used to do. The first one I came to, just to the right of the restaurant entrance, displayed several touristy gift items. I asked the sales person what they said, to which he didn't know! But I bought it anyways. Finally!

It was that time of life where I became obsessed with questioning who I was, why was I here, what is the meaning of it all ... etc etc etc. (damn it anyways!) I joined meditation groups, studied Gurdjieff, Sat Nam Rasayan energy healing and Feng Shui. And for that little space in time, I pursued the intention of self growth and evolution.

A few years into my search, I became involved in a most wonderful relationship, totally present and all that goes with it… the good as well as the "Oooo No, not again!" stuff that seemed to happen a lot. Mostly me embarrassing me. A big part of learning, growing, etc. since if you are not able to "see" the "it" then how can you change and oh, the risk of that is great. Heck I'd been studying "it" for a few years by then, feeling all "yeah I got it" when POW!!… this new level of risk and awareness was happening. They say we attract what we need and he was the "it" of the moment for me. The relationship lasted many years filled with lots of mirror images filled with great passion — then we went our separate ways…both still bringing risk and growth into our lives.

However, during one of our moments together he noticed the little Chinatown gift item, he could read Chinese, and I heard him say… "Embarrassment is Wasted On The Lost." kinda hit me like the saying "Only Then When I Am.!"

I moved on to other forms of growth encouraging activities, always looking for the next level of observation and risk. I started writing about the things that meant something to me and giving back, like bringing attention to Bullying with the Bebuddies.com; a Parenting book; and publishing books about life moments, and stories from a special group of people in Southern California.

Now as the years pass, growth is as normal as sneezing and often times feels like a sneezing-fit! Daily I risk the fears of participation, and the growth oriented embarrassing moments continue to happen. They bring the 'what is' to life for me. Some moments are more awakening than others, but all are not "wasted" as there is learning that allows me to "see" the me "I Am." and whether I like the behavior or not, I know deep inside, I will grow from it…assured I am not lost!

And risk Love.

http://www.karrieross.com

P.S. I want to thank all the Southern California artists who are in this book. Their participation has been, yet again, another learning experience of fear and the risk of allowing actions to be filled with embarrassing moments that feed my need to be seen and heard and grow through participation.

www.ingramcontent.com/pod-product-compliance
Lightning Source LLC
Chambersburg PA
CBHW021403170526
45164CB00002B/482